Are You a Christian Or Are You Just Playing One?

A Yardstick to Help You Measure Your Christianity

Are You Really Living the Christian Life that God the Father Desires of You?

Real Christian Books ™

Second Revision

Copyright 2008, 2009 Brian Schaefer
ISBN 978-0-9819418-0-6 Paperback
ISBN 978-0-9819418-1-3 Hardcover

All rights reserved, including translations. This book or any parts there of cannot be reproduced without written permission from the copyright holder.

Manufactured in the United States of America
Distributed by Real Christian Books Publishing, Inc
Author: Brian V Schaefer

Preface

The title of the book is intended to be controversial. Why? This book needs to bring about a significant emotional event in your life. This is the only way you can personally have behavioral modification! What is Christianity? What is your Christianity? Is it even remote to what Christianity meant when the term Christian was first coined in Antioch? Society has blended the word into something, but it isn't Christianity.

Take socialism. If you call yourself a socialist but believe in open markets and owning your own businesses for personal gain are you really socialists? No, you are a capitalist. If you call yourself a capitalist, but believe that the federal government should own everything and that it should be shared by all, are you still a capitalist? No, you are a democrat (bad political joke)! I mean, you are a communist!

If you call yourself a communist, but know in your heart the major means of production and distribution should be owned, managed, or controlled by the government or state, by association with the workforce. Are you really a communist? No, you are a socialist. You can identify a capitalist, socialist, and communist by the philosophy that they follow. So, what makes you believe that you and your friends are Christians? Is it just because you call yourselves Christians and attend a church that tells you not to work your way to eternal life? A Christian can only be a real Christian when he or she lovingly follows the guidance provided by God.

The thought process of this book is based using the entire Bible as if it is a "completely accurate" representation of books delivered to man from God. When I say completely accurate you will note that I am implying that there could be books within the Bible that are not accurate at all, and thus should not be used to guide your life's journey. This I believe to be true, but until I wrote my second book, *The New Testament: The Facts and the Fiction*, I really did not know how this would effect a real Christian's walk.

This book is based on the complete Bible. The whole point of this book is to help you understand why you need to read the entire Bible for yourself. This book guides you on lessons about true biblical values and doesn't use a verse here and there to drive home a point taken out of context. If you believe that you are living a Biblical life, I will hazard to guess that you will learn you have been misled. But as most Christian's feel that they are living their lives according to the Bible, lets just take a quick look.

You will not look at your future Bible study in the same way again. If you are wanting to live a life pleasing to God the Father, you will want to focused on a line by line study from Genesis Chapter 1, Verse 1 through Revelation Chapter 22, verse 21. Why? Because you will have learned that the denominational focused studies have led you astray.

It's very simple. If you follow your Bible literally, then you can claim the promises given to a Christian. Turn the page. Take the challenge. Measure your life to the "Bible." Are you a "Real Christian" or are you just playing one?

Table of Contents

What is Your Christianity Founded On, and is it Worth Laboring for?	1
Let's Talk Bible	12
What is God's Word and How Should You Study It?	14
Is the Bible the Inerrant Word of God?	20
Is the New Testament Trustworthy?	36
The Books of Luke	50
Is Paul taken out of Context?	59
Christian Living	71
Does the Old Testament Apply Today? After All, I am a New Testament Christian?	72
Do Today's Christians believe as the Early Church Did?	76
The Law, Works, Faith or Grace?	83
What is Sin, and What are the Consequences of Sin in My Life?	94
Christian Worship	101
What is the Trinity?	103
When was Jesus Christ Crucified?	113
What is the Sabbath and Does it Matter?	126
Christian Myths	141
Are You Really Saved? Can You Loose It? What About Once-Saved-Always-Saved?	143
Am I Pre-, Mid- or Post-Tribulation?	153
Who is the Bride of Christ?	158
Are the Dietary Laws of the Old Testament Current Today?	161

Who is Lucifer?	169
What Should I Give as Tithes or Offerings and to Whom?	172
What are the present day gifts of the Holy Spirit?	177
Author's Thoughts	182
What are the Hard to Swallow Facts for Christians	183
So, What is Wrong with My Church?	194
How Do I Know if I Love God and Why Don't I Fit Comfortably into Modern Society?	199

What is Your Christianity Founded On and is it Worth Laboring For?

What is your personal view of Christianity based on? A belief has to be rooted in some type of foundation or it is little more than a fairytale. You may say that you have 2,000 years of tradition and that is good enough for you. What did the early church have for their foundation? Wasn't it just hearsay from the early apostles? No, it was the miracles.

The Bible tells you that God the Father provided for the early church the ability to heal the sick, cast out devils, and bring back the dead. Those unbelievable powers or gifts gave them credibility. What gives modern day Christians credibility? What about the Bible?

Doesn't that give us all we need to know? Yes, but have you really ever read the Bible to understand it? Besides those catch verses you hear Christians constantly regurgitating, have you ever read the whole thing from front to back to understand God's credibility?

If you read your Bible through a couple of times and tried to live the life your loving God would have you live, you wouldn't need to be challenged. Most so-called Christians hide behind the doctrine they and their chosen friends have accepted and think God will "see it their way" after they pass from this life. Whether you want to believe this or not, that thought process just won't hack it. God expects more!

Do your Christian values allow you to work (labor) toward your salvation? If not, why not? Haven't you heard the old adage, "anything worth having is worth working for?" Instead, you hide behind modern Christian tradition. It goes something like this: Christian life is all about "faith" and you can do nothing to add to it! Right? Wrong! I will show you in a couple of hours reading that God (the true God of the Bible) expects you to work towards your true knowledge of Him and then live it. Your not earning anything. You are lovingly obedient to your Heavenly Father.

Before we go any further you should understand that Jesus tells you of these so-called traditions that modern religion has placed on you and has "warned" you against them. Do you remember the story where Jesus speaks of religious traditions in Mark Chapter 7? It's in the first 13 verses of the chapter. If you don't know it well, set this book down right now and go pick up your Bible and read it for yourself. Don't read any further in this book until you do so.

The average person would have just kept reading along. Why? Because most are too lazy to go find their Bible and read the story. This is because we are all too lazy to read the Bible for ourselves. We blindly follow along behind the teachings our pastor or minister has set before us and refuse to read it for ourselves.

If you are one of the rare ones that went back and looked up the story for yourself, it shows that you don't mind doing a little work to learn more of God. It also shows that you are a little more like the Bereans. Paul stated in Acts Chapter 17, verse 11 that they were better than those from Thessalonia, as they would listen with all earnest, and then would go back to the scriptures to see if it was true.

My mission for this book is to get you to read your Bible and then follow it. I will show you the facts as they are in the Bible. If you don't like them, tell God! There really aren't any gray areas in God's word. It is black or white, sinful or righteous. All Christian churches teach that God is, was and always will be.

That means that He is all knowing and does not learn. He has no reason to say one thing today and then change His mind and tell you to do something different tomorrow. If He was able to change His mind (or requirements), how would you know if your salvation was secure?

If He wasn't constantly the same, He might change His requirements for everlasting life. But, He doesn't. That is because if you read your Bible, you would understand that from the beginning of time He has always been the same. Why would He change from the Old Testament to the New Testament?

If the Old Testament was for the Jew only, what about those that lived before the Jew? Why do all the New Testament writers, and even Jesus Christ, quote from the Old Testament? Because it is just as relevant today as it was when God spoke and it was put down on parchment or papyrus. In fact, Paul (the one person more misquoted than any other) uses the Old Testament as his proof for <u>ALL</u> his arguments.

You are either a Christian or you are playing Christian. What is the difference? Real Christians spend their lives, out of love, looking for the lifestyle that is pleasing to the Lord. There are plenty of examples of this in the Bible. Someone playing Christian is the kind of person that does on the outside what he feels is expected and doesn't change inwardly. How can you change inwardly without an understanding of what God wants from you?

Man, in the name of religion, has polluted the message of God into what we have today. You no longer live the Christian life, you play Christianity with your chosen peers. Those peers are the

"Christians" that choose to play as you do. Playing Christianity doesn't necessarily follow the life that God has presented to you through the Bible. It is living a lifestyle that chooses various verses from the Bible to support their values to meet the needs of the type of Christianity that they choose to play.

It is impossible to follow guided studies from the Bible, designed by those with preconceived agendas, and ever really understand who God is. You must have an understanding that can only come from true study. Don't look for the type of box you want God to be in, but understand that He cannot be placed in a box.

This kind of study has to be from the beginning of the Bible through to the end. Don't read the commentary at the bottom of your study Bible. Just read the words as they are written. If you have a concern about the meaning of a word used in a sentence, look it up in the concordance.

For those unfamiliar with a concordance, it can be purchased at most book stores and any Christian book store. It lists every English word used in the Bible and then gives the original Greek or Hebrew word for the English translation. Using it will be covered in a later chapter along with using an interlinear scripture analyzer. Both of these powerful tools are essential to truly understanding the Bible authors' meaning.

Once you have looked up the word, continue reading. It may take a few times through, and this may take a couple of years, but after a while the entire Bible will begin to line up for you. Nothing will be out of place.

Wouldn't it be good to know if the scriptures were really written by the "pen" of God? After you understand how the Greek or Hebrew actually reads, you have to ask yourself, could the original translators have mistranslated a scripture passage or verse? Why would I ask?

Sometimes even using the concordance you will find that some passages from the New Testament seem to contradict the Old Testament. How could this be if the Old Testament is just as relevant today as the day it was placed on parchment? Has it ever occurred to you that the Bible may have mistranslations? If you say "no" to that question, I have to tell you to "get a grip."

For a great example of this, let's look at my favorite modern evangelical scripture most quoted to help them ignore the Sabbath. Read Colossians Chapter 2, verse 16. In the King James it goes like this: "Let no man therefore judge you in meat or in drink or in respect of an holyday or of the new moons or of the Sabbath days." From that translation it sounds like Sabbath is over!

What does the Greek text exactly say: "No then any you let be judging in feeding and drinking or in part of festival or of young months or of Sabbaths."

It would be a real stretch to say this verse in it's original tongue is telling you not to let someone judge you in food or Sabbaths. In fact, I could easily make the case from the words presented that you will be judged by how you are celebrating these events! In the Chapter *Is Paul Taken Out of Context*; you will see that Paul himself, the author of Colossians will counter the notion that these events are not required and he actually embraces them. If Paul embraced and kept them, why wouldn't you? Oh yes, that's because they may go against your present traditions.

Its funny, I have been reading my Bible earnestly almost every day since 1994. The more I read, the simpler the message becomes. The simpler it becomes, the easier it is to see what God wants from those that choose to follow Him.

True Christianity follows the same message throughout the Bible. In the New Testament, Paul explains in the Book to the Romans that the Jewish nation was the Holy Olive Tree. Some of the Jews were pruned out and many of us Gentiles were grafted in. Christians are not a new sect to God. We are an extension of His holy people.

That makes the entire Bible relevant to those of us grafted in. Are you grafted in? Do you think it is important to be grafted in? If you're not, what are you? What is a Christian if he or she is not part of the Holy Olive Tree?

<u>ALL</u> of scripture is relevant. There is <u>NO</u> commandment in the Old Testament that has been removed in the New Testament. When you pick and choose the scripture you want to be relevant to you, you are doing as the Children of Israel in the time of the Judges. Where you read "Every man did right in his own eyes (Judges 17:6 & 21:25)." By the way, that verse is quoted later in the Bible as a scriptural slam (Proverbs 12:15).

Many of the Modern Evangelical Church (MEC) teachings are not scriptural. Their way of interpreting scripture is mainly based on the misquoted writings of Paul. It isn't that Paul was incorrect, in fact he is my favorite author. It is that he states things that if you take just one or two verses from a chapter, without reading all the surrounding verses, you can be easily misled.

Christ's Apostle Peter even warns you of Paul's letters being hard to understand, and that the scriptures (Old Testament) have already explained all things. The way Paul is being interpreted by some is false and will lead to their destruction (2 Peter 3:15–18). I have already shown in my demonstration of Colossians (2:16) that some of what Paul is quoted to tell you is at the very least, a questionable translation.

This book is similar to all human endeavors. Even Paul stated that he was responding to the Corinthians "as a man" in 1 Corinthians. In his second letter to them, he corrects one of his positions from his first epistle to one showing a lot more lenience. With that said, even Paul explains that he makes errors in his letters. I try my best to accurately show what the Bible states about various hot topics. Face it, man is fallible. He is also selfish. That is why Christianity today is so easy. It is designed to keep you coming back, whatever it takes.

As I stated, I will do my best to accurately show you what the Bible "exactly" explains. This will actually be impossible as much of the New Testament contradicts itself. This is my first major revision since this book was printed for release to the public. Since that time I wrote a book that was to be an expansion of one of the chapters within this book. As I wrote it, I realized that much of what is found in the New Testament is questionable. But, that is another book with a different focus. This book will utilize the entire Bible for your yardstick. It is a great way to challenge your faith to see if you truly know what is written for your direction in the Bible.

I expect you to read the scriptures for yourself. God has given us a life long jigsaw puzzle to work. Each piece is found in the Bible, both Old and New Testaments. Once you have mastered the picture that He has placed on the pieces, you can start to put them in place. There is only one place for each piece, and each piece is necessary to put the puzzle together.

This book should give you enough doubt about your own Christian values that you will be forced to read your Bible to see if you are really living a lifestyle that is pleasing to God. When I state "read your Bible," there is only one way. Start at Genesis Chapter 1, verse 1 and end at Revelation Chapter 22, verse 21. Then start over again. I read every morning for about 15 – 30 minutes before I start my day. The more you read it, the less pleased you will be with the church you are attending.

Then, like me, you will be forced to talk to others about the real Christian message and help them to begin to diligently search the scriptures daily to see how God wants us to live our lives.

One more thing on Paul's letters, except for Romans, they are all pretty short. If you focus on the message from his books, they are usually about not taking on an external show of Christianity. His letters don't denigrate the Old Testament and/or the Law. He shows that if you are following them outwardly and not inwardly you have gained nothing. He actually states that the Law is holy, righteous, and just (Romans 2-3). Does that sound like something a real Christian should be taking notice of?

Why not read Romans Chapters 1 through 3. It shows you why we were given the Law in the first place. Then he explains faith and saving grace. Ah, grace. With that one word modern Christianity has thrown out the entire Old Testament. But wait! What does he state at the end of Chapter 3? "Do we then make void the Law through faith? God Forbid: yea, we establish the Law!"

How then have we as Christians, managed to throw out the Law and works? Oh yes, that brings me back to Mark Chapter 7 and Jesus. We have started to substitute traditions made by man for those "works" ordained by God.

Many false ideas that are presently offered by the MEC will be disputed with scripture in this book. Take the previous paragraphs. I offer a chapter called *"Is Paul taken out of context."* It will show you the misleading statements that are used by the MEC to explain why they don't believe that they, or you, can do anything to "add to your salvation." You really can't add to your salvation, but have you really made the choice to be saved?

I feel most people that call themselves Christians are misled. They are misled because they rely on a pastor to lead them to the truth about salvation. Your pastor was taught while attending seminary (or Bible college). They all learn the same way, and unfortunately it isn't scriptural, but it does sell. Is that how Jesus Christ would have taught? If you don't read the Bible for yourself you will never know.

I have attended many churches and have never found one that is scriptural. They all say they follow the Bible as close as possible. Some are close but then add their own opinion of what they would like it to have said or those opinions of their "prophet" to make it what they want it to be, not what God Almighty has already ordained.

Do you call yourself a New Testament Christian? Why don't I think the New Testament is enough? Find one New Testament writer that states "his is the definitive word of God and the only thing you need to be saved." All the writers point you to the scriptures as proof of what they are stating. They were Jews and of the "Holy Olive Tree" we now call Christianity. When they quote from the "scriptures," they are quoting from what we call the Old Testament. After all, the New Testament wasn't even written yet.

If you don't have an understanding of the Old Testament, how can you claim the promises of the New Testament? Paul stated that the Bereans were better than the Thessalonians because they listened to what he stated and then they tested his words with the scriptures (Acts 17:11). If you choose to take a verse here and there from Paul's writings as "all you need," have you searched the Old Testament to back up those verses? I can guarantee that after you have read your Bible thoroughly, you will no longer hold those poor values you have today, if you are a real Christian.

Saying a few words and "presto" you are in, is only a modern evangelical idea. This wasn't practiced by the early church. All the New Testament authors talk about works and being judged by your works. Read all the other writers before you read Paul, and then ask yourself, did Paul get it wrong? No, Paul points out, that your works and/or the Law do not save you. You are saved by grace, through faith. Then, what are works? They are the natural outpouring of your life when you are truly saved. It comes from God's love within you.

Are you doing works? If not, why not? Isn't it the natural outpouring of your love? Read the entire Book of James in one sitting. It will take less than 15 minutes. Faith without works is dead. It isn't faith at all. So, what are you calling faith, if you don't have works? According to James it really isn't faith at all! So, if you don't have faith because you don't have works, how can you be saved by grace through faith?

If you read Paul completely, you will understand that he felt the Law (found in the first five books of the Bible) was the schoolmaster, teaching you what sin is. All the other New Testament authors agree. If you read your Bible you will be able to identify sin. Don't you ever wonder what is meant when your Pastor states that you should "stop sinning and repent?" I agree with that statement, but what is meant by sin? All writers in the Bible state that it is the act of breaking the (Mosaic) Law.

How can you be a Christian and knowingly sin? If you haven't read your Bible, you have to believe the guy in the pulpit telling you what sin is. Not one MEC will teach you what sin is because not one MEC will teach you the LAW. Instead, they teach something more in the line of …"you will know you are sinning because the Holy Spirit will place it in your heart." That frequently quoted statement in this situation is hogwash.

That statement is from scripture, but as usual it is taken out of context. It is found several times in the Old and New Testament. It is true that in the future we will not have to tell our brother the Law as the Holy Spirit will place it on his heart, but that time is way in the future. Does the child place his hand in the adder (snake) hole today? Have the nations beaten their swords into plowshares yet? Look, that time is after the Lord returns for the second coming, not present-day life. But then, you would have to have a handle on the scriptures to have that knowledge.

Sin is anything that is contrary to God's Law! Are you keeping God's Law? If not, you are sinning. If you have read the Law and you are not keeping the Law, then you are knowingly living in sin. Can you be saved, and knowingly live in sin? The answer is No!

Even the writer of the Book of Hebrews tells you that, "For if we sin willfully after that we have received the knowledge of the truth, there remains no more sacrifice for sins, but certain fearful looking for of judgment and fiery indignation, which shall devour the adversaries (Hebrews 10:26-27)." That sounds scary, but then have you really made the choice to be saved yet? If you diligently read your Bible you will begin to decide, do I love God, or the world?

If you read your Bible, but still love the world you will not change. You will still have the lusts of the world. Jesus stated that if you look upon a woman, you have already sinned (Matthew 5:28). What does He mean? He means that the commandments are extended beyond the physical act of sin, to the desire within your heart to commit the sin. Lusting after another woman is sin in your heart. A Christian, through prayer, will begin to place those or any other sinful thoughts behind him.

Sure, you will be tempted to sin, but humble yourself and ask God for strength. This is the type of prayer, when asked in earnest that will be answered. Could the MEC's opinion of Christians be correct? Are we all sinners, living in a sinful world. Can Christians do nothing about it but say a few words and then they are saved?

If this was so, is it any wonder why the divorce rate is so high in the MEC? It is as high as the world around them. Is it any wonder why they have couples attending their churches living together out of wedlock? That is because these churches basically have the same values as the world. They aren't a Christian Church. They are playing Christian values outwardly, but accepting worldly values inwardly.

Far too many times Bible verses are quoted by the MECs to add validity to an argument. Over and over these verses are quoted and believed. Many times these are taken out of context, and when challenged by non-believers the argument falls apart because they don't really correlate or are obviously not connected. This is because most Christians have never read their Bible from front to back for themselves. They allow themselves to be led along like poor evangelical sheep.

A great example of this is the name "Lucifer." It has nothing to do with Satan, and the name is mentioned only once in the Bible. Yet we hear the names Lucifer and Satan used interchangeably. The one time the name Lucifer is used, it is talking about the King of Babylon. Yes, he really did think he was supernatural. Just read Daniel (about an hour read). With that stated, why do Christians refer to Satan as Lucifer, when he already has the "God" given name of Satan?

Or, when Paul states, "I can do all things, but all things are not expedient for me." Most all MECs claim that this is further proof that we are not under the Law, as Paul could do anything he chose and would still be saved under grace. Paul was only referring to the fact that he could eat meat that had been dedicated to idols, as he knew that an idol was not a real god. The reason it was not expedient for him, if you read the rest of the chapter, is because he knew that it might damage another's conscience, seeing him eat it! Go back and read the whole chapter for yourself. Better yet, read the Book of 1 Corinthians completely!

This book has many scripturally led discussions. They are definitely opposed to modern evangelical teachings. They will border on blasphemy to most modern Christians. Don't get mad at me. It is totally scripturally based. Modern evangelical teaching is not! I try not to quote a verse here and there unless it is a verse the MEC tries to use as a proof text for improper teaching. Rather, I will quote it and then give you the real meaning. Usually the original author's meaning will come from the same book.

Understand that each of the books of the Bible were not segregated into verses and chapters originally. They did not have punctuation. Why is this important to know? The punctuation can change a statement into a question. So, read it slowly and ask yourself, what did the author really state? The verses and chapters were added later by the Roman Catholic Church for easier memorization.

The entire New Testament and most of the Old Testament was in letter or manuscript form. So why not read each book in one sitting? Have you ever received a long letter in the mail and started reading it only to set it down several times before you were finished? No, you read it through completely or you might loose the meaning.

To understand what the author wants you to know from the letter, you must read it in its entirety and preferably in one sitting. Then ask yourself, what was he saying? Nothing in the Bible is complicated. It kills me that there are commentaries out there to tell you about the hidden meanings in the scriptures.

Take the Book of Romans. Most evangelicals will tell you it is a "deep" book. It's only deep if you want to complicate the simple message Paul was communicating to the small church in Rome. It was a book intended to strengthen their faith. Did they have those commentaries to help them decipher Paul's true meaning? No! They read it and grew from the message, and so will you. The only thing hard to understand is the translation from Greek to English. That is where a good concordance and/or a good interlinear scripture analyzer will help you to see the real words used by the author.

Which brings me to one last false pretense of the MEC. They teach that you can't keep the Law. The Law does not put additional burdens on you, it only limits certain bad behavior by you. Sure, you will sometimes fall selfishly into sin. But, as a Christian you do not have a license to commit sin. All sinful acts should not be tolerated within the body of true believers.

Before you can understand the love God has for you, you have to know and trust your Bible. Can you really trust what it is telling you? The answer is yes, but you may not like what it has to say. First, you have to throw off the trappings of modern Christianity that teach the Bible is a document that was penned by God Himself. It wasn't, but it is trustworthy if you understand its roots. You will have to use some common sense. God gave us creation. He is order. This means that He is the author of common sense. Why not allow your common sense to kick in as you read this book to learn more of how you should read His book, the Bible.

Where did it come from? How accurate is it? How can you be sure if what you are reading is what the original author wanted it to say? Once you have a good understanding of the material you can see what God is telling you.

When you have established what is truly authentic and a correct translation, ask yourself "Is the Bible the inerrant word of God?" You know, are there errors in the Bible and how does that affect the message? Why would a church teach it is inerrant, if it isn't?

Then ask yourself from what is documented in the New Testament, how did an early Christian live? Isn't that the way you should be living today? What did they hold sacred? Did the New Testament (letters) replace the Old Testament? Did they follow the teachings of the Old Testament?

These understandings (What is the accuracy of the Bible; is it inerrant; and how did the early church believe) will frame the rest of your ability to relate to God. Either your faith has a true foundation, or it is just non-factual unscripturally supported hope. It is kind of like the house built on a rock or the one built on the sand. Someone who wants a soft-gentle Christianity will jump straight to the chapters that interest them, but without a good foundation, they will probably learn very little.

Who are you trying to worship, God the Father, or Jesus Christ, or both? Are they the same? Is Jesus Christ God? When I pray, who am I praying too? Shouldn't I pray to Jesus? As a Christian, you should understand who the Christ is! What makes you think the Father, Son, and Holy Spirit are One? Is that scriptural? No. That is why it is an early chapter. You have to know who and why you worship, or it is little more than idolatry.

Once you have been grounded, you can look into questions that will haunt you as you read the Bible. After all, you are trying to live a life that is acceptable to God. You have to ask yourself: What is sin? Do I really have to keep the Law? What is living in sin? Is my present Christian walk taking Paul out of context? How do I know if I have eternal life? What ever happened to the Sabbath? Are Christians pre-tribulation?

All these are very plainly spelled out in the Bible. Unfortunately, true Christianity comes with obedience to God. After all, Christ was obedient unto death! But, obedience doesn't sell well in our out-of-control world. So, if you are not prepared to do a little "work" for God, or give up the sin in your life, put down this book and give it to another so-called Christian for a read.

Don't forget, it's not good enough for God that you just do the "works" that he has shown you in the Bible, you have to lovingly live them. If you read your Bible through a couple of times this will scream at you. The Book of Zechariah is the Old Testament book that foretells of Jesus riding into Jerusalem on an ass and a colt, the foal of an ass. As a super excited, over emotional Christian, does this book have relevance in your life? It should, it validates Jesus Christ's triumphal entry. But what else does this book teach?

Starting in Chapter 7, Zechariah has come before the Lord to ask about the fasts and feasts in various months of the year. God explains that He gets no joy out of them, because they are doing it for their own gratification. They have missed the heart issue God had intended.

What are you doing for God? Are your Christian activities something you are doing for God, or yourself? How can you feel you are saved by Grace and continue living a lifestyle that opposes those things God has made clear He expects from you? More importantly, if you are living those "works" He has ordained, do you do them lovingly, happily, and joyfully? Or, are they a burden to you?

So, are you a real Christian, living a life that is continuing to look for how God wants you to live and think, or are you just playing Christian, and doing the minimum you have been taught, and relying on the odd out-of-context verse that states that "Grace" is all you need?

Let's Talk Bible

Before a good salesman can sell a product, he should understand what he is trying to sell. Before a construction crew can build a house they should understand the plans. With this type of logic, how can a Christian claim the truths of the Bible if he or she is not familiar with the product or understands how it has ended up in their hands in it's final form?

The Bible is made up of a series of letters from various authors. The original writings had no punctuation. Punctuation was added much later. These letters were analyzed for authenticity years later and placed into the format we call the Bible, but people still try to add to or take away from these older manuscripts.

Haven't you ever wondered where it came from? Why are there so many different versions of the Bible if it is from God? If you don't know where it came from, how do you disregard, or worse, accept fantasy versions likes those found in books like the DaVince Code?

As stated earlier, I believe that a Christian needs to study the Bible for years before it will really come to life. This is a daily devotion that is led by a nondenominational theme, your Bible. Why not try reading it from cover to cover?

Once you have read it you will learn, if you have any retention, that it does disagree with itself. This is because the Bible is a human endeavor to put on paper what God has taught or spoken. The New and Old Testament will show to be in error. These errors might, or might not disagree with God's truths, but they are there if you take the time to look at them. There are passages and teachings that the author even tells you are not inspired.

These help you better understand that you cannot trust your salvation to a pet verse here and there, usually from Paul's writings. This is why I constantly try to reinforce that you need to read an entire letter in one sitting before you draw conclusions as to what the author is trying to say.

Understanding how we got to the document we have today should be important to those that calls themselves Christian. Understanding where the error potential is in this document will assist you in deducing what is true when there is a difference in scriptural verses.

Finally, learning different author's writing styles will help you better understand what they are trying to say. After all, Paul is the one author taken out of context more than any other. Once you learn to read all that Paul has to say about a subject you will better understand what he is really saying.

The following chapters will give you a jump start to better understand your Bible. You need to be like the Bereans as Paul explained in the Acts of the Apostles Chapter 17, verse 11. Read what I have to say and then judge it with the scriptures to see if it is true. Once you do you will better understand that the Bible isn't the inerrant word of God, some of the New Testament authors are more correct than others, and Paul is definitely taken out of context.

As a quick side note: Paul believed that a Christian would follow the Law, not for salvation, but as Christians he believed that you would not sin! You can't avoid sinning if you don't know the Law.

What is God's Word and How Should You Study It?

There are several resources I believe that you need to understand God's will in your life. You really need a good Bible, a concordance and an interlinear scripture analyzer. I never recommend reading a study Bible for understanding. Although mostly correct, they all slant towards the author's own desire for what they feel is meant by the scriptures. If someone has strong convictions, as I do, don't you think they will try to slant their writings to their beliefs?

With that said, am I going to try to convey to the reader what I want the Bible to say? I would not be human if I didn't. But, the difference is that I believe, and will prove, that the Bible has been taken out of context. My belief is that the "whole" Bible is important to you. All other Christian religions and authors do not believe this. All will say that they do, but then explain that some New Testament books have verbiage that releases "us" from following God's ordained direction. This direction could come from the New or Old Testament. Why not read the Bible for yourself and then you decide?

Your first and best resource to God's word is your Bible. Where did the information come from that has been translated into what we call the Bible? The Bible was made from taking the Old Testament (scriptures) and letters (epistles) written by New Testament apostles and then compiling the whole thing into one book. Most of what we call the Bible has been packaged together for about 1700 years, as we know it today, but was originally in Greek. The word "Bible" is the Greek word for "book."

We have some Greek and Hebrew texts of the books that make up the Bible. But, no original written material by the original authors has survived. Only copies, of copies, of the original letters. Early in Roman Catholic history, bishops got together to try to figure out what was authentic and what was fake. Since then many discoveries have shown that they were pretty good at their job.

Some of the earliest manuscript copies have been discovered in recent times. These prove that the original copies used were accurate. A great example of this is the Dead Sea Scrolls. But, without getting too deep, as I would prefer to be very shallow on the origin of each book, the earliest copies of the New Testament texts come from about the third century. These were compiled into a Greek text and then into various languages.

Christians kill me. They have so much faith in the book they call the Bible without even understanding where it comes from. Most, if not all Bibles have their roots in one of two compilations of the old Greek texts. These are the Textus Receptus (TR) and the Westcott and Hort (W&H). The TR was the first compilation of the Greek text put into a sellable format (its all about the money). Erasmus originally produced it, but he used very few original manuscripts and the oldest came from about the 10th century.

A compilation is just that. A studious individual or individuals find all the information about a subject and then compiles, or organizes it, into a single document. That is what the Bible is. The TR was our first compilation and was utilized for the King James Version (KJV) of the Bible. The W&H was out much later but was done with much more research. The W&H was a more thorough document using manuscripts back to (they believe) the 2nd century.

Go peruse the internet for yourself. The W&H is a much better compilation of the known scriptures than the TR. With that said, most Bibles that say they are based on the W&H are written in a softer gentler Christianity that is not in either compilation. For that reason, I read the KJV of the Bible and cross it with the W&H when there appears to be a scriptural contradiction.

Since we are talking about the Bible I use, what Bible is the right Bible for you to read? As stated earlier, the version I like most is the King James Version (KJV). He was an English King that commissioned this translation from Greek to English several hundred years ago. It is a bit of a hard read, but was considered the standard for years. It has gone through four major revisions improving the language.

Newer translations of the Bible are a better read, but most of them leave out the parts they don't like. The NIV Bible is notorious for this. I understand the Jehovah's Witness even wrote their own Bible so that it could be quoted as they saw fit (although it may be very close to the W&H compilation). The New King James Version is a little better read, but I have stuck with the original. After time, you will get used to the thee(s) and the thou(s).

Understanding that the KJV is based on the TR compilation of the Greek manuscripts may not make it the best Bible if you don't want to be misled a little.

I recommend that you read your Bible for at least 15 -30 minutes each day. I do it in the morning. Start in Genesis and work through Revelation. What then? Start all over. How many times? How about, until He calls you home? The more you read it the more you find both inconsistencies and constant chains of thought (threads). The threads help to reinforce those truths that you will hold to be "real truths."

Those inconsistencies will lead you to research why there appears to be "problems" with the text. It took me 10 years of earnest reading my Bible before I really started noticing problems that I had to understand. After understanding the history of the Bible and the Roman Catholic Church's (as well as newer Protestant religions) influence a little, you will be able to better understand what is real scripture, written by the original author, and what has been added or changed by the translator(s).

A great example of a thread found throughout the Bible is that the husband and wife are "entwined as one." God never separates the husband and wife union. Do you remember Job? He was a righteous man found in the Old Testament scriptures. God allowed Satan to take "all that he hath; only upon himself put not forth thy hand." God allowed Satan to take all his worldly possessions, even his children and his health. But Job still had his wife.

This thread appears broken in the New Testament when Jesus states in Matthew 19:29, "And everyone that hath forsaken houses, or brethren, or sisters, or father, or mother, or wife, or children, or lands for my name sake, shall receive an hundred fold, and shall inherit everlasting life." It appears that the wife is just something else that man can "leave or discard" for Christ. But, if you look the text up in the old original Greek, the word "wife" is not mentioned. Yes, it was added to our modern translations.

Another great example of just plain adding words to the text is found in 1 John 5:7-8. Read it in your Bible. Most will read as follows: "For there are three that bear record in heaven, the Father, the Word, and the Holy Ghost: and these three are one. For there are three that bare witness in earth, the Spirit, and the water, and the blood: and these three agree in one. (KJV)." Doesn't that sound like it gives conclusive proof to the existence of the "trinity?"

It has been in the King James Version and most other Bibles since they were printed in English for several hundred years. But, the original text doesn't really say that. The added words are: "in heaven, the Father, the Word, and the Holy Ghost: and these three are one." They were added in the Textus Receptus (TR) compilation. All the original manuscripts only show that there are three that bare witness in earth: "the Spirit, the water, and the blood." The trinity "stuff" isn't mentioned because there isn't a trinity!

The above wording (John 5:7-8) was in the Latin texts of the day when Erasmus wrote the TR, but when researched in the original Greek, these words just weren't and still aren't there. Even Erasmus explained this. The Latin was a liberal translation from the Greek by the Roman Catholic Church. Why would the extra words have been added to it? The Roman Catholic Church had elevated Jesus Christ to God and needed proof texts.

Later, better, compilations of the Greek texts (W&H) have removed this and other added passages from the previously accepted biblical text. Newer Bibles that use these compilations and look at the old manuscripts for themselves show the same. The Good News Bible shows the wording of this one example properly (although I do not recommend this translation). So, once you have learned that your Bible is a compilation of old Greek texts, how do you tell if the printed word is what the author wanted it to say?

A good start is to get a really good concordance. I use the Strong's latest revision. A concordance will help you understand the translation better. If you come to a passage like "the first day of the week" (presumably Sunday) you can look up each word to see how they got to that translation. It is kind of like a translation dictionary. You can see the translation of each word of the biblical text from their original Greek or Hebrew words. Then you can see how the translators translated the same Greek/Hebrew word later in the Bible. Many times it is different.

If something in the New Testament sounds too much like it was trying to fit into a controlling monarch's or papal web, you have to look it up to see if the translation is accurate. As I am reading, especially the New Testament, and come to a passage that seems to disagree with another passage in scripture, I look critically at the action words used in the passage. It is an easy process to look them up in a concordance. I've heard that there are 6 mistranslated passages in the King James Version of the Bible. That's ridiculous, I'm sure there are hundreds, if not thousands. Many of which were done purposefully to suit the translator's wishes.

Here is a really good example of mistranslated words: In Acts Chapter 12, verse 4, you find Peter is in prison and scheduled to be executed after "Easter." This sentence adds validity to Easter as a real Christian holiday. But the writer of the Book of Acts wasn't writing about Easter at all. The word Easter was translated from the Greek word "pascha." Pascha is the Greek word for Passover. It is used 28 other times in the New Testament and it is always translated into Passover.

Why did the translators translate the Greek word "pascha" into the English word "Easter" in Acts Chapter 12, verse 4? Because the Church of England had it's roots from the Roman Catholic Church. Easter was a combined celebration from Christian values in Christ and pagan beliefs back in the 3rd century. The people of England had celebrated Easter for years. They had to throw it in somewhere to show its significance.

Look at the word "charity." What does it mean to you? It is used a dozen times in the New Testament. Take the line from Paul in 1 Corinthians Chapter 13, verse 13, "Faith, hope and charity, the greatest of these is charity." Doesn't it sound like you should be taking care of the poor? Well, you should take care of the poor, but that is not what he is stating.

If it looks wrong, look it up. In all cases where the New Testament translators used the word charity, it is the Greek word "agape." Yes, that is the very word we say is the "Love of God," and it is translated into "love" in 57 other places in the New Testament. So, Paul really stated: Faith, Hope and "God's Love," but the greatest of these is God's Love. Now that makes sense.

Greek is a very specific language that has several times as many words as the English language. So, there should really only be one English word for each Greek word. Take the word we call Love. There are three levels of love in the Greek vocabulary. This is important to know, because it shows you that the translators are guessing sometimes as to the meaning of an old Greek word. The Westcott and Hort compilation only used one English word for each Greek word encountered.

With the Bible and concordance alone you will begin to understand that the Bible has been mistranslated in many passages. Remember that a concordance is looking at the Greek compilation for the Bible you are referencing. The Strong's that I use is for the King James Version. It will be based on the TR. If the TR is a bad translation for that passage, then the concordance can be a little misleading.

If you don't mind a little challenge, try an interlinear scripture analyzer. This is your third resource. You can find them hardbound, but there is a very good one on the web that is free at the time of this book's original release (www.scriptures4all.org). This is an awesome resource. It will give you the original Greek and Hebrew words in their native symbols and the English words for that symbol (ie. Alpha and Omega). It then gives you the translated words to each of the original words (ie. Alpha = First alphabetical letter; and Omega = last alphabetical letter), followed by the translated passage. The above interlinear scripture analyzer is based on the W&H Greek compilation.

Take an earlier passage I quoted "the first day of the week". You will find it several times in the New Testament and is accepted to mean "Sunday" by modern Christians. Go look it up for yourself. It is two Greek words "heis" and "sabbaton". Heis is almost always translated into "first" or "one". "Sabbaton" is the word Sabbath. Everywhere that you find the word "Sabbath" it is the Greek word sabbaton. You really need to look up those scriptures that appear to contradict God's Law of the Old Testament.

Speaking of research, the Internet can be your friend. Once you have a biblical basis to stand on, you need the resources provided by the Internet to better research each problem area. I use it often after I have read. A lot of information out there is just plain junk, but every now and then you may find a jewel.

I need to throw in something here about the "Gnostic gospels." You know the "Book of Mary" and others. Dan Brown (who appears to be trying to start some sort of religious movement) uses these heavily in fictional works like "The Da Vinci Code". Do some research for yourself on the Internet. The Gnostic Gospels were written starting about 300 AD.

The Gnostic gospels were fiction themselves, trying to denigrate the known epistles (New Testament). How could someone who lived several hundred years later than an event write a first-hand experience? They are just fictional stories that the Gnostic author would have liked to be true, but they weren't! Do your research!

In a nutshell, read your Bible from front to back, without skipping a thing. If you come to a verse that seems out of place, look up the words and see why it doesn't fit. All the truths will line up. If there appears to be a contradiction in Biblical truths, it will be a translator error or addition if it does not line up completely with the rest of scripture. And, if your present Christian walk contradicts the Bible, something has to give. Either change your walk, or throw out the Bible and stop calling yourself a Christian.

One last thought, the most important thing you can do to understand God's word is to pray before you begin to study, and have Him earnestly help you understand His will for your life! You will find over and over in the scriptures that all knowledge and wisdom comes from God. So, why not ask Him for it!

Is the Bible the Inerrant Word of God?

Before you answer this question, have you ever thoroughly read your Bible from front to back completely? Did you give it a critical read? If you haven't, then you should not even give comment to the inerrancy of the scriptures. Once you have completely read the Bible through, did you ask yourself, why are there inconsistencies in the Bible?

Let's look at it a little differently before we get into the issue. If you want to believe in creation, can your belief convince an evolutionist that his view is incorrect? No. Can an evolutionist convince a creationist that his view is incorrect? No. Why? Because both believe that what they believe is founded in fact and the other view is fantasy. But neither belief can truly be proven with facts. They are both beliefs.

I believe in creation because "I believe." Some Christians believe that the Bible is the inerrant word of God, written by the pen of God through a man's hand. But this again is not a fact, just a belief, but unlike creation it can be shown to be wrong.

There are inconsistencies throughout the Bible, but mainly in the New Testament. Face it, it just disagrees with itself. How can an inerrant word of God be inconsistent? It can't if it is inerrant. The Bible is not inerrant. That is just a new saying by so-called Christian leaders trying to control their flocks with a few pet verses. Take the New Testament. It is basically believed to be a series of letters written by God-fearing and inspired men, but their pen could not have been guided directly by the Holy Spirit, or there wouldn't be errors.

If I can prove this to be true, should this shake your faith in the relevance of the Bible in your life? No, it just demonstrates that God expects you to continue to study to understand what He is trying to teach you through these many writers. Start with the question, "have you ever thoroughly read the Bible." If you are a Christian you should be looking for a closer relationship with God the Father and His Son Jesus Christ. How can you claim that you are a Christian if you have not taken the time to try reading the only words written that will cement your relationship?

Why would all the modern churches of today teach that it is the inerrant word of God if it isn't? The answer is "control." If they can quote a few verses (from the "so-called" inerrant word) here and there to make their point, then they can convince you that they are the leaders of the flock and you should continue following them. And oh yes, don't forget to pay your tithes. But, what about the other words (in the scriptures) that teach contrary to their doctrine? They skillfully walk around them. If you attend church, any church, you will never be taught the doctrine of the Bible.

Let's hit this inerrant Word of God head on.

What is meant when Christians state that the Bible is the inerrant word of God? I have heard it stated that the Bible is written with a man's hand, but guided by the Holy Ghost. It is explained in evangelical circles that it is infallible and each jot and tittle (Hebrew punctuation) are placed there on purpose by the hand of God. Nothing is out of place. Surely one would attest to the fact that with time the truths and stories of the Bible are being proven correct. Many worldly scholars of times past stated that people like King Nebuchadnezzar never existed, only to find artifacts found in our lifetime that attest to the credibility of the Bible.

Before we go on any further with this discussion, I must warn you of the Modern Evangelical Church (MEC) shuffle. This is where they tap dance around an issue that could be a little painful if truly investigated. They look at verses they like as "literal" and others that contradict their doctrine as some sort of allegorical comparison. The problem with this type of hunt and peck for your scriptures is that it makes it a little like the way a lawyer prefers to look at the law-his way.

I have heard it stated that if there is even one error, a Christian would not know what parts to believe and/or disbelieve. I have had a woman almost sobbing over the fact that any error would leave her devastated. These are unfortunate conclusions raised by people that should know better or for some reason they refuse to accept the truth when they read their Bible.

Truth is true. Inerrant literally means "without error." I guess it depends on what your definition of an error is. Haven't you ever wondered why they call the science of defending Christian values, Apologetics? It's because they should be apologizing instead of making an excuse for taking the Bible out of context. You can't have it both ways. Either the Holy Spirit penned the Bible through man and you have no errors, or the Holy Spirit didn't. If there are errors in the text, then it wasn't actually written by God, but by Spirit-filled men, who do occasionally make mistakes.

I need to add this one thought right here. How accurate of a Bible translation do you have in your hand? Let's say the Bible author's pen was guided by God's hand. Is that what you are reading? It is an emphatic no! The oldest copies of manuscripts that we have today come from around the second to fourth century. None of the early manuscripts line up exactly, and none are complete. In fact, these are rewrites by monks of the Roman Catholic Church. Do you think a monk of the Church would leave in passages that were forbidden by the Pope? Many of the passages that you have in your Bible have been added and can't be found in the early manuscripts.

If this is true, and I will show that it is, how can it be the inerrant word of God? Most Bibles have their roots in one of two Greek compilations of the early manuscripts. As stated in the previous chapter, they are the Textus Receptus (TR) and the Westcott and Hort (W&H). The King James is TR, but the WH is much more accurate. If the W&H is much more accurate, then what makes you believe that the King James could be the inerrant word of God?

I believe and will show you that the Bible isn't inerrant, but it was penciled by man. They were Spirit-filled men. Errors do exist, but not in the truths. When a writer of the Bible is in vision, I believe the message is error free, but there are even errors in the visions. More importantly, the facts and truths do not contradict one another. The advantage of understanding that it was Spirit-filled men who do error, is that it limits the damage that the MEC does by taking a single verse out of context and building doctrine on it, usually from the apostle Paul.

Even Paul states in his writings at times, that he is writing to them as a man (Romans 3:5), but one that is inspired (1 Corinthians 7:25-40). These types of statements leave room for error in the scriptures. In the Book of 1 Corinthians, Paul tells the church at Corinth how to handle a matter with a man that is sleeping with his father's wife. In II Corinthians, he explains that he was too harsh about how he told them to handle the matter in his first correspondence. So, if the Bible is the inerrant word of God, with the same sinful matter happening in the MEC, would we handle it the way it is explained in I or II Corinthians?

Neither; the MEC would say it's OK if they love each other and keep paying tithe (just kidding). But the reality is that you really don't know, because there are two different responses explained by Paul for the same sin. This simple fact demonstrates that you can't just take one set of verses to build doctrine. And, one or the other of Paul's statements is correct. As he had two different judgments for the same sin, one is in error.

To be inerrant, the entire scriptures would have to carry the same message. **ALL**, not most, would have to be in agreement. If it states that $2 + 2 = 4$, everywhere that you have t $2 + 2$, it must equal 4. The teaching must be the same, or one is in error and hence not inerrant. There are too many examples of the non-inerrancy of the scripture.

What about when Paul was writing in II Timothy Chapter 3, verses 16-17 and he states that "all scripture is given by inspiration of God, and is profitable for doctrine, for reproof, for correction, for instruction in righteousness: that the man of God may be perfect, thoroughly furnished unto all good works?"

Modern Christianity tries to hang your salvation on Paul's previous verse along with a few he wrote that appear to say "Saved by Grace no matter what." After all, they teach Grace overshadows everything else in the New and Old Testament.

If you believe this MEC teaching, you have already shown the Bible not to be inerrant. Take the few passages by Paul that they want to take out of context, when teaching that all you have to say is "Lord, forgive me for my sins and dwell in my heart (or however they want to state it that day)." The MEC teaches that this is all you have to do to be saved. Presto you are in "saved" company. No one can take it away from you. You can't be unsaved if you want to be. Its interesting, this warm and fuzzy feeling of free security is contrary to everything that the Bible teaches us.

But, this teaching is in direct disagreement with the rest of the Bible authors. Even Jesus Christ stated, "If you love me keep my commandments." But to an evangelical, keeping His commandments would be doing "works." And if you are doing works you are committing heresy to the MEC.

To a MEC, there is no Sabbath of God (4th commandment), you are not limited in your diet (Food Laws), and there are no consequences to your current sinning. These teachings about scripture run totally opposed to the end time prophecy found in both the New and Old Testament. You really won't know until you have taken the time to read your Bible from front to back and then start over again.

Let's just look at scripture. The Old Testament has fewer errors than the New Testament. Compare II Kings Chapter 8, verse 26 and II Chronicles Chapter 22, verse 2. Both these passages tell the age of King Ahaziah when he became the King of Judah. If you note the verses before and after this passage you will understand that it is the same King with the same mother, Athaliah, and father, King Jehoram (King of Judah) and he only reigned in Judah for one year. How old was he when he began to reign?

Go figure, it's a different age in both accounts. In the Book of Kings he is 22 years old and in II Chronicles he is 42 when he assumes the throne. Moreover, what makes it worse, in the Book of II Chronicles it states that all of King Jehoram's sons are killed except Jehoahaz. This is found in II Chronicles Chapter 21 verse 17. So there are two errors in very few verses.

Surely, if the Holy Spirit had penned it through the author, He (Holy Spirit) would have the king's age correct. What this tells you is not to accept everything blindly. Should this crush your belief in the Bible? No, just note that some errors are present, and thus it is not inerrant. This one set of errors alone makes the scriptures in error. Why is it so hard for modern Christians to understand that the Bible was written by godly men, but men just the same and able to error? This is an easy error to find, as it is a direct contradiction to itself! If either book had not been written, who would have known?

Take cherubims. What do they look like, or does it matter? In Revelation Chapter 4 you see four of them before the throne of God. They each have just one head with one face. One has the head of a lion, one a calf, one a man, and one an eagle; and they each have six wings. In Ezekiel Chapter 1 you see the cherubims, each with four faces: the ox, man, lion, and eagle; and they have six wings. These are similar, but different as Ezekiel sees them with four different faces each.

Here is the kicker. In Ezekiel Chapter 10 he again sees the same cherubims, and states so. But, this time they have the faces of a cherub, a man, a lion, and an eagle. This time they only have 4 wings. So, were they the same cherubims he saw in the earlier vision? Something is wrong as the faces have changed and now they have less wings, but he states that they are the same!

Was Moses a Prophet? Of course he was, and Jesus quotes him. The Bible states that Moses walked with God, and he was a friend of God. But, did Moses get it right on all that he wrote? God tells his prophets of things, or to do things, but sometimes they get it wrong. Why do you think God warned Moses to build the temple as he was shown on the mountain? Because we (humans) seem to leave out important parts, by accident or purposefully. Moses obviously got inspiration from God, but still wrote things that have errors.

You may have to do a little math to get some of the following, but don't you want to know if the Bible is the "inerrant" word of God? How old was Joseph when his mother Rachel died? If you turn to Genesis Chapter 31, verse 38 you will learn that Jacob, his father, lived with Nahor, his mother's father, for 20 years and in that time Jacob didn't have any children with Rachel until the very end. (Genesis Chapters 29-30).

After leaving Nahor, Jacob and his family, including Joseph lived for a short time near Shechem and then moved through Bethel to Ephrath. But during the short commute Rachel died during childbirth to Benjamin. (Genesis 34-35). So Joseph had to be quite young. Now read Genesis 37.

Joseph is 17 and has visions where all 11 of his brothers and his mom and dad give obeisance to him. His father even clarifies through a rebuke that his mother would be bowing down to him. Remember his mother died during childbirth to Benjamin, the eleventh brother. Can the dead bow down to someone that is alive? Both visions show that Joseph has 11 brothers, but his mom supposedly died several chapters earlier in the Book of Genesis, during the childbirth to Benjamin, the last of the 11 brothers, yet she is mentioned here!

Wouldn't you think Moses would know his own lineage? Before we work this one, do you know how long the Children of Israel were in Egypt? It was 430 years. How old was Moses when he brought them out of Egypt? He was 80 years old. So he was born when the Children of Israel had been in Egypt for 350 years. How many years did Levi live after he entered Egypt? It was less than 80 years as he died at 137 years old, and he was a much older man than Joseph, who was about 40 years old when he invited his family to come to Egypt.

Who was Moses' mother's father? Well we know that Moses' mother was Jochebed. Read Numbers Chapter 26, verses 58 and 59. It states that Jochebed was " the daughter of Levi whom bare to Levi in Egypt." Ok, the word daughter could be used for anyone on the lineage, i.e., we are sons of Abraham. But the passage states that Jochebed was bare to Levi while he was in Egypt. The word "bare" is the Hebrew word "yalad." It literally means to be "born" to someone, and we know that she was born in Egypt.

It is the same word used to show the direct birth of Cain, Abel, and just about everyone in the Old Testament. If the word "yalad" hadn't been used, then you could make the case that she was a descendent, but you can't. That would have made Jochebed a very old lady when she had Moses, something like 250 years old (plus). Do I really think that Jochebed was born to Levi while he lived in Egypt? From the age it doesn't make sense, but the word yalad was used in the sentence and probably shouldn't have been. But, if you want to say that it is the inerrant word of God, you have a problem.

To be plainer, read Exodus Chapter 6, verses 16-20. You will read that Levi has three sons, one being Kohath who lived a total of 133 years. Kohath has 4 sons, one being Amram who lived 137 years. In verse 20 it states: " And Amram took him Jochebed his father's sister to wife and she bare him Aaron and Moses..." This verse confirms to you that Jochebed was Levi's daughter!

If you haven't worked out the problem, it is something like this; Levi came to Egypt 430 years before Moses leads them out! How could Levi be Moses' grandfather? Forget about the fact that his father is Amram. Take Moses through his mother directly to Levi. Moses is what we call a direct grandson to Levi. Just by the ages that they all lived, Jochebed had to be somewhere around 300 years old when she gave birth to Moses! Something is polluted. It can't be factual. It is in error or better put, not inerrant.

How many years did David rule Israel? Does it matter? Only if you want to say that the Holy Spirit penned the scriptures. In 1 Chronicles Chapter 29, verse 27 it states that David ruled seven years in Hebron and 33 years he reigned in Jerusalem, for a total of 40 years. But, if you read II Samuel Chapters 12–15 you will find the story of David's son Absalom after David's affair with Bath-Sheba. So, this places him many years into his reign.

Absalom was already a grown man, and his half-brother had raped his sister. Absalom flees the country after he murders his half brother, but returns later. In II Samuel Chapter 15, verse 7 you learn that after all this, Absalom sat in the gate and judged the people and stole their hearts for **40 years** before he tried to overthrow King David. It was still several years after that before Solomon assumed the throne. Read II Samuel Chapters 11-15. It is in order of events. Yes, David probably ruled in Israel for 40 years, but that makes the statement about Absalom sitting in the gates and judging the people for 40 years to be false. Oh yes, that would make the scriptures to be in error.

Look you can't have it both ways. Either the Holy Spirit guided the hands of the writers of the Bible, or it was written by Spirit-filled men that did make errors.

Then there are the crossover verses between the New and Old Testament. If you are a New Testament Christian then you would surely trust that Steven was a prophet. It states in Acts Chapter 6, verse 8 that he "was full of faith and power, did great wonders and miracles among the people." He was our first martyr.

When Steven was before the Jewish council in Acts Chapter 7, he explains that Abraham lived with his father (Terah) until Terah's death and then moved to the land where the Jews now live. Some time after, God gives Abraham the covenant of circumcision, and later yet he begat Isaac. Pretty straight forward, but is it? Remember, all this is in the Book of Acts and a direct quote from Steven.

Moses also told us the same story about Abraham but one of them got it wrong. Both these men received power to perform miracles and yet one of them had an incorrect vision about Abraham. This knowledge had to be from vision as this had happened many, many years before, so how else would they have known if God had not told them?

According to Moses, Terah was Abraham's father who had three children by the time he was 70 years old. Abraham was one of them and you learn of it in Genesis Chapter 11, verse 26. Abraham then took his nephew Lot and his wife Sarah and wandered around Canaan for some time before he had his sons Ishmael and Isaac.

How old was Abraham when Isaac was born? In Genesis 21:5 you will learn that Moses wrote that Abraham was 100 years old at Isaac's birth. But if you jump back to Genesis Chapter 11, verse 32 you will learn that Terah did not die until he was 205 years old.

So, according to Steven's recount, if Abraham lived with his father until Terah died, this would mean that Abraham had to be at least 135 years old before his father died! How could he be 135 years old before he started his wanderings in Canaan and then many years later have a son when he is only 100 years old?

Does this make Moses or Steven wrong? Someone is wrong. Can the Holy Spirit guide a Bible author's hand and yet still make errors? No, of course not. It just shows that the Lord gave the revelation of history, and one of His prophets didn't get it down on papyrus too accurately. What does this prove? Only that the Bible is not error free.

Daniel is a real important book of faith. It shows that if you truly trust God and live in His righteous lifestyle you will be delivered from sin. But the book has errors. Chapter 1 states that Daniel and his four friends are in training for three years. The chapter explains that after this three year period, this is the first time Daniel is presented to King Nebuchadnezzar and is found to be wiser than all other wise men. But Chapter 2 states that Daniel interprets the dream of Nebuchadnezzar in the second year of Nebuchadnezzar's reign, and the king promotes him above all others in his realm.

How could this be, when you read that Jerusalem didn't fall until Nebuchadnezzar was already King of Babylon, and sometime after the fall Daniel was in training for three years just to learn the language? How could Daniel not be known to the king for three years, yet interpret a dream and be promoted in his first or second year of captivity?

It shows that Spirit-filled men wrote with some inaccuracy or the "word" we feel written by them was polluted over the years. If you accept either, then you have to conclude that it is not inerrant and you can't rest your salvation on one or two pet verses and be secure. After all, those pet phrases that seem to be out of context with a God that hates sin, could be polluted. You have to read the whole Bible and look for the bigger picture that God has painted for you.

Let's look at the New Testament. One of the best ways to show the Bible is not inerrant is to use the four Gospels. They all tell the story of Jesus Christ's life on Earth. There are many apologetics as to why they tell different stories of the same event, but any way you want to cut it, they tell different stories. If one author says it was three figs, and another author says it was two figs, then one author is incorrect, and thus, not inerrant. Better stated; not written directly by the Hand of God!

Were any of the Gospels written completely first-hand? You know, the author actually saw the event? Of course not. Matthew in the book of Matthew doesn't start following Jesus until Chapter 9. Mark wasn't even one of the 12 apostles that walked with Jesus. Luke was said to be a Gentile physician, so he definitely would not have been in Jesus' presence, and John doesn't meet Jesus until after His baptism.

We will discuss why each gospel is different in depth in the next chapter, but for the purpose of this chapter we will use several examples from them to show that they were not penned by the Holy Spirit. After all, if the Holy Spirit penned them, then they would give the same account, but they don't!

I wrote my second book on this very subject. It was intended to be an expasion of this chapter and is titled, *The New Testament: The Facts and the Fiction*. It was intended to show the differences between the Gospels and the Book of Acts to better understand the Life of Jesus and the early church. It is a very critical look that is time sequenced according to each author. What I learned was shocking, but that is a different book with a different focus. As stated earlier in this book we are focusing on what the present Bible, that you hold in your hand, actually has printed.

When Jesus Christ was baptized, did He immediately go to the wilderness to be tested by Satan? It really depends on what account you read. Read Matthew Chapters 3 and 4, Mark Chapter 1, Luke Chapters 3-4, and then John Chapter 1. In Matthew, Mark, and Luke the Spirit led Him into the wilderness immediately after the baptism. In John, the story has a very different turn. Up to verse 29 is a time before John the Baptist baptized Jesus. Verses 29-34 are of the day of the baptism. Verses 35 and on is the day after Jesus was baptized. But in John's account, Jesus never went into the wilderness. The following day after His baptism is when He meets two of his disciples and starts preaching.

Here is the problem. How many of the Gospel writers even know who Jesus is at the time of His baptism? Zero! Where did they get the first hand story of all things before this time? Who knows, but it couldn't be God as all four Gospels are so different. It was just hearsay. How can you make doctrine on it?

Speaking of Jesus' disciples, who were the first disciples of Jesus Christ, and how did Jesus meet them? Look at John Chapter 1 again. In this account it is plain that two (Andrew and another) came to Jesus to "ask of Him." Then, Andrew brought his brother Simon (Peter) to come along. This is still at the Jordan River. Look at the other three Gospels. Remember Jesus walking along the beach and making them fishers of men? What account is correct? Since John was supposed to be one of the fishermen who were called in the first three Gospels, don't you think he would have remembered how he met the Lord? They definitely don't line up. In fact, they are totally in disagreement with each other!

OK, they aren't quite exact. Why should that matter? It does if you want to build a doctrine on a single set of verses in the New Testament. Take the Book of John. "In the beginning was the word...." The first five verses of this book are used by the MEC to show that Jesus has been around as long as the Father has. To the MEC, the Father and Son are the same God. Just one big God, that also came to live on earth. But, these verses can only be doctrine if there are no errors. But John is at odds with the other gospels on many occasions. Although off topic, you may want to read *What Is the Trinity?*, found later in this book.

How many times did the rooster crow before Peter realized that he had betrayed the Lord? Does it matter? Only if you want to conclude the Bible is inerrant. Remember, to be inerrant the stories must all line up. In Matthew, Luke and John the rooster crows after Peter's third denial. But in Mark Chapter 14 Christ prophesies that the rooster will crow twice before the third denial. And in Mark it does. Once after Peter's first denial and once after the third denial, thus the rooster crows twice.

Here is the problem. In Luke Chapter 22 Christ prophesies that: "The cock will not crow this day until you have denied me thrice." This would mean that the cock would never have crowed, ever again, if Peter had not denied him three times. But in Mark the rooster did crow only after one denial. So, if the rooster "really" crowed after the first denial, that makes the other three gospels wrong! Or, it only crowed once after the third denial making the Book of Mark wrong! Either way, one or more is in error.

Do these stories line up? Not totally, but enough to understand that Jesus foretold of Peter's denial and a rooster was used to illustrate his shortcomings. But the two stories do contradict each other. In fact, since the rooster crowed after the first denial in Mark, it makes the Lord's words in the other three Gospels FALSE. And, this would be a problem if the Holy Spirit had penned the scriptures. But, the Holy Spirit didn't. They were penned by Spirit-filled men many years after the occurrence.

In Matthew Chapter 8 you read of two stories. The first is Jesus healing the centurion's servant and the second is Jesus casting out the legion of devils into the swine. In the past I have heard pastors tell these stories from the other accounts in the New Testament where they are similar, but yet different. They usually close with something like this, these stories, although not quite the same show…blah, blah, blah. Think what they are saying. They have already shown that the Bible is not inerrant. You don't remember the stories? Read Matthew Chapter 8.

In the story of the centurion, he is a man of the greatest faith in all of Judea and yet was a Roman, not a Jew or even a follower of Christ. He personally comes to Jesus to plead for the health of his servant. But in Luke Chapter 7 the centurion doesn't come to Jesus, but sends friends to Him. I like both stories and they are of the same event, but did the centurion come to Jesus, or did he send a friend?

Compare Matthew Chapter 8 and Luke Chapter 8. In Matthew we see Jesus casting out the legion of devils into the pigs. It was at the country of the Gergesenes, right after He stilled the winds with His command while the disciples are in the boat. There are two men possessed with devils, and after Jesus casts out the devils, the people of Gergesenes ask Him to leave their shores. In Luke Chapter 8 you will read how Jesus after stilling the wind lands at the country of the Gadarenes. He finds a certain man that is possessed with a legion of devils and He casts them into the pigs and they run down the hillside and die in the sea. The local people ask Him to leave and He does.

First, if you read the preface to both stories you will have to conclude that they are the same story. The two peoples, Gadarenes and Gergesenes could be the same so I won't argue that point, but was it one or two men that were possessed by the devils? You haven't a clue! Does it matter? Not to me, because I know the Bible was written by Spirit-filled men and errors are present. But the story still carries the same message. The advantage that I have over someone who feels the Bible is inerrant, is I can't be fooled into accepting sin in my life with passages like "I can do all things." I understand that you can't take a line here and there from the New Testament and live by them, especially if they are contradictory to the Old Testament.

Compare Matthew Chapter 9 and Luke Chapter 9. Jairus is a very important man that wants Jesus to heal his daughter. When Jairus finds Jesus, does Jairus believe that his daughter is dead or alive? In Matthew he asked Jesus to bring his daughter back to life (i.e. she is dead). In Luke we don't see a report of her death until verse 49 where it states, "while He yet spake, there cometh one from the ruler's house, saying to him, Thy daughter is dead, trouble not the Master."

These stories display a hugely different level of faith, although only subtly. In Matthew, Jesus is asked to bring back the dead, and he agrees. In Mark, Jesus is only asked to heal a very sick young girl. Once the girl is dead, Jesus reassures Jairus that He can still deal with the situation, and does. Even though the outcome is the same, they are very different stories and levels of faith. According to the Books of Matthew, Mark and Luke, Jews had seen healings before, but in Matthew's account, you have Jairus asking Jesus to bring back the dead.

Did Jesus eat the Passover with the disciples? Of course not. He was our Passover and was in the grave over this festival. But if you read the first three gospels they will either lead you to believe that the Last Supper was the Passover or state that it was, and Jesus partakes of it with them. Read the Book of John on this topic. I cover this topic in a later chapter, but John Chapter 18, verse 28, shows very clearly that the day they brought Jesus before Pilot to crucify him was the preparation day of the Passover. Which book of the Bible is correct?

John states boldly that it is the day before Passover. The other three gospels lead you to believe the Last Supper was the Passover. To be the inerrant word of God, they should all agree, but they don't.

Look, who was at the cross when Jesus was crucified anyways? John and Mary the mother of Christ are the only two mentioned in the accounts. Yet in John's account you don't read the multiple statements that are attested to be Jesus' last words. You don't hear the two thieves talking to Jesus. In fact, in John's account, Jesus carried his own cross to the crucifixion. In the other gospels you find someone else taking the cross to Calvary. What account is correct? Since John was there, I would trust him more. By the way, in John's account of the gospels, Peter didn't walk on water! Don't you think that if you were there and saw someone walking on water, when you were telling the story, would you leave something so supernatural out?

Let's look at more advanced Biblical truths. Do you believe Christ died for your sins, was buried and then rose again on the third day, ascended to heaven and now sits at the right hand of God? If you are a Christian you should. But what actually happened at the tomb and who broke the news to the believers that Jesus Christ had risen from the dead?

Look at Matthew Chapter 28, Mark Chapter 16, Luke Chapter 24 and John Chapter 20. They all start with Mary or They... then the story changes. In Matthew they find the tomb open with an angel sitting on the rolled away stone who proceeded to explain what has happened to Jesus. In Mark they find a man sitting inside the tomb. In Luke it is two men in shining garments that break the news. Lastly in John, it is none other than Jesus who breaks the news to Mary that He has risen. Which account is correct? They are all completely different.

If you think that is bad, look at what happens afterwords as to the recount of the ascension and compare it to the first chapter in the Book of Acts. In Matthew, Jesus only appears to them at a Mountain in Galilee. Whatever happened to the two meetings in the inner room or the assention from the Mount of Olives?

Whatever happened to Judas and the betrayal money? You know, the apostle that betrayed the Lord. Read Matthew Chapter 27, verses 3-8. It is clear from that passage that he repented of the sin and threw the money back at the Jewish leaders. Then he hung himself, and the Jewish leaders bought a field for the burial of foreigners with the money. Now read Acts Chapter 1, verses 16-19. Here is an account where Judas actually bought the field and then "fell head-long and burst asunder." Which one is correct? Who knows; they are totally different!

Did the Bible writers lie about the accounts? I'm sure they did not. They all died for their Lord and they all wrote of the memory they had of Him, but they all wrote in a human fashion. All correct in their own minds and all probably a little bit off. One of them could be 100% correct, but that makes the others in error. It can't be "inerrant" if there is even one error.

Maybe errors like these were guided by the Holy Spirit to ensure MECs can't take single verses out of context. Remember, in the Old Testament you needed two or three witnesses before you could testify to put someone to death. We are talking about eternal life. Are you willing to place your eternal life in the hands of one author (who in my opinion is taken out of context)?

The reason why the MECs want you to believe that the Bible is inerrant is to be able to take Paul's odd verse here and there out of context. If the Bible is inerrant, then these (out of context) verses must be true. Verses like…I can do all things…once in his hand you can't get out… Verses that back up once-saved-always-saved.

Sometimes even Old Testament prophecies are used out of context by New Testament Bible authors (or we may not have all the manuscripts that they were referring too). Take the name Emmanuel (God is with us) or Immanuel. We sing this name in many Christian songs. Immanuel is foretold in the Old Testament. The name is mentioned only twice and both times by Isaiah. Emmanuel (spelled with an "E" as it in in the New Testament) is not mentioned in any Old Testament scripture that we have today. Matthew quotes these passages (Isaiah, we think) as a foretelling of Jesus Christ, but it is spelled Emmanuel by Matthew. These are the only three times the word Emmanuel (or Immanuel) is used, but what did Isaiah say the "Immanuel" being was?

Let's look at the scripture. In Isaiah Chapter 7, verse 14 "Therefore, the Lord Himself will give you a sign; Behold a virgin shall conceive, and bear a son, and shall call his name Immanuel." Again the name is repeated in Chapter 8, verse 8. But if you read the prophecy starting in Isaiah Chapter 7 and ending in Isaiah Chapter 8 you will understand what God was about to do to the nation Israel. They were about to be destroyed. The nation of Judah was under attack from both Israel and Assyria.

God gave the prophesy to King Ahaz of Judah as proof that his kingdom would not fall to Israel and Assyria. Then, all that was predicted by God happened. There is even an account of a prophetess giving birth to a child in the leading up to the overthrow of Israel! So the prophesy was to reassure King Ahaz that all would be OK. After all, God just did something that was impossible (the virgin birth), so don't worry about a few adversaries. What good would a prophesy be to a king that went something like this: "Don't worry about the present concern. After all in about 400 years I will do something amazing."

By the way, the prophecy stated that the virgin would conceive a son and his <u>NAME</u> would be called "Immanuel." When the Angel appeared to Joseph and Mary, the angel told them to <u>name</u> the baby "Jesus" not Immanuel. So, was Emmanuel supposed to be Jesus? Matthew appears to be telling you that Emmanuel of Isaiah's prophecy is Jesus, but there is no other mention of this anywhere else in the New Testament.

He pulls another stretch of scripture when he quotes "Out of Egypt I have called my Son." This is supposedly a quote from Hosea Chapter 11, verse 1. If you read the verses in Hosea before and after this verse you will find that Hosea is definitely talking about the Nation Israel and not the Lord. As I stated earlier in these paragraphs, either there are manuscripts missing that have some of Matthew's footnoted material or it is not a quote guided by the Holy Spirit. One last possibility: Matthew just got it wrong.

After all, in the Book of Luke account of the virgin birth, the baby Jesus and His parents never go to Egypt and are not visited by the wise men.

Let's just take two chapters out of the Bible, Matthew Chapter 21 and Mark Chapter 11. This could be done all over the gospels, but if you haven't caught the fact that the gospels are really different (not the same, so not inerrant), you have shown that "you see and don't want to perceive." Did Christ come into Jerusalem on an ass with a foal, or was it just the foal? Did Jesus cast out the moneychangers on the day of the triumphal entry or was it the next day? Did he make the fig tree wither before or after he cast out the moneychangers from the temple, and how long did it take for the fig tree to wither? Read these for yourself.

How can you continue to blindly follow a proof text here and there and refuse to read the rest of the Bible? The Gospels in particular, are riddled with contradictions, but if you take the time to read the entire Bible a couple of times you will learn that it follows the same message. God loves you. He wants you to love Him. If you really love Him you will live a life that is acceptable to Him. He has shown you the things that He does not want in your life. Follow His teachings if you love Him.

Look, you can either whine to your pastor or grow up and study your Bible. I could go on and on about errors. The first error should be enough to understand that the Bible is not error free. So what? The Bible doesn't state anywhere that it is! The Bible is there for you to read and learn of the Lord.

Don't be fooled into believing that the odd out-of-context verse is there to save you while you continue to live a sin-filled life. Once you have read your Bible a few times you will understand the loving heart the Lord expects all that love Him to have. And with a loving heart for the Lord you will reject sin in your life. What is sin? Anything that is opposed to the Law!

Remember the earlier thread about wives being entwined with their husbands? Later translations added words that appeared to break this thread, such as the word "wife" in Matthew Chapter 19, verse 29. See if it is in your Bible. Is the Bible you hold in your hand still inerrant?

You learned from the previous chapter that there are great examples of just plain adding material as is found in 1 John Chapter 5, verse 7. Read it in your Bible again. Most will read as follows: "For there are three that bear record in heaven, the Father, the Word, and the Holy Ghost: and these three are one (KJV)." Doesn't that sound like it gives conclusive proof to the trinity? Remember, the added words are: "in heaven, the Father, the Word, and the Holy Ghost: and these three are one." If your Bible has these words, they are added to the original author's writings.

One last thought: Are you saved by Grace or Hope? If it is the inerrant word of God, I would hope that it would be just one word, but its not. Paul, the guy that gives you the "Saved by Grace" line that most Christians stick too, also tells you that you are "Saved by Hope." Yes, that's right, you are no longer saved by grace if you believe that it is the inerrant word. Read Romans Chapter 8, verse 24. It is clear as a bell! "For ye are saved by <u>Hope</u>: but hope that is seen is not hope: for what a man seeth, why doth he yet hope for?"

So, are you saved by grace or hope? It can only be one if it is truly the hand of God that is penning the scriptures, but it isn't. It is inspired men writing to others to inspire them.

So what book did I read that helped me find all these and many other errors and contradictions in the biblical text? None! I've never even talked with others to absorb material about this topic. It just comes from reading your Bible daily. I probably could write a book on the topic of the inerrancy of the scriptures. Should any of these above errors shake your faith?

Of course not! It is just there to show you that anyone that tries to convince you that the Bible is the inerrant word of God is just trying to fill you full of hogwash. They are teaching you this to help them sell a false religion that explains that God will allow "a little sin in your life" and "that it's OK."

If you are an evangelical sheep (asleep at the wheel), you need to wake up and read your Bible. If you did, you wouldn't follow along blindly behind some MEC pastor. Unfortunately, I am sure that some of what is written in this book will be used by lesser caliber, non-God-fearing, pagans to beat on baby unschooled Christians. The only advice I can give is to read your Bible. Could the Bible in its present form be the direct Word from God? No. If He could have preserved it for us, then He wouldn't have allowed the flaws to creep in!

That is what makes the way that modern Christians look at the Bible so wrong. They view the present Bible His direct word, and yet is if filled with errors. I view God as a greater being than most Christians. If it was God's direct Word, then it would be error free, and it's not. So that only leaves us with "the Bible is man's best effort to put down on paper what he feels God has revealed." As man's best efforts it will have errors, and it does.

If you cannot accept the fact that the Bible is not the inerrant word of God from the above mentioned errors, then you are "seeing and not perceiving." There is no reason for you to read any further in this book. It will do you no good to read endlessly if you do not want to learn. Why read your Bible either, you obviously have no intention of living as God wants you to live and will just skip over the parts you don't like.

For a Christian that believes or believed that the Bible is the inerrant Word of God, the errors in the Gospels will be the most mind blowing. I know, it blew my mind, but using common sense and a lot of prayer, I began to perceive the truth. It really isn't hard once you shed the false teaching of the inerrancey of the scripture and look at the authors that wrote each epistle that we call the Gospels. Let's look at the next chapter.

Is the New Testament Trustworthy?

As you have just read and hopefully tested for yourself, you know that the Bible, and especially the New Testament, is full of errors. This one fact is what seriously shook my early Christian faith. This is probably why most Christian leaders don't encourage their congregations to diligently read their Bible each day. They probably don't understand why there are errors in the Bible themselves.

There are many focused reading materials used by Christians as daily devotions. Most churches put together daily readings that they then preach from the next time they gather together. These types of daily reading materials skip over the errors and hence build your confidence in an untrue form of Christianity. None of these should be a substitution for a good front to back reading of the Bible.

When you do read it through, as I did, it will shake your foundation unless you pray a lot and keep reading. God will give you understanding if you work to show yourself worthy. The first time I went through the Bible I really didn't see too many problems. But the second time through, I was shocked. How can the Bible, that is the "Word of God" be flawed?

How do you reconcile the fact that the New Testament is riddled with errors? How do you rationalize with yourself when it is obvious that there are problems with the text that you feel you have to ignore? How can you ignore an error and still feel the "whole" thing is from God?

This is where you have to ask yourself, why? Why, if it is the Word of God, is it wrong? Most Christians look heavily at specific verses in the New Testament and discount most things they read in other areas of the Bible, especially the Old Testament, if they don't fit into the tidy little picture they think Christianity is all about.

But is this Christian version they have in their head even scriptural to the New Testament? It all depends on what New Testament verses you are clinging too.

What is the New Testament and how trustworthy is it? This starts a very slippery slope if you are not careful. If you know that some of it is wrong, where do you draw the line? What scripture do you put your faith in? The New Testament is a valuable resource if used correctly. I will break the New Testament into two areas. You have the Gospels along with the Book of Acts, and the others books which are purposely written letters. What is the difference?

The Gospels are the story of Jesus Christ's life and ministry while He was on the earth. The Book of Acts covers early Church history. They are written years after the events and some by people that weren't even there. Think of them as history books.

The rest of the New Testament were letters written by an apostle or early church leader to a specific person or group of people and they are usually about early Christian doctrine.

What is the error potential of the New Testament? It really depends on the book you like to quote. Ask yourself, was the person writing the message a first-hand witness to the event he is writing about? It also depends on the time frame between the event and when they put it in writing. As you will read, Mark and Luke are the least accurate of the Gospels. I have even written a chapter on the *Books of Luke*, as they are more questionable than the rest.

The Jews at the time of Jesus Christ were looking for a Messiah. This person would free them from the oppression and taxation of the Romans. All the New Testament writers were of this mindset.

The Gospels are all records of events, filled with good accounts of the events in Jesus' ministry, but you know if you have read them for yourself that they do not always tell the same story or in the same sequence. In contrast, the purposely written books have almost no contradictions so let's cover them first.

How did Paul do? Paul wrote more books in the New Testament than any other author. There is a complete chapter in this book called, *Is Paul Taken Out of Context*, and he is. That is why an entire chapter was written.

Without going into too much detail, Paul is probably the most educated of the apostles with the possible exception of Matthew. Paul is the only schooled apostle in the Old Testament scriptures. He was a Hebrew of Hebrews. But if you don't take a complete book at a time and read it through thoroughly, it can be misleading. This is because he explains what we were before Christ, and then what we will become through Christ. The latter is what he wants you to become and expects you to be. Additionally, he hasn't been translated too accurately at times.

Paul is the only New Testament writer that looks as if he is telling you that the Law has been done away with. This is why Peter is so helpful. You will learn that Peter has spent time with Paul. He has either read some of what Paul has written, or has been briefed on how it is being understood by Christians.

He tells you in 2 Peter Chapter 3, verses 15-18, that the way Paul's writings are being understood is wrong. That if you have already learned the scriptures (Old Testament), then don't be lead away by false interpretation of Paul's writings. He doesn't say that Paul is wrong, just that he is not being understood correctly. You may note that Peter believes that the way it is written in the Old Testament is the correct way.

James does the same thing. James takes several examples from Paul's writings and then adds to them to further expound them for clarity. In Paul's work it looks like you are saved solely by faith and that is all you need. James takes the examples of Abraham and Rahab from Paul's writings and further explains that if you have faith, as you must, then you will have works.

This is why you have to have a complete understanding of the scriptures for yourself. How many times in the last several years have you heard a preacher tell you that you need "works" to be saved? I would hazard to guess that you would say "zero." That is because modern Christianity likes to quote only the verses they like and they are usually from Paul.

So, Paul has written some very good books, but they need to be read completely, maybe several times, before you should form an opinion of what he is really trying to say. The other apostles, specifically two that walked with Jesus, have told you they love Paul, but his letters may lead you astray. Why wouldn't you heed their advice, especially when the way modern Christianity teaches is against the Old Testament scriptures?

One last point. As it will be covered more thoroughly in the Chapter, *Is Paul taken out of Context*, Paul will tell you at one point that he is writing his letter to the Corinthians "as a man." This means that he is telling them that his writings are not a direct reflection of God's will, although they could be. Even though he is a Spirit-filled man, he is letting them know that his writings could be in error.

That brings us back to Peter, an apostle and disciple, who wrote two good, but short books. We already covered some of what he wrote. There is also the Book of Jude, believed to be written by one of Jesus' half brothers. It has some very important truths if you read it. Last of the authors, other than the Apostle John, is the Book of James.

The Book of James we know isn't written by the disciple James, as he was beheaded earlier than the book was written (Acts 12:2). It appears to have been written by one of the other half brothers of Jesus. What makes James so interesting is that he appears to be the leader of the Church at the time. His word appears to be final, even for Paul. Why do I say this?

Read Acts Chapter 15. If Paul didn't care for James' opinion and that of the early church council, why did he come back to fight for the position that Christians didn't need to be circumcised? He would have carried on teaching as he believed regardless. In Acts Chapter 21 Paul enters Jerusalem and goes directly to meet James. He is then asked to purify himself and Paul does begin the process, before he is arrested.

In Paul's own words in Galatians Chapter 1, verses 18-19 he explains the relationship and honor he holds for both Peter and James. This is why the Books of Peter and James are so important. Peter explains that Paul is being misinterpreted and James stresses the need for a Christian to prove his or her faith through good works. This is so opposed to modern teaching.

When contemplating whether "works" are important in your life, you have to ask yourself, do I believe James, the leader of the early Christians, or the way modern Christianity is taught at church today? If you don't want to believe Peter, Jude, James and John you are in good company. When researching the Reformation and Martin Luther, I read that he wanted to discount them entirely as they didn't fit neatly into how he interpreted Paul. Funny, it is the same today.

Lastly, you have John, who like Peter was an apostle and disciple. He wrote the most accurate of the Gospels as you will see later in this chapter, but also three short books to the church. He also wrote the only prophetic book of the New Testament, the Book of Revelation. It is said to be hard to understand by some. It really isn't if you have an understanding of the Old Testament. And remember, it is a vision directly from God.

Revelation is a book that is quoted by most, if not all churches associated with Christianity. No church follows its teachings today. I will quote from this book many times and you have to ask yourself, do I follow its God-directed teachings? A quick example of this for all Pre-tribulation churches is found in Revelation Chapter 20. This chapter clearly explains that Christians are not Pre-tribulation. This is covered more thoroughly in the Chapter, *Am I Pre, Mid, or Post Tribulation*.

The above mentioned books and authors do not appear to write anything that is contrary to the Old Testament if read thoroughly. They do not write anything that is disputed by the other New Testament authors, just clarified. You also know that Paul is the most prolific, and yet I believe, is easily taken out of context. The other authors are solid as you can line them up with scripture. They help to control those out-of-context verses by Paul used by modern churches to say that you can "live as you were called," and "don't need to do anything to be saved."

A lot of what we call the Gospels are stories that were passed down, until they were put down on paper many years later. Let's take a closer look at these. Do you remember the game "telephone" (or whatever it was called) when you were in grammar school?

The teacher would tell a sentence into someone's ear and then each student would whisper it into the next student's ear until everyone had been told. At the end of the string of students, the last one would tell the teacher what she had first stated. Do you remember playing that game? How many times did the sentence stay the same by the end of all the students? Sometimes it did, and sometimes it didn't.

Use a little common sense here for a moment. If some of the Gospels were stories told to others and then over the years written down, don't you think that they would have inconsistencies? Of course they would. And as we have already pointed out, the Bible isn't the inerrant Word of God, so we realize that there are errors.

This isn't to say that there is anything wrong with reading hearsay. But if it isn't given to the author by the Holy Spirit, and it wasn't seen first-hand, then it is prone to errors. Does this mean that it should be discounted altogether? Of course not. It can add weight to another's observation of an event.

You will see, if you don't already understand, that the Gospels are an excellent source of information from God through an author's eyes. But, as you already learned from the previous chapter, it is not the inerrant Word of God. Even a first-hand witness doesn't see or hear everything.

Let's look at each Gospel and its author a little closer. Remember to reference them back to the Old Testament. If God is, was, and always will be, then He doesn't change. This means that He is consistent through time. So, authors should be consistent with God's "will," if it is to have relevance in your life.

The Gospels are believed to have been written by four different authors. Do they all carry the same authority? Of course not. Who was a first-hand witness to an event? That author would have to carry the most weight. Remember, the Bible was not written by the hand of God. If there was no first-hand witness, then you have to test the story to the truths we know of God.

As stated earlier in this revision, this book is written taking the entire Bible into account. The Gospels and the Book of Acts are used here as if they are "Gospel." But, once I wrote *The New Testament,: The Facts and the Fiction*, I learned that much of what I first believed to be true about the authenticity of the Gospels and the Book of Acts to be false.

I'm not saying that this makes these pages unnecessary, it is just that there are a lot of truths that are not found in modern Christianity that can be learned if you take a critical look at what each book is telling you.

The Apostle Matthew supposedly wrote the Book of Matthew. He was one of the twelve apostles of Jesus Christ. We know that he was an educated man as he was a tax collector (publican). He had to at least be able to document who and how much each patron had paid to the Roman State and others he managed. This writing ability may explain why he has such lengthy dispositions on the events that he was a first-hand witness too.

As an apostle he would have had first-hand knowledge of many of the events, but when did he become this very important witness? Matthew explains that he doesn't become a follower of Jesus Christ until Matthew Chapter 9, verse 9. So, where did Matthew get the information that he shares with us in the preceding chapters and verses?

Matthew flees with the other disciples at the garden when Jesus is arrested and then locks himself away with most of them until the resurrection has already happened. Where does he get the information that he passed on about the arrest, trial, and crucifixion? Remember these time frames when you want to contemplate his credibility to an event he writes about.

John Mark supposedly wrote the Book of Mark. Many modern theologians like to speculate who wrote the Book of Mark, but then, why not trust who the book says wrote it? Mark was a youth at the time Jesus was preaching, or maybe not even born as you learn of his youthful age years later when working with Paul in the Book of Acts. From this simple fact, where did Mark learn all that he wrote down about the life and ministry of Jesus Christ? It had to be from stories of others.

Let's try to work out Mark's age at the time of the Lord's crucifixion. Mark isn't mentioned in any of the Gospels. The first time you see Mark in the New Testament is in the Book of Acts, Chapter 12, verse 12. "And when he (Peter) had considered, he came to the house of Mary, the mother of John, whose surname was Mark..."

Whose house was it? Mother's didn't keep the house back then, it was given to the son when the Father passed away, unless he was not of age. The age of adulthood established by God is 20 years old. It appears that he is not 20 at this time in the Book of Acts. How many years have occurred since the Lord died?

Paul was not a Christian until after Steven was stoned (Acts 7-8) which was some time after the crucifixion. He then spent 3 years in Arabia (Galatians 1:16-19) and returned to Damascus before going to Jerusalem. Paul's own letter to the Galatians, states that the first time he went to Jerusalem he only met with Peter and James, no other disciples. He then doesn't return there for 14 more years and this time he meets with everyone. Once in Jerusalem, he caused an uproar among the Jews and was sent to Tarsus (Acts 9:30). Finally, Barnabas seeks out Paul and brings him back to Jerusalem where they assembled for a year before they take their first journey (Acts 11:25). All this happened before Mark is 20 years old!

Let's be honest, I do believe that this time frame is a little long as I have used Acts in the building of the time line. I believe, and so should you if you have looked closely at Luke's work, that it is usually a little unreliable. But from Paul's own words it was many years between Jesus' death and when Paul took Mark under his wing for their first ministry trip.

I like the Book of Mark as it does add to many of the events that are recorded in the other Gospels, but it can't be a first-hand witness to those events. Mark wimped out on his first ministry trip with Paul and Barnabas (Acts 13:13). This is why when Paul and Barnabas are to take their next trip, they separate ways as Paul will have nothing to do with Mark (Acts 15:36-41). You learn later in the Book of Acts and in Paul's later writings that Mark becomes a solid witness as he matures.

Even if you don't like my reasoning from the scriptures as to the age of Mark, you have to agree that he was not one of the 12 disciples and hence, would not have been privy to most of what he wrote about, even if he was older. The very fact that he was not there during the Gospel events explains why Mark's order of events and some contradictions to the other Gospels appear. The same is true with the Book of Luke.

Luke, the supposed author of the Book of Luke is said not even to be a Jew. The Book of Luke is supposed to be a legal document that was sent in defense of Paul when he was on trial in Rome. Isn't it odd that during all Roman encounters in the Book of Luke (and the Book of Acts, also supposedly by Luke) the Romans are the good guys? Was he a first-hand witness to anything?

I'm not saying that his accounts should be discounted, but they have to be looked at closely. His books are written the way they are because he never saw anything first-hand. These were letters to persuade a Roman, not Christians.

Mark and Luke are great documents to help clarify an event. If it is in one of their Gospels, it proves that they at least trusted the source that told them the story of the event before they wrote it down themselves. Just remember that they were not there.

This is why hearsay is not permitted in a court of law. Although hearsay may be based in truth, it is partial to errors. Modern Christian leaders try to explain the differences in the Gospels by saying that they are written to different audiences. That is just nonsense. If you look at the Books of Mark and Luke closely you will see many stories were told several times and they begin to blend together, or change, and definitely fall out of sequence with the other Gospels. Parts of one story are blended with parts of another.

The Book of John is the only pretty much fully first-hand account of all the Gospels. As you know, John was with Jesus shortly after His baptism. You would think that the Book of John and the Book of Matthew would line up during the time when the Apostle John and Matthew are with Jesus, but they don't. Where do Matthew and John differ? Unfortunately they really don't tell a similar story at all!

Let's look at a few of the differences between the Gospels to expand this explanation of each writers story. The previous chapter proved that the Bible was not the inerrant word of God using examples of contrasting accounts from all over the Bible to include the Gospels. But here we want to show the impact of having the stories told by other than first-hand witnesses to the event. Remember the truths will be the same, just the story will be told differently or out of sequence from when it is "needed" to be told.

In the beginning of Mark Chapter 7 you see the Pharisees starting the argument about washing your hands before you eat. Jesus' response is about what comes out of your mouth is what defiles you, not what goes into your mouth. The problem with this story is that the setting is all wrong. It is almost correct, but it appears to be a different time than when it happened in the Book of Matthew.

Do I think the story is true? Yes, it just didn't happen that way, and of course Mark left out Jesus' important parable and punch line. Mark leaves you thinking that food can not defile you, but that isn't what the story is completely about. It is that your heart will defile you, but eating with unwashed hands won't! This event isn't a license to eat Levitically unclean foods. Read Matthew 15:1-20 for a more accurate account of the event.

Matthew ends the story in Matthew Chapter 15 verse 20 with "...but to eat with unwashed hands defileth not a man." This is the problem with Mark and Luke. Mark's rendition is true and adds credibility to the event happening, but left out a very important part that leaves today's Christians believing that Levitically unclean foods can't defile you, and that's wrong!

Another example of leaving out the important part of the message can be seen in the story of Jesus being asked by what authority He is doing His miracles and teachings. Matthew starts the story in Matthew Chapter 21, verse 23. After Jesus traps the chief priests and elders He tells two parables, the two sons and the wicked vineyardmen. Mark and Luke both tell the same story with the parables. They start at Mark Chapter 11, verse 27 and Luke Chapter 21, verse 1.

So what is the difference between the stories? Read them for yourself. In Matthew, the point is made to whom the parables are directed after the first parable. These parables explain why the "so-called righteous Jews" didn't listen to John the Baptist, nothing more nothing less. The parables were directed at the leadership, not the Nation of Israel. If you read Mark or Luke's rendition of this story you may draw the conclusion that this story is 3 separate events consisting of 1 argument and 2 self contained parables by Jesus explaining why the Christians will be replacing Judaism.

Only Matthew pulls the 3 events together because only Matthew was there of these 3 authors. Mark and Luke constantly left out the important part of the message leaving Christian leaders, worried about their membership, to exploit these stories. These parables had nothing to do with Christianity in the future!

This is why you have to ask yourself how reliable are the books of Mark and Luke? I have heard these parables from Mark and Luke told over and over in Christian churches and yet, not once have I heard them use Matthew's account. Why? Because Jesus did not have anything against common everyday Jews that were looking for their relationship with God. He just hated any organized religion that was self-serving. Ask yourself, is Christianity today any different than Christ's day Judaism?

In Matthew Chapter 16, starting at verse 5 you find Jesus and His disciples have landed at the coast of Magdala, and he is warning them of the leaven of the Pharisees. Are they still in the boat? No! But in Mark Chapter 8, starting in verse 14, they are still in a "ship." It is the same story, but one account is still in a ship and the other is after they have come to shore. Both stories follow the feeding of 4,000 with the seven loaves.

Speaking of the feeding of the 4,000, Luke and John don't even mention it.

There is a story starting in Mark Chapter 9, verse 32, where the disciples are arguing who will be the greatest when they are with the Lord in His kingdom. Do I think that this event happened? You know, they are fighting for position. The Zebedee sons want to sit on Jesus Christ's right and left side when He is in His glory. The other disciples don't like the request. In Mark's account of this event James and John ask the question.

Matthew tells the same story in Matthew Chapter 20 starting at verse 20, but it is the mother of James and John that makes the request. Similar, but not the same. In both accounts it is the same response from Jesus, so was it the Zebedee boys that make the request or was it the mother?

Jesus puts them all down and explains that the first will be last and the last will be first. Or better put, the servant will become the greatest of all. Do I think that they had the argument several times over position? No, when it came up, Jesus put it down.

This type of placing a story in the wrong sequence of events or leaving out the important meaning of a story is all over Mark and Luke and parts of Matthew. It is because they were based in truth, but written down years later and by someone who probably didn't see the event.

If you read John's account of the betrayal in John Chapter 13, they eat the last supper and it is over. Jesus washes all 12 disciples feet. Judas is still there. During or directly after the foot washing, Jesus explains that one will betray Him. Peter asks John to ask the Lord who it is. It is a discreet discussion. This is why when Jesus gives Judas the sop it goes unnoticed.

Doesn't it seem strange in the other Gospels that they don't drag Judas out and stone him after Jesus gives him the sop? After all, it sounds like He announced the code to identify the betrayer to everyone. For that matter, if Judas new the code, why did he even take the sop openly. But that is because it probably didn't happen the way the other Gospels tell it. Remember the closeness of Peter, James, and John to the Lord. Read the stories again in the Gospel and judge between the accounts, recalling that only John and Matthew were there.

I had taken a close look at the Book of Luke right here, but the subject matter was so great that I had to make an entire chapter just to show how over dramatized and inconsistent the book really is. It isn't that I feel it should be discounted altogether, it is just full of half told stories and facts that don't line up with the other Gospels. Just follow the rest of this chapter and see where a consistent and accurate story line can be found. Then read the next chapter if you want a closer look at the *Books of Luke*.

This is why the Book of John is so important. It is basically a first-hand account. To see this better, why not look at how Jesus called His disciples in the first place? Look at each Gospel's account. The first three Gospels tell you that Jesus calls them, and then they follow. You remember, Jesus is walking by the seaside and calls them two by two and they drop their nets and follow him. Is this how it happened? Was Matthew, Mark, or Luke there?

But in the Book of John, Andrew and "another" follow Jesus and inquire of Him the day after His baptism. Why does John tell a different story than the other three Gospels?

Because John was the only apostle that wrote a book we call a Gospel that was there during the event. He was there when those we call the disciples met Jesus. Peter isn't in a boat, and Jesus doesn't tell him "I will make you a fisher of men." Peter is brought to Jesus by his brother Andrew (John 1:40-42). Read the Book of John and then the other Gospels and you will see that John, when he is the only first-hand witness tells a different story sometimes. When do you take John's word over the other Gospels? When he is the only first-hand witness.

Most of John's book is about the early days, last supper, arrest, trial and resurrection of Jesus Christ. Who was there during these events? Sometimes it was all of the 12, and sometimes it was only John, Peter and or James. How do I know? John only refers to himself as the "the one Jesus loved" in his Gospel.

When you see an apostle in John's Gospel that John references to in this way, you understand that it is he referring to himself. This is how you know that John was the other apostle that was with Peter when he went to see the trial of Jesus. There is no mention of Matthew, Luke or Mark being there.

So, if the Holy Spirit didn't pen the other Gospels, where did their versions of the trial and crucifixion come from? It had to be hearsay from either Peter or John. This is why the Book of John is different from the accounts in Matthew, Mark and Luke.

There are three accounts of Jesus calming the sea. They are in Matthew Chapter 8, Mark Chapter 4 and Luke Chapter 8. But John who was supposed to be in the boat doesn't make mention of it. Did it happen? Was there a first-hand witness that wrote of the event? No! Remember, Matthew isn't a follower of Jesus until Matthew Chapter 9. So where did the story come from?

How about the sending out of the 12 disciples to cast out demons and heal the sick. It can be found beginning in Matthew Chapter 9, verse 36, Mark Chapter 6 and Luke Chapter 9. Most peculiar is that Luke has a story of the sending out of the seventy, two by two. He is the only author to write of this sending forth. But if you read the story beginning in Luke Chapter 10, verse 1, you will see it is the identical words used by the Lord in Matthew Chapter 9, verse 36, when he sends forth the 12.

Isn't that odd that Luke has two "sending forths" and the other three only have one? Isn't it also odd that the words by the Lord on the sending out of the 12 are identical to the sending out of the 70 in Luke's second sending forth? What is worse, this is a supernatural power given by Jesus to men. John sees no reason to tell you of this sharing of power by the Lord, and so it too is not in his Gospel.

Once again, there are three accounts of Jesus and the Mountain of Transfiguration. They can be found in Matthew 17, Mark 9, and Luke 9. And again John, who was supposed to be there, doesn't make mention of this unbelievable supernatural observation in his Book of John. But to be fair, and I am fair, Peter does make mention of God talking to them from the "Holy Mount" in 2 Peter Chapter 1, verse 17-18.

Is Peter giving credibility to the story of the Mountain of Transfiguration? I really don't know, but he is telling us that he heard the Father speak of Jesus, although the words used in Peter's letter are different from those found in the Gospels.

John does help the others in the walking-on-water-by-Jesus event found in John Chapter 6, Mark Chapter 6, and Matthew Chapter 14. Unfortunately only Matthew makes mention of Peter starting and then failing to walk on water.

There are three accounts of Jesus being anointed by a woman before his burial. They can be found in Matthew Chapter 26, Mark Chapter 14 and John Chapter 12. Read the accounts closely several times and then ask yourself, are they the same event? At first I would have said no. After all John tells you it happened six days prior to the Feast of Unleavened Bread and the other two Gospels tell you it happened two days prior.

It is probably true that it happened in Bethany at Simon the Leper's house and Lazarus was there as a guest. Martha and Mary were there to help. Mary anointed the Lord. All three accounts could agree with these accounts, but when did it happen and does it matter? After all there are two witnesses that say that it happened two days prior to the feast.

If they were different events, it would be odd that they happened in the same town. More peculiar would be the fact that Jesus rebukes his disciples over their thinking of the anointings as a waste of money and then four days later has to rebuke them again for the same thing. Stranger yet, he uses the same words to rebuke them. No, it was the same incident. But was it six days prior or was it two days prior?

Here is where just because a witness is out numbered, he is not necessarily wrong. Remember, Mark was not there, he just wrote down what he was told of the event. From this point on, John is very thorough as to what is happening with Jesus. Look at how much detail is written by John from this point forward. John gives you seven more chapters of events before the crucifixion.

You really have to ask yourself, do I trust John's account, or do I trust Matthew's? As John's is much more thorough about events happening and linked in writing as to the days before the feast I have to side with John. Read the book of John. He actually chronicles the events happening in respect to the days before or after a major event. It is one of his signature writing styles. This is very important if you want to learn when Jesus was actually crucified and rose from the dead.

Actually, all four Gospels mention an anointing with oil of the Lord if you include Luke's rendition of a woman named Mary in a man named Simon's house in Luke Chapter 7. This Mary had been demon possessed, possibly a prostitute by the way Simon is talking of her past. Unfortunately, it has to be a different event. But then you do have the same man's house, the same woman's name, and an anointing with oil. If it is to be the same event, Luke is again very much off the mark for accuracy. I would have to question everything about this rendition of the story. But, as you will learn in the next chapter of this book, I believe that Luke has this habit!

Did you ever take a good look at the triumphal entry? It can be found in Matthew Chapter 21, Mark Chapter 11, Luke Chapter 19 and John Chapter 12. Go back and read the chapters. They are not really that similar. Did He enter on an ass, or a fowl the colt of an ass, or both? And where do you find Jesus explaining that the rocks would speak if the crowd didn't? That over dramatization of the event can only be found in Luke! The rest of the accounts have Jesus speaking rationally, yet firm about the praise.

All of the Gospels have something to add. Many accounts are mentioned in each of them that are true, but only to a point. Always remember who was the first-hand witness to an event. Then if you have to choose between two different accounts of the same event, <u>and you do have to choose</u>, pick the obvious best choice, the first-hand witness. If there are two first-hand witnesses with different accounts of the event, which one was more detailed? This isn't to say that Luke and Mark should be totally discounted. They may have something to add that the first-hand witness neglected to say, but they are not a first-hand witness.

This is why when I cover what day the Lord was crucified later in this book I will side with John's account of Jesus Christ's last days over the others. Why? Because he was the obvious first-hand witness, and chronicled his Gospel. Better yet, although John's account is lengthy, Matthew backs up John's accounts in the critical areas although they did not always agree on every detail. John was there all the time and Matthew was there at least part of the time.

If you think about it, the reason for the inconsistencies is obvious. If you take into account that half of these books were not written by the first-hand witnesses and none of the Gospels are completely first-hand accounts, you can understand why they don't line up. But Christians like to hide behind the statement that it is the inerrant word of God, penned by the Holy Spirit. That statement reminds me of the story "The Emperor's New Clothes" by Hans Christian Anderson.

If you don't know the story it is about a emperor that wears a new set of clothes that was prepared for him. But, they are not clothes at all. He is told they are special and so he acts like he puts them on. Every adult that sees him explains how nice they are. No one will admit the obvious. He is actually naked in a Parade. Finally, a child asks why the emperor is naked and then the illusion breaks down.

That is why Jesus tells us that we have to be as children. Don't put up false barriers to truth. Check your religious denominational weapons at the door. Read it as a child and then ask yourself why are there errors? These last two chapters can be summed up like this.

The Bible is written by Spirit-filled men that wrote what they thought was true. They never state that it is the direct Word of God, unless they are in vision. All written material by Bible authors needs to be verified as to what we know about God. He is, was, and always will be, so He can't change! If it is from God then it should be referenced by more than one author. Lastly, rely on the first-hand witness to an event for the most credible account of that event.

If you follow those basic rules to understanding your Bible, there really aren't any passages or contradictions that can't be easily explained. Face it, sometimes the Bible disagrees with itself, but now you should be able to discern what are the "real" truths over the fairy tales that are taught in your denominational church.

When I originally wrote this book, I truly believed what I wrote. Remember, earlier on in the first chapter that I wrote that I would give you my best shot at the information, but I am a man and man is fallible. As I have already written in this revision, I learned a lot when I wrote a book to try to expound on this and the previous chapter. It is called *The New Testament: The Facts and the Fiction*. If you want to learn a subject, try to teach it. The same is true when you try to write a book on a difficult subject.

Hasn't the errors in this chapter screamed at you? It did to me and I used this concern to write a book that would explain the errors. It wasn't to be a Christian apologetic that tries to explain it by telling a fib like, "They were written to four different audiences." I was trying to line then up and show that there was too much error to be Holy Spirit led and that there had to be a better explanation to the errors. What I found was truly shocking. It is probably too shattering for most so-called Christians to accept, but makes the entire thing understandable. Now that I understand, I have peace, but do you?

The Books of Luke

We have covered the fact that the Bible is written by men that were fallible. As noted in the last chapter, there are many errors in the Bible. So we can conclude that it is not written by the Hand of God. The New Testament is a compilation of various letters from church leaders to various groups of people for many different reasons. Finally, the Gospels are very different from each other in their recollection of order and happenings of events in the ministry of Jesus Christ.

Focusing more closely on the works of Luke, it can be surmised that he wrote two books, the Book of Luke and the Book of the Acts of the Apostles. These were purposefully written books, but not to edify the church. As mentioned earlier they were probably written in defense of Paul when he was in Rome. This is theorized by the opening in Luke Chapter 1, verse 3 "It seemed good to me also, having had perfect understanding of all things from the very first, to write unto thee in order, most excellent Theophilus..." This is a very formal opening to a Roman, possibly a lawyer.

By the time the Book of Acts is written, the author is on a less formal note starting the Book of The Acts of the Apostles like this: "The former treatise have I made, O Theophilus..." As you can see, both the Book of Luke and the Book of Acts were written solely for the information to get to a man called Theophilus. Acts concludes with Paul being at Caesar's Palace awaiting trial. This does bring the point home that they were both written for an event centered around Paul's first imprisonment.

So, the Books of Luke and Acts were not written for the Christian's edification at all. They were written as a persuasion to help explain why Paul believed as he believed. You can accept this argument or you can reject it, but you will have to conclude after reading this chapter that the events, as told by the author of Luke, are overly dramatized. Many of the stories we know of in Jesus' ministry are only told in the Book of Luke. But, after you read them and the other Gospels, ask yourself, are they true?

I have more doubts as to the accuracy of the Book of Luke than I do the Book of Acts. This is because he is a close associate to Paul, at least later on. The stories he writes down about Paul would have been first-hand hearsay or possibly even first-hand witness sometimes. In the Book of Luke, he is very much in disagreement with the other Gospel writers, and that is why I find the areas that only he writes about to be in question.

I know, I know this is the beginning of the slippery slope. If we doubt here, where do we stop? It is simple, look at it for what it was: a defense document written by a man that had no first-hand knowledge of the events he is writing about until later into the ministry of Paul. He is only mentioned two times in the New Testament. Paul writes of him in Colossians Chapter 4, verse 14 and in 2 Timothy, Chapter 4, verse 11.

In the Book of Colossians Luke is mentioned at the close. This is common in most of Paul's letter to give credit to those that are working with him at the time of the letter. If you read Colossians Chapter 4 you will see that Luke is not mentioned with the group known as the circumcision. This is how you know that Luke was not a Jew. Even if he was a Jew he would not have been accepted by Jews being uncircumcised. Hence, he would not have been with or around Jesus in Israel or Judea. You will also note that Paul tells you that he is a physician.

So where did he get all of those stories of Jesus Christ's life and the early church? Most of it had to be from Paul, who was also not a first-hand witness to anything that Jesus did or said. Remember the first time you see Paul mentioned is at the stoning of Steven and in that action he was working against the church!

Remember, the purpose of this book is to get you to read your Bible for yourself. You need to prove "truth" to yourself. Do not trust even me to accurately help you, even though I will do my best. This book takes the Bible for face value. As this is a revision, over time I learned many new revelations about the trustworthiness and authorship of much of the New Testament.

So, the million dollar question is this: is the Book of Luke accurate? If Luke was a Gentile, would he have the same understanding of Jewish custom, as say, one of the Apostles? Go back and look up what type of woman a priest could marry. She had to be a virgin of the Levitical line. She could have been previously married if it was to a priest that had died and they had no children.

Luke starts out with the story of John the Baptist and the conception of Jesus Christ in Chapter 1. John's father, a Levitical priest, and mother are old and beyond the years to have children. John's mother's name is Elisabeth. You should read the story before you read any more in this chapter. I enjoy the story, but have to question the author's Levitical understanding.

First you have the conception of John. Then you have the conception of Jesus. In Luke Chapter 1, verse 36, you read that Elisabeth is a cousin of Mary, the mother of Jesus. But here is where you start to have a Levitical problem. Mary's line is from Judah. Elisabeth is a Levite. In Luke Chapter 1, verse 5 it states "...and his wife was of the daughters of Aaron..." So this verse in the middle of Luke Chapter 1 has just stated that she was a Levite of the line from Aaron. There is no way they are cousins! Yet, Luke tells you they are. But let's not argue over blood lines.

If you read Luke's account of when Mary and Elisabeth meet in Luke Chapter 1, verse 41, the babe in Elisabeth's womb leaped. Elisabeth is filled with the Holy Spirit and prophesies. They stayed together for some time. Doesn't this sound like Jesus and John should have a close relationship, or at least John should know who Jesus is? After all, John knew who Jesus was while he was in Elisabeth's womb in the presence of Jesus while He is still in Mary's womb.

But John the Baptist questions whether Jesus is the messiah in the other Gospels. Even the Book of Luke in Chapter 7, verse 19 states "And John calling unto him two of his disciples and sent them to Jesus, saying, Art thou he that shall come? Or look we for another?" Did John's mother keep all that she knew of Jesus to herself? Did John not hear the words from heaven say "This is My Son in whom I am well pleased," when he brought Jesus up out of the water? I do believe that John sent and asked the question, I just have a hard time with Luke Chapter 1, although it is a nice story.

Before we leave Luke Chapter 1 lets go back to the Book of Matthew. How does Matthew say that Jesus came to live in Nazareth? Matthew Chapter 2 starts with "Now when Jesus was born in Bethlehem" (Judea); Matthew makes it clear that the journey starts here. Herod sends the wise men there and in verse 11 it states they (the wise men) came into the house, and fell down to worship Him. Matthew doesn't say anything about finding Jesus in another town, but lets not quibble. After this Matthew explains that they fled to Egypt. No mention of Nazareth yet!

Still in Matthew Chapter 2, verses 22-23 you find that they start their return home to Israel, but are warned in a dream and so they "turned aside into the parts of Galilee...and came and dwelt in a city called Nazareth." Matthew doesn't mince words here. They have come to a new location where they feel safe from Archelaus. They aren't returning to their old home, as they are worried about coming back to where they may be found!

But in Luke Chapter 1, verse 26 he tells you that the Angel Gabriel finds Mary at Nazareth and tells her the news that she will be the mother of our Savior Jesus Christ. In Chapter 2, verse 4 he tells you that Joseph abode in Nazareth. Start remembering here that Luke was not on the scene for many years after Jesus had been crucified. This letter was not intended for Christians, it was a story used to help explain why Paul believed as he believed.

If you read Luke's rendition, by the time you finish Chapter 2, you see that Jesus' parents lived in Nazareth, take a trip to Bethlehem where Jesus is born, and within 8 days of his birth they walk to Jerusalem to have Him circumcised, and then returned back to Nazareth. Luke doesn't understand that Jesus' family wasn't from Nazareth originally. They ended up there out of necessity.

What ever happened to Egypt and the Wise Men as recorded by Matthew? The account of Matthew would not have been received well in Rome. After all, in the Book of Matthew you have a Roman-appointed ruler that has just slain every male child under the age of 2 years old. This is where it becomes apparent that the Book of Luke is written to show that the Romans are the good guys and the Jewish leadership are to blame for the problems happening between the Jews and the early church.

If Luke's account is accurate and these miraculous events happened, why didn't Jesus' brothers and parents believe He is the Son of God? Jesus will do miracle after miracle. Just one of these accounts would have sold me, but miraculous events happen over and over, and yet, His family really never believed.

By the time you have read to Luke Chapter 2 verse 42, Jesus is twelve years old. He has stayed behind in Jerusalem and is discussing the scriptures with "doctors" of the Law. What a dramatic story. Imagine a twelve year old child that is talking the Word of God without education. Did it happen? I really don't know, but I believe if these events happened to my son, I would be worshiping him, and yet He is still not revered by His family.

In Luke Chapter 4 you find the story of Jesus returning to Galilee, but is not accepted as a "prophet" as they know His father was Joseph the carpenter. All four Gospels make mention of this. They can be found in Matthew Chapter 13, Mark Chapter 6, and John Chapter 4. But once again Luke goes into a dramatic account of the event that the others for some reason do not record.

Luke actually states in Chapter 4, verses 29-30 that they are about to throw Jesus off a cliff, but He somehow walks back through them and leaves. Jesus already has miraculous powers that all three other gospel writers display, but Luke seems to give Him more supernatural powers than the rest.

Just a side note, if Luke wasn't a Jew, then he wouldn't have understood the importance of how a Jew would take the life of someone who blasphemed God. In every other Gospel and throughout the Bible you will see that the Jews "stone" someone. They don't throw them off a cliff! Romans crucified on a cross, and the Jews stoned their convicted.

Look at the event starting in Luke Chapter 5 where Jesus tells Peter to let down his nets. Peter has been out all night with James and John. There are too many fish to haul into the boat. None of the other Gospels tell of this story, but it is almost an exact copy of the story told by John when Jesus appears to the same disciples <u>after</u> His resurrection in John Chapter 21. Once again, Luke tells a lot of dramatic stories, but they seem to be out of order and not totally on the mark.

Did you ever take a good look at the Beatitudes? They are found in Luke Chapter 6, starting at verse 20. These are also recorded in only one other place, Matthew Chapter 5, starting in verse 3. Did you ever compare the two? They are different. Which one is correct?

Well, to help figure out who is correct, look for the accuracy surrounding the story. Luke tells you that Jesus has already named His twelve disciples, also known as apostles in Chapter 6, verse 13. Does that matter?

Go back to Matthew, and you will find that Matthew doesn't even follow the Lord until 4 chapters after this event. Was Matthew there as an apostle? Matthew himself tells you he isn't there, and the apostles are not named yet. Were either Matthew or Luke a first-hand witness? No! How accurate are the Beatitudes? They aren't, as the only two recorders of the event were never there and they each tell a different story.

It is obvious that the Book of Luke has a high error potential. The stories are all close to the other Gospels but are out of order, or they over dramatize a situation. He even adds many of his own stories that no other Gospel writer writes about. Let's look at a few.

How about the story of the Good Samaritan? We all know the story of how a Samaritan (an outcast according to the Jews) helps a good man that was robbed, but the prim and proper of Judah pass him by. It can only be found in the Book of Luke.

How about the rich man in Luke Chapter 12 who brought in an exceedingly large harvest and tore down his barn to build a bigger one? But before he could enjoy any of what he was squandering away for himself, the Lord takes his life that evening. You guessed it, the story can only be found in Luke. For a guy that wasn't there, he seems to have more stories about the Lord than anyone, and yet the stories that do have similarities are different from the first-hand witness' account.

Take the time near the end of the Lord's life on the earth when He is in Jerusalem and sobbing over the city that has rejected Him and says, Oh Jerusalem, Jerusalem how I have wanted to gather you together like a hen gathers her chicks... It makes sense where it is found in the other Gospels, but Luke places it at the end of Chapter 13 where you are left asking yourself, what is this doing here? For that matter, start reading from Chapter 12 and you will find no fewer than 12 stories that are bits and pieces of other Gospel stories totally in the wrong place in Jesus' ministry.

How about the story of the 10 lepers that Jesus healed as He was on his way to Jerusalem starting in Luke Chapter 17, verse 11? All 10 are healed, but only one comes back to worship Him? What was the lineage of that man? Why would I ask that question? It is obvious that this letter is intended to slant the story against the Jewish leadership and people, and to show a favorable light on the "unchosen" who have come to accept Jesus' love.

Luke makes a point to show that once again it is a Samaritan that comes back. In verse 18, he even states that this one man is the "stranger" in their midst, showing the other nine to be Jews. Don't forget, the Samaritans were disdained by the Jews. And, just as in the story of the Good Samaritan, Luke is the only Gospel writer to tell this story.

Read Chapter 19. It starts with the story of Zacchaeus the publican. Obviously, the one job description hated most by the Jews. By this time in Luke's book publicans have been mentioned favorably many times. It is a touching story of a man that converts to kindness and is forgiven by the Lord. Why was the Lord happy that Zacchaeus was willing to give away half of his ill-gotten wealth, and yet he required the rich young ruler to give up all that he had? Did it happen? Or rather, did it happen that way? Why not read the other stories found in the conclusion of the chapter?

They start with the Lord's parable of the man that leaves three servants with money, 10 talents to one servant, 5 talents to another and only 1 to the servant that will be called "wicked" later. So, what is so special about this story? It is also told in Matthew Chapter 25. If you read the 2, they have many differences. Why this matters is that if Luke can not tell any story the same as the other Gospel writers, then what makes you feel he has written the stories that only he tells correctly either?

Did Luke get it any better with the Lord's triumphant entry into Jerusalem? You still haven't left Chapter 19. He affirms that the Lord came in on a colt. The story is located in Matthew Chapter 21, Mark Chapter 11, and John Chapter 12. John does not go into it other than to say that Jesus rode on an ass. Mark tells the same story as Luke, almost word for word, but remember, Mark was not there either. He and Luke are writing from hearsay.

To understand why Jesus didn't ride in on a colt you have to read Matthew's version. He explains that a colt was there, but gives the prophesy that Jesus was to fulfill. Matthew quotes Zechariah in Matthew Chapter 21, verse 5 "Tell ye the daughter of Zion, Behold, thy King cometh unto thee, meek, and sitting upon an ass, and a colt the foal of an ass."

Jesus was not to enter on a colt or He would not have fulfilled the Old Testament scripture found in Zachariah Chapter 9, verse 9. So Mark and Luke got it part of the way correct, yet missed the reason it happened, and so the story was not complete.

If you overlook the inaccuracy of not telling it the way scripture has prophesied that Jesus would enter, Luke makes up for it with yet another over-dramatization where he explains that the Lord states that if the people did not cheer as they did, the "stones would cry out." Yes, that is only found in Luke.

At this point, I have to ask, how much more do I have to show to drive home the point that the Book of Luke was an over-dramatized, usually incorrect version of the Lord's life on earth? Let me show my favorite over-dramatization error in the book and a few parting thoughts.

I used the story of Peter's denial of the Lord using a rooster that is different in all the Gospel accounts to show that the Bible isn't the inerrant Word of God in a previous chapter. But where was Peter when He denied the Lord for the third time? Better yet, where was the Lord?

Obviously, the accounts all differ, but John tells you that they had sent the Lord bound to Caiaphas in John Chapter 18, verse 24. Peter is still warming himself by the fire. So, is he with the Lord? No, Peter as yet hasn't left the palace, but the Lord has. John tells you by the time you read John Chapter 18, verse 27, that Peter has denied the Lord for the third time and the cock crows. So the Lord is off to see Caiaphas and Peter is still at the palace, totally ashamed.

But in Luke Chapter 22, verse 61, Luke affirms that the Lord turned and looked at him on the third denial. Is Luke right? Ask yourself, who is the first-hand witness? This just shows that Luke knew of the event, but not how it correctly happened. It is an over-dramatization of what actually transpired. Do I believe that Luke thought this was correct? Yes I do, but it is still wrong.

If you try to read the Book of Luke in just one or two sittings you will see that it really doesn't flow either. It isn't consistent. Remember that the chapter and verse numbers were added by the Roman Catholic Church. So one chapter should flow into the next chapter. It was a "Letter." But Luke doesn't flow like one. It is a whole lot of facts that are sort of true and yet don't belong. This is why when Luke is read in church they start at the beginning of a chapter. Even the Roman Catholics understood that they needed to add partitions or it didn't sound credible.

Take the story of the rich man and Lazarus at the end of Chapter 16. Read the whole chapter before the story of Lazarus. Do you read anything about children anywhere? Is Jesus teaching about children? Of course not. But right after this story at the beginning of Chapter 17 you read that Jesus is warning those that "offend one of these little ones." Where did that come from? There aren't even children mentioned in the group! It comes from a different story, but Luke really doesn't know the facts. This type of mixing up of the stories is all over Luke if you would first read the other Gospels and then read Luke.

You really have to take a good look at the Book of Luke. Why do I sound so skeptical? Because I am sure that much of the book is based in fact, but it really doesn't line up with any of the other Gospels. I enjoy reading it, but I won't use it over any other New Testament book to form or support doctrine. Luke seems to be the only author of many of the stories that we tell about Jesus and yet, he is so easily proven wrong. There is not enough space to show each of the inconsistencies and over- dramatizations in the Book of Luke.

So, are the other stories that Luke tells accurate? You really don't know as you do know the stories he tells that are in the other Gospels are full of errors. But Luke does have some of the best stories and parables not told in the others. I have enjoyed them for years and until I took a little more critical look at the Bible, I never noticed that they were only in the Book of Luke. Let's just take a short look at the list.

There is the raising of the widow's son in Chapter 7. What is so important here is that Jesus is raising the dead so early in His ministry. The Good Samaritan is found in Chapter 10. It is the ultimate slap in the Jew's face. The Prodigal Son is in Chapter 15 and teaches unwaiverable love by the Father no matter how bad we have behaved. And then there is the Rich Man and Lazarus in Chapter 16. It teaches that if you don't share in your plenty while you are on earth you will hate life after death.

Obviously, I have condensed these stories down and they have a much larger message. But, how accurate are the stories? Did they really happen?

At the Cross, only Luke quotes Jesus as saying "Father forgive them." Only Luke shows that one thief repents and asks Jesus for forgiveness, and only Luke tells you that He and the thief would be in paradise. Did Jesus ask to have "them" forgiven, and did the thief repent? You really can't be sure as only John was at the cross and he doesn't make mention of it.

The Book of Acts doesn't have another book that it can be tested against accept at the beginning of the book. It covers some of the closing events around the time just after Jesus' crucifixion. All the Gospels tell a different story, and so does the Book of Acts.

After the ascension in Acts Chapter 1, verses 16 – 19 you read the story of how Judas dies. It is explained to have been from a fall, and he burst asunder. But in Matthew Chapter 27, verse 5 you find Matthew's understanding that Judas passed away by hanging himself. Think about it: Matthew and Judas "hung" around together for years. Don't you think that he would have known how one of his 11 closest associates had died?

I have already shown earlier in this book that the author of the Book of the Acts of the Apostles has a discrepancy in the age of Abraham when he had his son Isaac. In Acts Chapter 7, verse 4 you read that Abraham lived with his father Terah in Charran until his father dies, then he goes to Canaan.

But if you read Genesis you will see that Abraham was born to Terah before Terah was 70 years old. Abraham's father lived 205 years. As Issac was born to Abraham when he was 100 years old it would mean that Isaac was born in Charran, and we know this was wrong. So either Steven was wrong, or the author wrote it down wrong!

There isn't too much more in the book that you can collaborate on or test. But the early stuff is just as much off-target as the Book of Luke. I'm confident that the events around Paul would have been a little more accurate if the author of Acts is Luke the physician, as he supposedly worked closely with Paul.

Remember to look for two witnesses for any truth. I say this because of the damage that Christians do by leaning so heavily on the council's decision found in Acts 15. It is a story that is used by Christians, wanting a little sin in their lives, to justify almost anything. I cover it more thoroughly in the chapter *Is Paul Taken Out of Context*. Under the new found freedom that Christians claim by using this chapter, you could commit murder or a number of other sins and still be saved.

I tell you this because I want you to look for a second witness to claim this freedom. There isn't one found anywhere in the New Testament. It is only found in the Acts of the Apostles, and this appears to be a legal document written for a purpose other than the edification of the church.

Yes, I do like the Book of Luke and the Book of Acts, but it is very easy to see that they are not too accurate, at least before Paul hits the scene. Read the books a few times and compare like events with the other New Testament books and you will have to agree that these are probably the least accurate of the New Testament accounts of events.

Is Paul Taken Out of Context?

Paul is my favorite author. Think about it? He was probably the best educated of all the New Testament authors. He was one of the big-men-on-campus for the Jews before his conversion. He persecuted the early church, and for good reasons (he felt). Paul held the coats during the stoning of Stephen (our first martyr). Jesus personally talked with Paul (Saul) on his way to persecute the church in Damascus and he was immediately converted. Lastly, he wrote more of the books of the New Testament than any other author.

I have hinted around in almost every earlier chapter that Paul is taken out of context by evangelicals and most Christian religions for that matter. Why is it so important then to understand that Paul is taken out of context? Because Paul is the one author that sounds like he states that "a little sin in your life is OK if you are saved." But that is the farthest thing from the truth. Paul believed that you are saved by grace or hope (Romans 8:24), through faith. And because of our love for God we would live a life that is as sin free as possible.

The modern evangelical church quotes Paul in many instances to show that not only are we "not under the law," but that it has no relevance to us as Christians. Once again, that can't be farther from the truth. Paul does teach that you are not under the law for your salvation, but he also teaches that since you are saved by grace you will strive to live a sin free life.

What is a sin free life? Paul explains, in agreement with all other New Testament writers, that sin is anything against or contrary to the Law. So the law has relevance in your life, as it is a tool to teach you what sin is. If you are struggling with my last statement then you obviously haven't read your Bible. Reading your Bible isn't following a list of scriptures that will guide you to a conclusion that the author wants you to draw. It is from Genesis Chapter 1, verse 1, to Revelation Chapter 23, verse 21, and then start all over again.

Read all that Paul has to say before you draw a conclusion as to what he has just written. If Paul felt that there is no reason to keep the Law, and taught that way (misleading by picking and choosing verses from his writings), do you think he would have kept the Law? If he kept the Law, and taught others they did not have too, wouldn't that make him a hypocrite?

For some reason the translators took certain specific Greek words that Paul used and translated them differently for Paul's work. Take the word "charity." What do you think Paul meant when he stated "now abideth faith, hope and charity, these three, but the greatest of these is charity (1 Corinthians 13:13)." Paul is translated to use charity in his sentences over 20 times. If you look the word up in your concordance you will find that it is literally the Greek word "agape`." The exact word that we commonly use for God's love.

Why didn't they just use the word "love" as in all other translations for the same word? This is why you must look up words in your concordance when a passage looks like Paul is teaching something that may contradict the Old Testament. Before we look at some quotes from Paul, lets look at a few facts.

We are reading Paul's return mail in most of his letters. Most of what he wrote are his responses to letters or questions posed to him from various churches. You do not know exactly what they asked, although you may have an idea. Most of your ideas to what he is answering come from the teachings you have received over the years from Modern Evangelical Churches (MEC). I believe that much of the teaching is incorrect. The posed questions they suppose, are used to guide you toward their doctrine of "living in sin is OK because you can't do anything about it."

Paul explains that he is answering their questions "as a man" (Romans 3:5). This demonstrates that some, if not all, of the answer is coming from him and not given to him by God. He was a Spirit-filled man, but even Spirit-filled men do not always see eye-to-eye. Take his disagreement with Barnabas over Mark. This matter split Paul and Barnabas' working arrangement forever. Barnabas took Mark under his wing and Mark eventually became a mainstay of the early Church (Acts 15).

Take a look at the first book of Corinthians. Paul makes a decision over a matter of a man sleeping with his father's wife. In his second letter to the Corinthians he changes his mind. Which corrective action that he gave is the correct one? Who knows? He told the Corinthians he was giving them his best advice both times. If the Holy Spirit guided his every thought, especially those he wrote down for us to read today, why was there a softening of his rebuke?

There were many rituals and traditions kept by the Jews that we do not understand or have total knowledge of today. Take unclean foods. What made a food unclean? Many flesh items are Levitically unclean, but any food item was considered unclean to the Jew of the day unless you had prepared it in traditionally cleaned cookware. Also, if you had not washed your hands in a certain fashion it was considered unclean. These preparations for cleanliness were only traditions of man.

Paul writes many times about unclean food being clean, but he can never be quoted that unclean "flesh" is clean. The word flesh is important, as the word "meat" in your New Testament is the translation for any type of food, where flesh is only from animals. Take the meat offering in the Bible, it was finely ground flour! Do you think Paul ate pork? The answer comes later.

Paul advised on many local church concerns that didn't matter anywhere else in the world at that time. A good example of this was the wearing of head coverings by the women in Corinth. If you read Corinthians, he explains that the women of the church should wear a head covering. If you read the passage you will not find that he is limiting it to Corinth. Does your mom or wife wear a head covering while in public?

If you take this passage literally, Paul would require all women to wear a head covering. It has been explained that it is widely known there was a temple to a goddess in Corinth. There were prostitutes that worked in the city for the temple. If you didn't have your head covered, you would be taken for a prostitute. Obviously, Paul didn't think it was a good idea, and let them know. The previous scenario is modern teaching, and if you read the passage over and over you will have to start questioning this reasoning of the passage.

I've read this passage a number of times but have to conclude that Paul literally wanted women to have their heads covered. Why? It was a sign to show that they were in subjection to their husbands. That whole chapter is about position in the hierarchy of order. Do I think women need to have their head covered today in western society? No. But I do believe that this passage shows that a man is the head of the household and his wife is there to support him in his role. This view is not politically correct. So what! Read your Bible, use your concordance and interlinear scripture analyzer and then you decide.

Remember, you are gambling with your eternal life and death. The only person that the MEC will quote to give them the freedom they feel they have to live a life in sin, is Paul. I know, your church never openly states that you can live a life in sin, but then, do they condemn all things that are considered sin in the Bible?

If we are talking eternal death, lets look back at Deuteronomy to see what it took to condemn someone to death. It took two or three witnesses. One was not enough. If you take what Paul states, and usually out of context, he is only one witness. You may use several verses from various books, but they are all Paul's. I don't think he got it wrong. Either we just don't know the questions he was really answering or we never took the time to read the entire book he wrote, in one sitting, to see what he was really saying.

But if you believe, as the MEC would have you believe, that Paul shunned the Law and the traditions that God (not man) had handed down through the Jews, why does he boast of these in his life? He explains that they are nothing when compared with Jesus in his life. But, Paul states over and over of his Jewish values as a Hebrew and Israelite that he still lives by. Read 2 Corinthians Chapter 11 and Philippians Chapter 3 and other passages.

Peter can add some light to this matter. Christ's Apostle Peter even warns you of Paul's letters… "being hard to understand, which those that are unlearned and unstable wrest (wrestle with), as also the other scriptures, unto their own destruction." He further explains that… "they understood before so don't be led away with the error of the wicked" (2 Peter 3:15-18). What Peter is explaining is that the scriptures (the Old Testament) have already explained all things and the way Paul is being interpreted by some is false and will lead to their destruction.

Not only does Peter refer you back to the scriptures, but so does Paul in Acts Chapter 17, verse 11. Paul states that the Bereans were better than the Thessalonians, because they listened to all he had to say and then searched the scriptures to see if it was true. In other words, they would listen to him, and then go to the synagogue and open the scrolls. They didn't judge him about what had been stated during or after the time when Jesus was on the earth (New Testament), they looked in the Holy Scriptures, what we call the Old Testament.

Paul knew what he was saying could be cross-referenced in the Old Testament. He was proving Jesus and the Christian life with the Old Testament scriptures. That is why early Christian life was so much like Jewish life, but with a twist, no man-made traditions! Much of what was taught by Jewdeizers was not in the Law of God, but merely traditions of the Jew of the day.

Paul constantly quotes the Old Testament as his proof for all things that he taught. How is it that the MEC tries to dishonor the Law by teaching that Grace has replaced the Law? Go back and read Romans. It will take a slow reader about two hours. Focus on what Paul writes, not what you want him to say. By the time he shows how Grace will justify you, he has already told you that we must embrace the Law as it leads to a righteous lifestyle. Does he say to pick and choose those areas you like? No, he tells you at the end of chapter 3 to establish the Law in your life!

Let's go back to our original question about Paul that I posed. If Paul felt that there is no reason to keep the Law, and taught that way (misleading from his writings), do you think he would have kept the Law? Why would he? If he was under grace and the Law meant nothing, then he was free from following the law. But…we know that Paul not only kept the law, he taught others to do so. And when they broke the Law they should repent and do the works of repentance. Do you see? This is how we know what sin is. It is the breaking of the Law. Grace does save, but breaking the law is sinning and he did everything he could to avoid sinning.

The story starts in Acts Chapter 21. Read the whole chapter but focus on verse 24. The chapter shows how followers in Jerusalem are glad Paul has come to town, but are worried because many will say he is teaching against the Law. Verse 24 states: "Then take and purify thyself with them, and be at charges with them, that they may shave their heads: and all may know that those things, whereof they were informed concerning thee, are nothing; <u>but that thou thyself also walkest orderly and keepest the Law</u>." Did he do what was requested? Of course he did! Why? Because Paul did not want anyone to perceive that he did not keep the law.

Now jump to Acts Chapter 25 and read through the end of Chapter 26. Paul has been arrested and stands before Festus and King Agrippa. Paul tells Festus (and you) that "neither against the law of the Jews, neither against the temple, nor yet against Caesar, have I offended anything at all (Act 25:8)." And to King Agrippa he explains that he was sent to all to teach them that "they should <u>repent</u> and turn to God, and do the works meet for repentance." (Acts 26:20)

It is a very interesting read. Read both chapters in their entirety and you will have to conclude that Paul kept all of the Law, both God's and man's. Did Paul lie to the Kings to save his hide? Or, did he keep the Law? It is impossible to read anything into this story. Paul kept the Law!

Think about it. The Jews wanted to put him to death. Many of the Jewish Laws were "unto death." The only fault that the Jews presented was that Paul believed in Jesus Christ and that He had risen from the dead. Subsequently, he reiterates this again when he is in Rome later in the book. Breaking the Sabbath was a law unto death. But, he never broke the Sabbath. In these few chapters he has just affirmed that He hasn't broken even one Jewish Law.

As a parting thought that you should keep in mind when you read the rest of this book and your Bible, Paul is appearing before these dignitaries (King Agrippa and Festus) after he has written the Book of Romans. This is certain as he will be in Rome and meeting with everyone that will visit him. It is clear from the Book of Romans Chapter 1, verse 13 that Paul has never been in Rome when he writes the Roman epistle. So, when you want to pull at straws from Paul's work to say that he felt a certain way, remember that after these books (Romans and others) were written, he testifies that he has never broken a Jewish Law.

The MEC would like you to believe that Paul can be quoted to say that we are not under the Law and hence it does not pertain to us. This is a half truth. You are not under the Law for salvation since you have already failed, but it still shows you what sin is and that makes it relevant. Take any one of Paul's letters and read it from front to back in one sitting. Take notes of the truths he will teach you. Outline it.

He usually points out that Christians will no longer live a life that accepts sin in their lives. Christians will understand what sin is, as that is what the Law will teach you. Christians will unfortunately sin, but that is what Jesus Christ has done for you, offered himself as a sacrifice. Paul states that Christ's sacrifice is for our **PAST** sins (Romans 3:25). That means that we can no longer live in a sinful lifestyle. Find one passage where Paul states that Jesus died for the sins you know you will be planning to commit. Sorry, there isn't one.

In 1 Timothy Chapter 1, starting at verse 5-13, Paul warns of those that are teaching the Law as an outward show, but then state that it (the Law) is good if used Lawfully. He further states "The Law is unneeded if you are already righteous." Are you righteous? But then he gives a list of those who definitely need the Law. One of these categories is "sinners." The MEC would have you believe that you are a sinner and I believe they are correct in this statement. So, according to Paul, as a sinner you need the Law to guide your life.

Read the chapter, or letter for that matter, several times and it will always come back to sinners needing the Law to guide their lives. Do you try to follow the Law? If you are playing Christian instead of being one, you probably don't.

Although discussed later to explain whether the Old Testament Scriptures are needed for modern Christians, I must quickly cover this here. What about when Paul was writing in II Timothy Chapter 3, verse 16-17 where he states that "all scripture is given by inspiration of God, and is profitable for doctrine, for reproof, for correction, for instruction in righteousness: that the man of God may be perfect, thoroughly furnished unto all good works?" Doesn't that mean that we can take what appears to be "Saved by Grace no matter what (as some would teach)" in the New Testament and discard those Old Testament rules?

Remember, he was obviously talking about the Old Testament. Just read the verse prior to those quoted. II Timothy Chapter 3, verse 15 "And that from a child thou hast known the holy scriptures, which are able to make thee wise unto salvation through the faith in Jesus Christ." The New Testament consists of letters from the early church leaders to other churches and members. They weren't compiled for years into something we call scriptures. Timothy could not have read them as a child as they hadn't been written yet. Paul didn't say to Timothy, "read my epistles as they will make you wise." On the contrary, he told him to read the Old Testament and use it in his life as a guide.

Even the writer of the Book of Hebrews (we think it is Paul) tells you that, "For if we sin willfully after that we have received the knowledge of the truth, there remains no more sacrifice for sins, but certain fearful looking for of judgment and fiery indignation, which shall devour the adversaries (Hebrews 10: 26-27)." Hey, what is sin anyway? Paul tells you if you read the book of Romans that it is ANYTHING that is contrary to the Law. Does the author of the Book of Hebrews feel you can be saved and still sin? No!

In fact, the MEC tries to portray God as a different God than in all known biblical accounts. Their God is a New God that loves everyone even if they are still sinning. If you believe that, it is a form of idolatry, because that is not what is taught about the God of Abraham, Isaac, and Jacob. They do this by trying to read a deeper meaning into these letters by Paul. There isn't a deeper meaning. Who did he write to? Paul was writing to people that he wanted to understand his message. Although his letters do apply today, they were written to people less educated than you. How could there be a deeper message? No one would have understood it. He told then that he wanted "fruit" from them.

These letters are so simple that you don't need anyone to help you interpret them. Just read them a couple of times and they will come alive to you. Don't be fooled by a church that allows you to live in a sinful lifestyle. Just read the Bible for yourself and apply it to your life. The only way that Paul is hard to understand is when you take him here and there. It becomes complicated because it appears as if he states contradictory statements to scripture. This is because you haven't read each epistle from start to finish in one sitting. If you do, it will not contradict itself or any other Bible passage and message.

Now, lets take a few of the better-known passages by or about Paul that the MEC would use to suggest that we have the freedom to sin. Why do I say "freedom to sin?" Because if you lower the bar of what you consider to be sin, then you may not be sinning by this new lower threshold. We will see what each of these passages really teaches you.

The first incident of this freedom to sin focuses on Paul, but is noted in the Book of Acts which is believed to be written by Luke. This passage is one of the most quoted freedom statements to the Gentiles. In Acts Chapter 15, the MEC would have you believe that the council in Jerusalem is called together because Paul came back to the council to plead the case that Gentiles shouldn't be under the Law (Acts 15). Thus, Gentiles were accepted into Christianity if they followed a few basic rules.

Acts Chapter 15 starts with the belief that a Gentile Christian was required to be circumcised. This is truly the only issue of this chapter in the book, but liberal churches try to create an all or nothing decision about the Law with it.

Christians are plainly not Jews. There are only four sinful acts that most modern churches believe this chapter tells Christians that they must not do. They are to abstain from four things: pollution from idols, fornication, strangled things, and blood. If these are the only Christian requirements, then I guess we can wife-swap, commit adultery, embezzle, steal, murder, covet, and the list goes on.

Read Acts Chapter 15, verse 21 closely. Right after the four above mentioned requirements there is the statement: **"For Moses of Old time hath in every city them that preach him, being read in the synagogues every Sabbath day."** The following verse (Acts 15:22) states that this pleased the council and so they sent the word of their findings to the various Gentile churches. Do you understand what this means? It means that the early church didn't believe in the extra rules that the Jews of the day were living, but they did expect them to live by the Law delivered by Moses **and four more things**. These were not precursors to salvation; they were simply identifying what sin is and what to avoid. This is called "obedience."

Too many modern churches hang their hat on this chapter. If the decision was "God-sent" and written by God's hand, you could make the case that a Gentile Christian is not under the Law at all. Obviously, you have to forget that Acts Chapter 15, verse:21 is located right in the middle of it, but let's say that you desire a more liberal read to this chapter, as most modern Christian churches follow. Was this a decision ordained by God?

What about when the city of Gibeon duped Joshua and the entire Israel leadership not to destroy them in Joshua Chapter 9? What does this have to do with Acts Chapter 15? Many times in the Bible, holy men make decisions without going to God through prayer. Sometimes these decisions are a stumbling block later in their lives.

Paul didn't think the decision from the council was God-ordained later in his ministry. Paul believed that he could eat meat (flesh) that had been offered to idols. We will show this when we cover the next out-of-context statement by Paul. So, if Paul later believes that he can eat meat offered to idols, what else was wrong with this "Council" decision. They should have prayed before they made it!

What you can conclude from this discussion of Acts Chapter 15 is that Paul didn't believe that a Christian needed to be circumcised, but still needed the Law. Later in his ministry he understood that at least some of what the council had decided was in error.

Read 1 Corinthians Chapter 10, verse 23. Paul has many statements that are similar. "All things are lawful for me, but all things are not expedient, all things are lawful for me, but all things edify not." The MEC would like you to believe that the word "all" used would clearly indicate "all things that the Law would classify as sin." So, they would have you believe that Paul was telling you in this passage, as well as those that he wrote that use similar wording, that Paul was not concerned about what he did as he was guided by Jesus and was not under the curse of the Law for sinning.

This can only be used if you ignore all other passages where he tells us that a Christian not only refrains from sinning, but also shouldn't dwell on the thoughts of sinning. Thus, there is a contradiction. But, there is an answer! If you take the whole chapter and look at it in its entirety you will learn that the MEC's interpretation is false.

In Chapter 10 Paul is talking about food dedicated to idols being of no consequence and then transitions into how if someone thinks Paul is giving reverence to these foods, it is better to not eat them. Read the entire chapter and leave out the *italicized* added words (i.e., wealth). It is pretty clear that it has nothing to do with Paul feeling he can "do all things" without any consequences. It is clear that Paul was simply stating that he knows he can eat flesh that was dedicated to an idol, as there is only one true God.

1 Corinthians Chapter 6, verse 12. "All things are lawful to me, but all things are not expedient: All things are lawful for me, but I will not be brought under the power of any." Once again this sounds like Paul is telling you he can do anything, and so it is taught by the MEC using this verse. This kills me. You can only agree with this thought process if you haven't read the verses leading up to it.

Read 1 Corinthians Chapter 6, verses 9–11. Paul teaches that there are many classes of lifestyles that will <u>not</u> enter into the kingdom of God. If you are having sex out of wedlock, have any idols, have sex with your neighbor's spouse, if you are gay, a sadist, steal from others, longingly lusting after what others have, drink to excess (I would imagine this would also include drugs today), be a brawler, or extort from others; all these classes will not enter into the Kingdom of God. Don't take my word for it, look it up.

So, how can Paul tell you that those who commit such acts are exempt from entry, but he (Paul) can do them? All Paul is telling you is that you have choices, as he does. And if you choose a worldly lifestyle, you will not enter into eternal life. And although he could do those acts, he chooses not to, hence they have no power over him and his eternal life is secure.

1 Colossians Chapter 2, verses:16-17 "Let no man therefore judge you in meat, or drink, or in respect of an Holy day, or of the new moon, or of the Sabbath which is a shadow of things to come." This statement does sound like he is telling them that there is no significance to any of these. But you have to have read Paul's letters completely through a couple of times, and the Book of Acts to have a better understanding of how Paul felt.

In many of his letters he was trying to get back to Jerusalem in time for one of the holy days. Why? Because they were special to him. But read the entire chapter before you are drawn into believing Paul took no notice to what he ate and drank and Sabbath worship. In verse 22, he explains that those rituals that he is telling them to take no notice of, are "commandments and doctrines of men." Remember the punctuation (?) was added by the translator. There is no punctuation in the original manuscripts. The chapter even talks about worshiping of angels.

So, Paul didn't state not to take notice of the "Commandments of God," just the commandments of men. Could it be that ritualism had already crept into the young church and many new customs had been imposed?

Just like Jesus Christ, Paul lashed out at the religious leaders of the day that added outward ritual to prove holiness. The only thing God cares about is our inward righteousness. But, let's take it a little farther. If you drink alcohol, are you sinning? The answer is no! But many churches teach that you are. It is the excess of alcohol that is sinning. Paul writes many times on this. But, if you take 1 Colossians Chapter 2, verses 16-17 as a modern translation for ending Sabbath worship, then it also states that you can't be judged for drinking and it doesn't give a limit. If you take this literally, it contradicts Paul's statement that drunkards are not living in the Spirit, and thus are of the world.

So, Paul isn't giving license to eat and drink whatever you want. Nor is he telling you that the holy days and Sabbaths are of no concern. He is just stating not to take notice of the external limits and rituals placed by religious leaders, as they are adding to what God has already stated.

Always look up questionable scriptures with an interlinear scripture analyzer. The above verse (1 Colossians 2:16-17) reads literally in the Greek: "No then any you let be judging in feeding and drinking or in part of festival or of young months or of Sabbaths which is shade of the being about the yet body of the anointed." I know it sounds blocky, but are you really sure that the Bible you read today is a correct translation?

Paul warns you of those that would deliver a gospel other than the one he is delivering. Why is this so important? He is telling you about false prophets or ministers. He states in Galatians Chapter 1, verse 8 "But though we (he even includes himself), or an angel from heaven, preach any other gospel unto you than that ye have received, let him be accursed." Now read 2 Corinthians Chapter 11, verse 14. You will note that Satan can appear as "an Angel of light." Why is this so important? Paul has told you how to test a prophet or your local church leader.

This brings us back to understanding what Paul really taught. In many of his letters when he is rebuking something, he explains "As you already understood," or "As I taught you when I was there." You really have to pick up your Bible and read all of his letters and the Book of Acts to understand what Paul really taught. And, unfortunately for those that want a little sin in their lives, you will have to draw the conclusion that Paul felt there was no sin for those that are saved.

So, can you rest your salvation on a few of the above passages like, "I can do all things?" Is there any way to be certain that Paul wasn't stating that he could do "all" things? You know, Paul thinking that he was saved, and believed in once-saved-always-saved. Could Paul let sin into his life (sin according to the Law) and still be salvation bound?

Of course there is an answer! In over half of Paul's letters, he tells you of groups of people that are definitely not salvation bound. In fact, he tells you that they are meant for sure destruction. With that said, could Paul commit these sins and still be salvation bound? Of course not! Otherwise he would have stated "I can commit these sins, but you can't." No, he says "all these are not meant for salvation." Guess what, most of these categories are not listed in the four things listed as sin to Gentiles in Acts 15. Maybe that is because those four sins were additions.

Read: Romans 1:27-32
        1 Corinthians 1:6-11.
        Galatians 5:19-21
        Ephesians 5:1-5
        Colossians 3:5-8
        1 Thessalonians 4:3-8
        2 Corinthians 12:19-21.

Don't be fooled by those church leaders that want to bend the Commandments of God to meet their desires and doctrine. Just read the Bible for yourself from front to back. You will begin to enjoy Paul's letters in the way he intended for them to be read. No secret messages, just obedience to the Father with love. Yes I know, not many of your so-called Christian friends will agree with you. Take it from Jesus Christ, "narrow is the path to eternal life and few shall find it. Broad is the path to destruction."

To conclude the above exhaustive study, Paul is quite clear on how to live a Christian life. He also tells you how to ensure that a prophet is of God (and I see no prophet since Paul that meets the test). First, all doctrine will agree with the Old Testament (2 Timothy 3:15-17). Secondly, all doctrine will be as he, Paul, taught it or it is not from God, even if it is received from what appears to be a heavenly angel (more likely Satan in disguise). And lastly, don't cling to added commandments made by men to make your life more "Holy" (Colossians 2:22). The Commandments of God are what you need in your life.

You have a choice to make. Will you follow your Christian peers in a quest to enjoy "some" world values at the expense of your eternal life?

Christian Living

Now that you have a better understanding of your Bible and some of it's authors, do you want to be a "Good and Faithful Servant?" What does God really expect? Most Christians have a good understanding of the pet verses taught in the New Testament. They may even try to live their lives by them, but is that enough for God?

Do you believe that you can live by the words of Jesus Christ only? How many actual words that He spoke do we have written down? Do you believe that He understood the Old Testament? If He did, doesn't that beg the question, shouldn't it be important to you? You may say that after His crucifixion and resurrection all things changed. We are under a new covenant.

If that is true, how did the early church live? Is there enough in the New Testament to prove either position? There really is, and it may surprise you. The million dollar question is, if you see them living differently than you live today, will it change your life choices?

What about sin in our lives? As a Christian, doesn't Grace take sin off the table? Sin has consequences. Sin leads to death. The following chapters will nail down for you how the early church lived and what they believed. These chapters will explain why Grace is the important Salvation instrument of God, but under Grace you will not accept sin in your life.

What sin will you reject? All sin if you are truly saved by Grace!

Does the Old Testament Apply Today? After All, I am a New Testament Christian.

In a nutshell, YES! First, you've got to ask yourself, what is the Bible and where did it come from? If you understood this, you would never have to wonder about the first question. The Bible is made of the Old Testament and the New Testament. The Old Testament are the scriptures that are referenced by Jesus and the rest of the New Testament writers.

So, when you read in the New Testament that someone is referencing the "scriptures," he is referencing the Old Testament. The authors do refer to other epistles of the New Testament (very few times), but they just refer to them as "letters," not scriptures.

The Old Testament is made up of the Law and the Prophets. The Law is the first five books of the Bible. The Prophets are the rest of the Old Testament. When Jesus Christ would say…"it is written"…what was He referring to? He was referring to some passage in the Old Testament. And you can look up those Old Testament passages for each time He referenced them.

When Paul would stated that the Bereans "searched the scriptures to see if it were true," what was he referring to (Acts 17:11)? The Bereans would go back to the Old Testament scrolls in the synagogue and see if what Paul was telling them about Jesus was in the scriptures.

In fact, most, if not all of the New Testament books reference the Old Testament for some kind of proof of their authority. Then, what is the New Testament and why do so many Christians believe that it is all we need?

As stated earlier, the New Testament starts with four accounts of Jesus Christ's life. Although not quite the same, they all carry the same message. We call them the Gospels and they were written some time after Christ's resurrection, maybe as much as 50 years. The last book of the New Testament is the only prophetic book other than those in the Old Testament. It is Revelation, and it was written by the Apostle John. There are hundreds of Old Testament prophetic illusions in this book. For those that have a hard time reading Revelation, just read the Old Testament a couple of times and Revelation will become very clear.

The rest of the books in the New Testament are called the epistles. These are letters from the apostles or church leaders to various churches and other church leaders. Although very important documents, these are not "scriptures." Many in the Modern Evangelical Church (MEC) try to give them the same or higher authority than the Old Testament. There is no place in the New

Testament where an author downplays the authority of the Old Testament. In fact, the promises that the MEC try to claim come from the Old Testament.

Although stated earlier in this book, what about when Paul was writing to Timothy and he states that "all scripture is given by inspiration of God, and is profitable for doctrine, for reproof, for correction, for instruction in righteousness: that the man of God may be perfect, thoroughly furnished unto all good works (II Timothy 3:16-17)." Isn't this good enough proof that we need the scriptures in our lives? Do you remember what scriptures Paul was talking about?

We know Paul was referring to the Old Testament. Just look at the proceeding verse. II Timothy 3:15 "And that from a child thou hast known the Holy Scriptures, which are able to make thee wise unto salvation through the faith in Jesus Christ." The Holy Scriptures Timothy learned as a child could only be the Old Testament. The New Testament wasn't compiled for years into something we call scriptures. Paul called the books we refer to as the New Testament, "epistles." Paul didn't say to Timothy, "Read my epistles as they will make you wise." On the contrary, he told him to read the Old Testament and use it in his life as a guide.

But the Book of II Timothy was written with many other warnings. Go back to Chapter 2 of the same book and you will learn how Paul felt Timothy should handle his daily life. Paul instructs him to "study to show thyself approved unto God." Study what? The only thing Timothy could study would have been the Old Testament. Do you study the Old Testament? Do you want to be "approved unto God?" Don't you think from these two passages to Timothy that it shows he felt the Old Testament is essential in all our daily lives? Of course he did.

Do you believe that you are of the Holy Olive Tree, or do you think that a Christian is "something else" or something better? In the New Testament, Paul explains (Romans 11) that the Jewish nation was the Holy Olive Tree. Some of the Jews were pruned out, and many of us Gentiles were grafted in. Christians are not a new sect to God. We are an extension of His holy people. That makes the guidance given to the "Holy Olive Tree" relevant to those of us grafted in. What was their guidance? The Old Testament.

Do you believe that you are of Abraham's seed or do you think that a Christian is something different? Look up the word "Abraham" in your concordance and see how it is used. Everyone that we would class as "saved" in the New Testament is claiming to be of his seed. But all of his "seed" are not saved. Yes, God has pruned some out, making way for some of us to be grafted in.

What about when you hear that Jesus has fulfilled the scriptures? Doesn't that mean that we no longer need the Old Testament? First ask yourself, Did Jesus really fulfill all the scriptures? At His first visit with mankind He did fulfill a lot of the Old Testament requirements, but not all.

There are too many Old Testament prophecies that are still waiting to be fulfilled. Let's just take one book of the Old Testament and then you decide if the Old Testament has anything to offer you.

How many churches teach that there will be a Battle of Armageddon? I don't know of any Christian church that denies it will happen. Where does this story come from? It is found in Ezekiel Chapters 37-39. Has this prophecy been fulfilled yet? No, of course not. It is in the future. So, does this book of the Old Testament still apply to you? I would hope so. God will overthrow evil with Jesus Christ at the front of the charge. Do you discount this book? Of course not. But what happens after Chapter 39 in Ezekiel?

You will read of a temple to come. Yes, there is another temple. Out of the throne will begin a flow of water that will grow into a river. Read the account in Revelation 22. They are very similar. Why? They are both end-times prophesy. But if you read Ezekiel 40 through 48 you will learn that the "Chosen" will still keep the law, the Sabbath, and it does appear that there will be sacrifices. How can there be sacrifices if we are all "New Testament" Christians and we don't believe in them anyways?

Where did you get that idea? I don't profess to understand the sacrifices either, or I would explain it right here. But, did all sacrificing end for Christians with the death of Jesus Christ? I really don't think so. None of the other writers in the New Testament talk about the issue in their letters. Only Paul appears to talk about it.

But if all the "God-ordained" celebrations of the Old Testament that we teach have gone away and/or are not required, why was Paul so concerned with returning to Jerusalem to attend them? Read Acts 18 (verse 21) and others.

Or if it wasn't important to keep the Law, why was Paul so ready to prove that he "kept the Law" by purifying himself in the temple with four other Jews in Acts 21 (verse 26). This is even more important when you realize that Paul was also providing the offering. This would have been a sacrifice.

Modern Christianity explains that the outward display of Judaism (circumcision), is not required by Christians, so why did Paul circumcise Timothy in Acts 16? After all, Timothy's father was a Greek. This is really odd as this occurs after the council in Jerusalem agrees that a Greek doesn't need to be circumcised. Now, Timothy's mother was a Jew, but does that matter? Back then, women meant nothing in regards to lineage. Don't be fooled by your "friendly" Christian counselor. Just read your Bible for yourself.

The more you read your Bible the more you will understand that there is a lot there that we don't understand. More importantly, the more you read your Bible the more you will understand that Christianity today is not the Christianity of Paul's day.

Today's Christianity is an easy, simple, Christianity where you do nothing at all, and are still saved. If you claim to be a New Testament Christian and disregard the Old Testament, why not read each book of the New Testament in one sitting and ask yourself, "Did the author of this New Testament book tell me I can throw out the Old Testament?" The answer will be No every time.

Do you sin in your present life? Is it acceptable to God? Is that what your church teaches you? Why not read the Book of Romans in one sitting? It will teach you that you are saved by grace. You know, Jesus died for you on the cross and if you have faith that He died for your sins, you will be justified by that faith. Paul further teaches in Romans that sin is anything that is contrary to the Mosaic Law. You also learn that as a Christian you will not live in sin. But in the same book, Paul teaches that if you are under grace you will embrace the Law (end of Romans 3).

Do you really think you can claim "saved-by-grace" and continue to live a life that is knowingly sinful? Of course not. Read Romans again. Now, to understand what sin is you must read and understand the Old Testament. So how can you claim to be saved-by-grace, if you are living in sin? And how can you understand what sin is without understanding the Old Testament?

So, if Jesus and the rest of the New Testament writers referred to the Old Testament as their authority for their controversial doctrine; the promise for everlasting life comes from the Old Testament; Revelation needs the Old Testament to make sense; do you think that you can understand the Love of God by being a "New Testament only" Christian?

I guess I could sum up a conversation with someone playing Christian like this: Oh, you don't really want to know how God wants you to live? Then don't read your Bible. Oh, you don't read your Bible? Then you are just playing Christian, you really aren't one.

Do Today's Christians Believe as the Early Church Did?

Are you kidding? Of course not! This should be summed up by now if you have been paying attention to this book. That is the problem with the Modern Evangelical Church (MEC) and all other older denominations today. Look, these institutions are a product of years and years of tradition. They are concerned with membership.

The early church didn't worry about membership. The Holy Spirit took care of that. Read the New Testament Book of Acts. To be like the early church, all you have to do is read your Bible. Start with Genesis 1:1 and end at Revelation 22:21. Then read it again. Are you tired of me telling you this yet?

You will see that the early church believed very much as the early Jew (several hundred years before Christ). All the New Testament writers pointed out that you should avoid sinning. They also point out, that to do this, you would keep the Law. They taught that keeping the Law did not save you, but that if you were saved you would no longer sin. The Law points out what sin is!

So, what is different from the early Church to what we have today? They were obedient to God, they lovingly took care of one another, and they sacrificed their lives to share the Gospel. Let's look at these three points before we look at how so many changes became accepted by the MEC and older denominations.

Nowhere in the New Testament do you find an example of anyone breaking God's Law or the local laws of the land. I don't think that you should ever find yourself in that position. Take paying taxes. Do you avoid paying your taxes? Do you fudge them a little? Do you believe the early church paid their taxes? Even Jesus paid taxes (Matthew 17: 24-27). God will always give you enough to do His will and allow you to be a good servant to the country you belong to.

Look at keeping the Sabbath. It is in God's Law and the early church kept it. Can you find an example where any of the "saved" of the New Testament worked on God's Sabbath? No! You will not find them breaking the Sabbath, as that would have been sin. But today, we find all kinds of reasons not to keep the Sabbath. Instead, we keep the "Lord's Day." Is keeping the "Lord's Day" as a replacement for the Sabbath of God scriptural? Show me!

Take eating unclean flesh. Can you find any examples of any of the "saved" eating unclean flesh in the New Testament? No! For that matter there is no place where you can find any of the "saved" in the New Testament breaking any of God's Law. There are places in the New

Testament where Paul is quoted to say it is OK not to "live" under the Law, but then, you don't find Paul breaking the Law of God anywhere. No, the early church did not break God's Law.

They were so "Jewish" that they were considered a sect of Judaism by the Gentiles, and realistically they were. They kept the "Laws" of Judaism with one twist. They believed that the Messiah had come. Read your Old Testament. When the Messiah came, were they to change their belief in God? No! But the Jews didn't accept the early church because they were looking for a different Messiah, one that would throw off the Roman rule.

Although discussed earlier in this book, the modern evangelical church quotes that Paul came back to the council in Jerusalem to plead the case that Gentiles shouldn't be under the Law (Acts 15), and thus the Gentiles were accepted if they abstained from only four things: pollution from idols, fornication, strangled things, and blood. This is idiotic. Although partly true, read the whole chapter again. It starts with the believed need that a Gentile Christian was required to be circumcised. That is the act of removing (cutting away) the foreskin from males. This was the act, or sign, required by man to show his acceptance of Judaism. Christians are plainly not Jews.

Next, take the four requirements. If that was all Christianity required, then I guess we can wife swap, as that is adultery, not fornication. We can embezzle from work, as that is only stealing. If we like our neighbor's wealth, we can kill him and take it, as it is only murder and covetousness. Read Acts 15 again and focus on verse 21. Right after the four above mentioned requirements there is the statement: "For Moses of Old time hath in every city them that preach him, being read in the synagogues every Sabbath day." The following verse (Acts 15:22) states that "this pleased the council and so they sent the word of their findings to the various Gentile churches."

Do you understand what this means? It means that the early church didn't believe in the extra rules for man to live up to as the Jews were currently living, but they did expect them to live by Moses' Law and four more things. These were not precursors to salvation; they were just identifying what sin is and what to avoid. This is called obedience. The only problem is, this may not have been a God-ordained decision. Could the Council have made a non-God-ordained decision? It happened before, and I believe it happened right here.

Read Joshua Chapter 9. It is the story of the "wily" leadership of a city called Gibeon that duped Joshua and the entire Israel leadership. They enter into a pact together without presenting the facts to the Lord for guidance. Since they gave their oath of peace, they could not wipe out this city as the Lord had commanded. Not wiping out the inhabitants of a pagan culture was the beginning of idolatry working into the Children of Israel. So, what does this have to do with Acts Chapter 15?

Where do you see the Council's leadership coming together to pray and wait for guidance from God? You don't, they are just arguing about why each side believes that they have it correct. These are Spirit-filled men making a decision. But they got it wrong.

How do I know? Because Paul states that he understands that he can eat foods that have been offered to idols later in his ministry. Where does he say this? Why not read 1 Corinthians Chapter 10? It is in other passages by him also, but one example should be enough here.

My next point about how the early church members lived is they sacrificed all they had for one another. Read the Book of Acts. Then do it again. You will see what sacrificing for others is all about. They were a persecuted church. Their spiritual lives were in secret, or they were put to death. They lost all they had. The early church reminds Paul to bring back money for the poor.

In the Book of Acts you will also learn what living for your Creator would be like. Take Stephen, James, or Paul. They all suffered over and over, and were finally killed for our Lord. All the early church knew was why they were here, and it was to spread the word of our Lord. Not to create a beautiful building or increase membership.

Jesus stated that the path to eternal life is narrow and few shall find it. Attending a church club is not entry into eternal life. From your reading of Acts Chapter 5, look back at Ananias and Sapphira. They attended the church and gave a lot of money, but they didn't really live in their hearts as they verbally expressed. The Lord will not be mocked. Do you think they were saved? I bet they said the spiritual words of the day… "Jesus Christ come into my life and forgive me of my sins." Do you believe in once-saved-always-saved? From that story, it doesn't appear that they will be with me in eternal life. John didn't think so either.

So, how did we get so far off from where the Lord would like us to be? Take a look at early church history. This is not meant to be an all-encompassing history lesson. If you really want to understand it, look it up on the Internet for yourself. You may have to sort out the fiction and it will take work, something most evangelical sheep (always needing to be led) will not do for themselves.

The church was persecuted by Rome until about 300 AD. Then the church became the government's church, hence the name, the Roman Catholic Church. To congeal the pagans and Christians, we took a little and gave a little. This is called compromise. Do you think God wants you to compromise His values for an easier life on earth? From that point, bishops got together to make decisions on how Christians would live.

We took the Christian's God and celebrated on the pagan's day. It was so easy, we got Sunday worship (the Lord's Day). We took a pagan rabbit (the symbol of fertility) holiday, added Christ's death and "presto," you got Easter. We took the pagan celebration of the winter solstice and the yule log, added Christ's birth and we got Christmas.

Look up the "Council of Nicea" on the internet. The Catholic bishops proudly explain what they decided the scriptures meant. This was the council where they decided Jesus' divinity and gave themselves the authority to change the Sabbath (Friday sundown to Saturday sundown) to the Lord's Day (Sunday worship).

A lot of the Roman Catholic Church's authority comes from the claim that Peter was the first Pope. Once again, this is just stupid. Peter was persecuted by the Romans before 100 AD, died, and was buried in some obscure place, as were most early Church members. Peter being the first pope is about as daft as finding Jesus' true burial place. This would and does create idolatry. Why would you worship a location or relic? Catholicism didn't even begin to exist before 300 AD.

Think about how dumb it is to believe that some bishop in the 300s AD would have some link back to the early Church of 33-70 AD. It would be something like you having a link into the understanding of how George Washington and others really felt, during the Revolutionary War. Only, we have a lot of writings from the 1770s and super computers to help sift through the documents out there. The early bishops had nothing more than what we can read today about the early church, and that was if they could read!

In the 1600s, the Great Reformation took place. It was the birth of the Protestant Church. They began to ask themselves, why do we do things the Roman Catholic way? Why not the Bible's way? Why not Grace? It was a great falling away from Catholicism. Only, under peer pressure, many of the great reformers kept the scriptures to themselves. They feared a great uprising if they changed too much. Far too many people were and are more concerned about the negative outcome from living and teaching a biblical life.

Did you ever wonder why there are so many denominations that call themselves Christian? I think it is all about money and control. Someone corners the market on some verse of scripture, and a group of people get together and think it is the one awe-important part of the Bible. Others agree, and voila (that's French for BAM), a new denomination of the Christian Church emerges.

Funny though. I believe they all have it wrong. It stems from man's selfish nature. Would you be a member of the town "club" if they looked down on you when you showed up for an event? Probably not. You must fit in to be a good member.

It is the same with Christian denominations. They all have their list of rules. The problem is, it is a "church club." I love churches that have Bible study on some day of the week. They all sit around and read scriptures and then, when they find something their church is doing wrong, they ignore it! It's pathetic. Why even have a Bible study if you are not there to learn, grow, and love the Lord? Have you ever run into this? If not, you probably haven't sat in a group and read your Bible line-by-line.

The early Church understood who they were worshiping. Do you find any New Testament author, or any early believer calling Jesus Christ, God? Jesus is referred to as a man, as the son of man, as the Son of God, and Holy, but not God. Read the New Testament again. Then ask yourself, am I holding to the faith of the early Christian Church? Probably not.

We all know the story of Jesus Christ entering the wilderness after His baptism, but what is the significance of this incident? We don't need to look deeper into it, but one thing is very profound.

Jesus had been fasting and praying for a long time. Then Satan tempts Him to follow his lead. Go back and read the exchange. It can be found in Matthew, Mark and Luke.

The tempting starts with the required action Satan wants Jesus to do, but at times it is followed by Holy Scripture quoted by Satan. This is the profound part. It isn't just a desire planted by Satan as a temptation to the Lord. It also comes with scripture to back it up, to say, the action Satan has requested from the Lord is OK.

Why is this so important? For anyone who thinks they live by the scriptures, it shows that if we want to partake of almost any selfish desire, we can take scripture out of context to back up the action. Obviously, the Lord listened and then re-quoted scripture to show the real intent of what God the Father desires.

But before you say, "I live by scripture," ask yourself, do you? Take the writings of Paul. Many things written by Paul appear to allow us out from living under the Law. And, by picking and choosing the lines we want to quote, we are. Paul never states that the Law is null and void. He just stresses that the Law cannot save you, and it can't. But he also tells you that it is Holy, and shows you what sin is. The Father hates sin. When you live contrary to the Law, the Father hates that action in your life.

Are you purposely doing things in your life that are contrary to the Law? My favorite two that oppose MEC mission statements, as you have probably observed by now, are the Sabbath and the health/diet laws. Do you keep the Sabbath? I really don't care what day of the week you go to church, but do you work on the Sabbath? Read your Old Testament and ask yourself, is it the Jews' Sabbath or God's Sabbath?

Do you eat pork? Yes, there are many other foods God stated were an abomination to eat, but this one is my favorite. When Jesus cast out the Legion of devils from the man in the tomb, where did they go (Mark 5)? They asked, and He sent them into some grazing swine. What are swine? Pigs! No, I don't believe that pigs are filled with devils, but He didn't cast them into cows either.

What makes it significant is that He did allow the devils to enter into the pigs. Pigs were and are unclean, and hence a good place to send a devil. In the New Testament you will find many places where even Jesus talks about what goes into your mouth isn't what defiles you, it is what comes out of your mouth.

All of these teachings can be linked back to the added rituals given by man to make their food more pure. It had to do with the washing of hands and cleaning of pots. Paul even tells you regarding food, that he can do all things, but this is only referring to eating flesh that had been offered to an idol. Lots of scripture on this will be presented further in this book.

Remember it is a heart issue to God. But, if you don't try to keep at least the outward appearance of the Law set by God, how can you say your heart is keeping the Law? Remember the Beatitudes? God wants more than the external show. But how can you have an inward desire if you are not fulfilling the outward display?

Depending on what church you attend, there will be many issues they believe and teach that are not biblical. Take the rapture. Are you pre-trib? Where is your biblical proof? There isn't any. Only an obscure way of looking at Revelation Chapter 4, verse 1 where we hear a voice from heaven calling John up to heaven. This was a vision. Next in the vision, John is looking down on the things to come with God. You can infer what you want from the scriptures, but most things are spelled out pretty clear if you would read your Bible from front to back a couple of times.

Where do you find that living a homosexual lifestyle is OK? This life choice is accepted by society, but is it accepted by God? It is only called an abomination in the Bible. Look up the word sodomite in your concordance. Why not read Romans 1, focusing on verses 26 and 27? It is obvious that when man sleeps with man or woman with woman, it is sin and an abomination to God. But is this sin any more of a sin than a man cheating on his wife? No, both are unacceptable to God and they should be an unacceptable life choice for a real Christian.

Why do we find it hard to understand that God never ordained women to lead men in Church? Paul, the apostle used by most churches to beat back the Law explains it several times, but best in 1 Corinthians Chapter 14, verses 34-35 and 1 Timothy Chapter 2, verses 11-14. Paraphrased, it is because the woman (Eve) was deceived. In other words, women follow emotions. Those are feelings. There is no reference to women leading men in worship anywhere in the New Testament!

Feelings are great, but God requires obedience no matter how you "feel" about it. Read those chapters and verses carefully and ask yourself, is there any wiggle room in allowing women to teach men in church? The answer has to be "No." Yes, women and men are equal, but different. Both can be saved and loved by God, but women are forbidden to teach!

Modern Christians seem to "feel" they have to love and please everyone. This includes accepting other non-God-fearing lifestyles. Sorry, that wasn't how the early church practiced and so why should you?

The list goes on and on. Being a Christian and leading a life that is pleasing to God is not followed by any church that I have found. It isn't a life that will be totally accepted by your peers. But, you have to ask yourself, do I want to please man or God? Why not read your Bible, and when you come to a "Thou shalt or Thou shalt not" ask yourself, did God change His idea of what is sin? My God doesn't change. He is the same yesterday, today and tomorrow. If He is changeable, then my salvation is questionable.

The Law, Works, Faith or Grace?

You are saved by grace through faith. End of story. But do you love God the Father and Jesus Christ His Son? How do you know if you are loved by Them? If you aren't loved by Them, can you be saved? As a parent, when my child obeys my rules and does as he knows I want, I know he at least respects me. I hope that it is truly love. If I love God, why wouldn't I want to do the things I know He has asked of me and reject those things that I know He hates?

Should the Law be important to Christians? This would not be an issue if it wasn't for modern evangelical teaching taking Paul out of context over and over again. You will learn after reading your Bible front to back that it isn't the Law or Grace, it is the Law and Grace. Can you be under grace and knowingly do a sinful act? If you answer yes, then you need to read your Bible again, or maybe for the first time.

A later chapter in this book helps you understand if you are really saved. It is interestingly titled, "*Are You Really Saved, Can You Loose it, What about Once Saved Always Saved.*" It will help you understand if you are truly saved by "Grace" on a personal level. But, does Grace alone save you? Are the works of the Law needed in your life? Is it Grace alone?

Christ could not make it plainer when He stated: "If you love me, keep my commandments." He never stated or discussed the removal of any commandment(s). Please read Matthew Chapter 5. It starts with the "Beatitudes." He is plainly explaining how we should conduct ourselves as His followers. He then goes on to explain that He isn't here to remove the Law or the prophets, just to fulfill it. In fact, He stated that not one yot or tittle would be removed from the Law until all be fulfilled (Matthew 5:18). What does the word "all" refer to in that statement?

Modern Evangelical Christians would like you to believe "all" is fulfilled. You know their saying, "Jesus has fulfilled the Law." How about Jesus Christ's second coming? That hasn't happened yet! There is a lot of Old and New Testament scripture that has not yet been fulfilled, but He did start to fulfill it on His first coming. For those that cling to "Jesus fulfilled the law," read the first thing in Matthew Chapter 5, verse 18, that must happen before the Law is finished, "Till heaven and earth pass away." Jesus Christ stated it Himself!

No, that hasn't happened yet either. But it will. Read of it in the New Testament Book of Revelation. There will be a fire, then there will be a new heaven and a new earth. Jesus never stated that He has fulfilled all the Law, and explained through this verse that it will be some time to come before this will happen. Hence, the Law is still a tool for your life.

But He goes on to explain how those that are to enter the kingdom of heaven shall live. Matthew Chapter 5, verse 20 reads, "For I say unto you, that except your righteousness shall exceed the righteousness of the scribes and pharisees, ye shall in no case enter into the kingdom of heaven." You will find that He further explains in the rest of the chapter how to exceed their righteousness. It must be a heart issue. He expects us to live without even dwelling on the desire to sin.

This one chapter in Matthew is solid proof that Jesus Christ felt that all of the "saved" living on earth, until its destruction by God, would live a righteous lifestyle. That is a life without sin. Sin is anything that opposes the Law and the Prophets. Isn't Jesus Christ's plain language on this matter good enough for you? If you don't believe Jesus Christ, who are you believing in for your salvation?

Law and Grace are two different things. Certain promises are made for those that try to keep the Law and do so. With the same promises come curses for those that try to keep the Law and fail. No one wants to be under those curses, especially those evangelical Christians. In fact they would like to discount the whole "Law" thing all together.

From the beginning of the creation of Man there was the Law, maybe not totally what is in the Mosaic Law, but a Law just the same. When you read Genesis you find that Adam and Eve were forbidden to eat the fruit of the Tree of the Knowledge of Good and Evil. They broke the Law and we will all see death as a consequence.

The Law is mentioned by all the New Testament writers. It is a list of requirements given to Abraham, maybe even earlier. We first read that God placed these requirements on man when He makes a promise to Isaac in Genesis Chapter 26. God explains the reason He had a binding contract with Issac's father Abraham.

God states in Genesis Chapter 26 that Abraham obeyed His voice, kept His charge, kept His commandments, kept His statues, and His Law (Genesis 26: 3-5). Moses wrote Genesis. The same Moses that wrote in detail the Law of God in the Books of Exodus and Leviticus. If it was a different "Law," don't you think that Moses would have stated it somewhere?

Fortunately, Isaac took up the challenge. This is why you read in the Old Testament about the God of Abraham, Isaac and Jacob. Jacob's name was changed to Israel by (we think) Jesus, hence the Children of Israel (Genesis 32:28). All the New Testament promises you want to claim trace back to the promises given to Abraham and other Old Testament prophets.

Do you read your Psalms? Why not read Psalms Chapter 105? It again affirms this idea that the Law started back with Abraham, not Moses. Psalm Chapter 105, verses 9 and 10 actually state God made a covenant with Abraham, gave an oath to Isaac and confirmed the same unto Jacob for a <u>Law</u>. The chapter then takes you through the growth and joy of the people and ends with them in the land where they keep His statutes and keep His <u>Law</u>. It doesn't state that it was a different Law! I find it funny that so-called Christians try to state that the Law started with the exodus from Egypt. Why not read the Bible closely and look for the truths for yourself?

Jesus is foretold in the Old Testament. Have you ever looked up the references for yourself? Do you trust these prophecies? How can you "not" believe in them if you are a Christian? Have you read the rest of the book that the prophesy is found in? If not, why not? How can some of the prophesy be true, but not the rest?

Do you believe in Jesus' birth? Was he born in Bethlehem? Was He prophesied to be born there? What makes you believe that fact? Once again, your faith has to be founded in some fact or it is little more than a "wish to be true." Jesus' birth in Bethlehem is prophesied by Micah Chapter 5. This is the same Old Testament book that prophesies of the beating of swords into plowshares and spears into pruning hooks in Chapter 4.

If you don't believe that these prophets are important to you, then what are you really believing in? If you read the complete Book of Micah you will learn that the beating of these warfare weapons into agricultural devices will occur in the last days. Read Chapter 4. You will read in verse 2, "And many nations shall come, and say, Come, and let us go up to the mountain of the Lord, and to the house of the God of Jacob; and He will teach us of His ways, and we will walk in His paths: for the Law shall go forth of Zion, and the word of the Lord from Jerusalem."

Micah is telling you that in the last days we will be able to seek council from God in Jerusalem. We sing those songs, "We're marching to Zion, beautiful, beautiful Zion..." Why do we sing those songs? It is a hope that we will be able to be with Him there. But what comes forth out of Zion at the end times? Go back and read verse 2, the Law!

How about the Books of Zechariah and Malachi? Have you ever read them? They are also prophesies of Jesus Christ and the end times. How can you be sure that Jesus Christ is your savior if you don't have an understanding of these books? Zechariah foretells in Chapter 11 of Jesus' betrayal for 30 pieces of silver and then the sum being cast back into the temple and the purchase of the potter's field with the silver. In Chapter 12 you learn where the Christians get the statement "and they shall look upon me whom they have pierced." Isn't this obviously about Jesus Christ's crucifixion? This is a book a real Christian should understand.

In Malachi you learn in Chapter 1 that the Lord's name will be great among the Gentiles. That's us! Chapter 2 has the statement "The law of truth was in His mouth, and iniquity was not found in His lips: He walked with me in peace and equity, and did turn many away from iniquity." That's Jesus, our loving Savior. In Chapter 3 verse 16 you see the Book of Remembrance being opened. Do you want to be in that book?

Who will be in that book? And what does that have to do with Christians who believe that all they have to do is believe in "Grace" and nothing else is important? Read Malachi Chapter 4. It is the last chapter in the Old Testament. It is a final crushing by the righteous who were in the Book of Remembrance. Verse 4 states, "Remember ye the Law of Moses my servant, which I commanded unto him in Horeb for all Israel, with the statues and judgments."

It is too clear. You may want to claim "Grace," but God expects you to live a righteous life. That life is found in the Law. And it is perfectly clear that the Law is what you find written by Moses to include the commandments, statues, and judgments.

Paul, the New Testament writer most quoted to show that we are not under the Law for our salvation is correct. Why? All men have sinned. If you have failed once, you deserve death. Only Jesus lived a sin free life. That is why we must receive Grace to live. We deserve death, but through His payment, we receive life. How can this simple idea be polluted into something more like "Christians have a license to sin under Grace?" Do you believe that there is a commandment that doesn't apply to you? If you do, then you believe that you have a license to break that commandment. Or better put, you have a license to sin!

Many times, Paul's statements are used in a misleading way. If you understand that we are under Grace, through faith, then you cannot be under the Law for salvation. But, if you love God you cannot continue to live in sin. Paul puts it best when he states at the end of Romans Chapter 3, "Do we then make void the Law through faith? God Forbid: yea, <u>we establish the Law</u>."

If you knew for sure that the early Christians kept the Law would you? If you say no, then I have to ask you, why not? It is hypocritical to state that you want to live the life Jesus wants you to live in one breath and in the next breath state that you won't live it.

Do you remember the Christian that Jesus Christ instructed to return Saul's sight (later Paul) in Damascus? Read Acts Chapter 9. Ananias is sent by Jesus to convert Paul and teach him of the new way. Isn't this the life you would want to live, a life where Jesus would actually instruct you on things to do with your life? But this story really doesn't tell you if "they" kept the Law, or does it? From your reading in Acts, did Ananias keep the Law? Was it the correct way of life for a Christian to live?

Read Acts Chapter 22. This is where Paul is taken into custody in Jerusalem. When he is stating his defense on the steps to the castle in verse 12, he states that Ananias was a devout man according to the Law. This statement alone makes the case for keeping the Law too plain. The movement, called the "Way," that later is referred to as the Christian movement, still believed in keeping the Law. Paul is making it abundantly clear here!

There is no individual in the New Testament anywhere that specifically states that they did anything against the Mosaic Law. Once again, early Christians didn't confuse the traditions of man, that had become as law to the Jew of the day, with the Mosaic Law.

Christian, ask yourself: How can the Law exist for Abraham, Issac, Jacob, the Children of Israel, King David, Jesus, the early Christians, and to be foretold of during the end times, but somehow modern Christians don't feel it is needed today? This is a mind blower, but simple to answer. Most Christians would fall away from the church they attend if they couldn't live the lustful life they are apparently living. Church revenue would drastically decline and many religious leaders would have to get a real job. So, they tell you that you are living an OK lifestyle to God if you have faith, so just keep attending.

I guess we could put this to bed if you asked yourself, "Am I righteous or a sinner?" Paul felt we would all be righteous if we had his level of faith. Do you attend a church that reminds you that "we are all sinners and your best efforts are as filthy rags?"

You have to read 1 Timothy Chapter 1. Start focusing on verses 3-11. Paul is warning of those teaching externalism and the Law. What does it say in verses 8 and 9? "But we know that the Law is good, if a man **uses** it lawfully. Knowing this, that the Law is not made for a righteous man, but for the lawless and disobedient, for the ungodly and for **sinners**..." So, I guess from what Paul teaches, you don't need the Law if you are already righteous. Of course you wouldn't need the Law if you were righteous, because you would not be sinning! Hence, you would not be a sinner.

In fact, Paul was so sure that we need a stick to measure our righteousness, even if we are not aware of the Mosaic Law, that he explains that for those that don't have the ability to know the Law, the Holy Spirit will place it in their heart. These people's conscience will either justify them, or condemn them for whether you follow it. Read Romans Chapter 2 and focus on verse 15.

Many Christians today try to state that the above verse gives them license to ignore the Old Testament as the Holy Spirit hasn't placed it in their heart to honor it. That argument could then be used to do any polluted act that one so chooses. Go back and read the entire chapter and see if you can really make that argument. No, Paul makes a clear distinction between those that can read the Law, as you can, and those with no possible ability to obtain it. Each of us will have a Law to follow and we, those that have free access to the Bible, will be judged by how we kept it.

So what you really need to ask yourself is, "Am I a sinner?" If you are a sinner and living a life that has sin in it, then you are not living a righteous lifestyle. I love the way modern evangelical churches control their masses. This almost brings us to the "faith" or "works" question. Do you believe you are saved by faith "only?" Is your faith giving you "Grace" without "works" or the Law?

Where is your proof? The Book of Hebrews has a chapter that explains the great faith of the early patriarchs. But James actually clarifies it a little for you. It appears that if you read Hebrews, and then the Book of James, he is clarifying some things that can be misquoted. James tells you that if you have faith, then you will have works. If you don't have works, then you really don't have faith (James 2:17)! So, what is wrong with trying to do those works?

Romans Chapter 1, verse 17: "The just shall live by faith." There it is. That is all you need, but is it? If all you need is faith, then you can ignore the entire Law and works in your life, but can you? What was Paul referring too? Many would like to say that he is quoting Habakkuk Chapter 2, verse 4. What is actually written in Habakkuk? Look it up in your concordance.

The word "just" is referring to a righteous man. But the word "faith" is the Hebrew word "muna." It is used a total of 49 times in the Old Testament. It is only translated into "faith" once, and that is here in Habakkuk. Usually it is translated into faithfully, truth, or faithfulness. It isn't the word "faith" as a Christian would use the word. Read Habakkuk, it is about a five minute read.

So Habakkuk was stating that a just man shall live faithfully in truth or faithfulness. Paul was not trying to state a new meaning for "muna," just that Jesus Christ's followers would be lead by "muna" or better stated; truth, and faithfulness.

Paul does believe that we are saved by Grace through faith in Jesus Christ's payment for our sins, but he is not saying that it is a substitution for a righteous lifestyle. Don't forget how Paul felt a righteous man would look at the Law later in the same book, "Do we then make void the Law through faith? God Forbid: yea, <u>we establish the Law</u>."

Did faith or works save Abraham? Remember how Moses quoted why God saved Abraham in Genesis Chapter 26, verse 5? These were the things that Abraham did, and we have to call them "works." Now, jump back to James Chapter 2, verse 21. Read the whole Book of James, but you will find that James makes the case that Abraham was saved by "works." James also uses the story of Rahab to show the same point.

How can you be saved by grace through faith if you don't have the "works" that are found in the Law? It is impossible. Take out your concordance and look up the word "work" or "works" just in the New Testament. It is mainly used as something a Christian will do, "...unto good works." It is used over and over some 20 times by many New Testament authors.

How is it that we have made "doing good works" something evil in today's Christianity? Have you ever heard the term "a works trip?" As if, trying not to sin and living a righteous lifestyle, that God has ordained, is a bad thing. The MEC calls these practices a "works trip." They say you are trying to earn your way to heaven. It's kind of like being asked, "are you holier than thou?" for not bending the rules. And, Christians sheepishly follow along because they don't want to appear to be judgmental.

What does the Bible say about our "works?" Has it ever occurred to you to read your Bible intensely to see what is written? Who will be saved? Those that have faith alone, are they saved? Can their faith without works save them? Why not read Revelation again? Remember that it is the only prophetic book a "Christian" has ever written. If you don't want to listen to the Old Testament prophets, let's see what John says Jesus told him.

It is all summed up in a couple of verses. Read Revelation Chapter 20 and focus on verses 12-13. You will be judged according to your "works." It doesn't say anything about your faith, just your works. It talks about the books being opened and you will have one of two fates. You will either live with the Lord God Almighty and Jesus Christ, or you will be cast into the lake of fire.

Go back to our conversation of the Old Testament prophets. Remember the Book Of Remembrance? After it is opened, the righteous trample the wicked. Just like in the Book of Revelation!

It is pretty simple. Either live a life that includes good works unto God, or be cast into the lake of fire. How do you find the life that is pleasing to God, that brings you to good works? Jesus told you to Love God and man. He told you that if you loved Him, you would keep His commandments. Not the external additional rules given to you by religious leaders, just those provided by God and found in the Law of the Old Testament.

Let's say you are really hard nosed and a "soft, loving" Christian wanting to have an easy life. You believe that you have to do nothing, and are saved by "Grace," and take a loose translation to the above mentioned two commandments: Love God and love man. If that is the case, you probably believe that the Law does not apply to you.

Many New Testament Christians have concluded that when they say they are not under the Law, they are referring to the Ten Commandments. If you are not under the Ten Commandments then it would mean that you don't have to worry about the Sabbath, and for that matter any other commandment. But if it wasn't important to follow the commandments of God, wouldn't Jesus have just stated it plainly?

What is the most important commandment? Jesus Christ already answered this for you, but did you ever think of the significance of His answer? First, let's look at the question and circumstances leading up to His answer. Read Matthew Chapter 22. It begins with the Pharisees trying to trap Jesus with His own words, but as usual, He flips His defense to an offense and they immediately back down. Then, one of the scribes asks Him, "Which is the great commandment in the Law?"

In a nutshell, Jesus tells him it is to Love God. He then states that the next important commandment would be to love your fellow man. This is about as far as most Christians want to read. This is why they cling to "Grace" and love God and love their fellow man, but He also says, "On these two commandments hang all the Law and the Prophets."

There are two truths here that are not very apparent. Christ has just told you that the Law is not the Ten Commandments, although they are in the Law. Many people would like to substitute the Ten Commandments for the Law. The Law is the first five books of the Old Testament. It was, and is, sometimes referred to as the Mosaic Law. Jesus has just quoted from a passage in Deuteronomy Chapter 6, verse 5 and Leviticus Chapter 19, verse 18. He is certifying the Mosaic Law as commandments to men from God.

The second part of His statement shows that loving God and loving man sum up the entire commandments of God. But, we are selfish and try to squirm our way into believing what we want. This is why there is the Law, as it gets rid of our wiggle room. Jesus does not say that they replace the Law, just that all the Law hang on these two commandments. So, you can condense all the Law down to these two commandments, but you can also expand these two commandments out to the Ten Commandments, and then even more if you want to know how God wants you to live.

Why would you want to expand the Ten Commandments? You don't want to add man-made rules to explain the commandments of God. After all, that is what the Jews did which led to some ridiculous rules in Jesus' day. You don't have to do it for yourself, as God has already done it for you.

If you read your Old Testament you will find "thou shalt(s)" and "thou shalt not(s)" all over the place. I have heard it stated that there are over 600 of them. There are a lot of them, but if you look at each one of them, they will all fit into one of the Ten Commandments.

If you look at the Ten Commandments, you will see that Commandments 1-4 are all about love and respect to God. Commandments 5-10 are all about loving your fellow man. So, all the 600 plus commandments of the Old Testament will fit into either love God, or love your fellow man.

If I do those 600 plus commandments, am I keeping the Law? Here is where it gets a little sticky. Go back and read the Sermon on the Mount in Matthew Chapter 5. Jesus explains that it isn't just the physical act that God is looking for, it is the emotional desire to do the right thing. If you dwell on an unloving act, you have already committed it in your heart. So He is telling you not to even dwell on those sinful acts.

There are those that want to back themselves into a corner and state that they don't care how plain it is and will only follow: "Love the Lord with all your heart, mind and soul; followed by, love thy neighbor as thy self," in their own way. They want to feel that this is good enough for God, after all, they don't want to be on a "works trip." If you believe this way, then you are ignorant. Read the question posed to Jesus again that brought His response.

It wasn't "make us up a new commandment to follow," it was "what is the greatest commandment?" Go back and read it for yourself. Both verses quoted by Jesus have descriptors in the text that He is quoting to explain how to do these actions. In Leviticus the very next words are "I am the Lord, Keep my Statutes." In Deuteronomy Chapter 6, verse 2 it states, "That thou mightest fear the Lord thy God, to keep all His commandments, which I command thee, thou and thy son..."

In fact, the phrase, "Love the Lord thy God with all thy heart" appears over and over in Deuteronomy and it is either prefaced or followed closely by "doing His commandments" as proof of your love. These are the "works" God is looking for in your life.

It can't be more plain. Doing the "works" of the Law demonstrates that you love God. So it really isn't the Law or Grace. It is the Law and Grace. It is Grace you receive from God because He loves you. If you love Him, you will do the works He has shown you in the Law. It all begins with discontinuing sin in your life and repentance.

Why not read the following chapters that surround these statements about God's commandments found in the New Testament:

1 Corinthians 7:19 Circumcision is nothing, uncircumcision is nothing but the keeping of the commandments of God. (In other words, it isn't an outward display, it is an inward obedience to keep the commandments)

1 John 2:3-4 And hereby, we do know that we know Him, if we keep His commandments. He that saith, I know Him, and keepeth not His commandments, is a liar, and the truth is not in him. (Point blank, if you refuse to keep His commandments, you do not know God)

1 John 3:22-24 And whatsoever we ask of Him, we receive of Him, because we keep His commandments, and do those things that are pleasing in His sight. And this is His commandment, That we should believe on the name of His Son Jesus Christ, and love one another, as He gave us commandment. And he that keepeth His commandments dwell in Him, and He in him. And hereby we know that He abideth in us, by the Spirit which he hath given us. (It isn't good enough just to keep His commandments, we must also accept Jesus as our Savior)

1 John 5:2-3 By this we know that we love the children of God, when we love God, and keep His commandments. For this is the love of God, that we keep His commandments: and His commandments are not grievous. (Brings you full circle to ensure that you understand that the commandments that John has been talking about are not only about loving Jesus. They are rules placed on your life, but if you love God they will not be grievous for you to keep.)

2 John 1:6 And this is love, that we walk after His commandments. This is the commandment, That, as ye have heard from the beginning, ye should walk in it. (you can't have love if you refuse to follow the commandments, and they have been around since the beginning)

Revelation 12:17 And the dragon was wroth with the woman, and went to make war with the remnant of her seed, which keep the commandments of God, and have the testimony of Jesus Christ. (Who does Satan fight against? Christians that keep the Law, the rest are already fallen. Do you keep the commandments of God?)

Revelation 14:12 Here is the patience of the saints: here are they that keep the commandments of God and the faith of Jesus. (This one verse tells you that the saints are those with Faith, but also must keep the commandments of God)

Revelation 22:14 Blessed are they that do His commandments, that they may have right to the tree of life, and may enter in through the gates into the city. (There is no discussion of "grace", but simply keeping God's commandments)

Do you know the commandments? They are listed throughout the Bible. Don't the above passages beg you to keep the commandments of God? If you are not keeping the commandments of God, then you are sinning! The following chapter should help you sum up sinning in anyone's life.

What is Sin, and What are the Consequences of Sin in My Life?

I think that this is the most important topic, if we are to live a righteous lifestyle. Do you think that it is possible to live a righteous lifestyle? Many people in the Bible are said to have lived a righteous life, Abraham for one. Living a righteous lifestyle doesn't mean that you don't ever sin. It means that if you do, you repent and do the works of repentance. Paul explains this when he is testifying before King Agrippa in the Acts of the Apostles Chapters 25-26.

Remember the destruction of Sodom? Lot, Abraham's nephew, was living there. The two angels could not destroy the city until they got him out. Why? Because he was righteous. Did his life in the Old Testament accounts look righteous to you? It doesn't look too apparent to me, but the Apostle Peter explains that Lot was righteous in his epistle, II Peter.

Why don't you think you can live a righteous lifestyle? Because you probably attend a Modern Evangelical Church (MEC). I equate them to the Pharisees of Jesus Christ's day. They have a list, that if you complete it, you can pretty much ignore the commandments of God. They will tell you not to sin, but then they don't really explain what sin is.

When discussing Sabbath with a Lutheran minister, who was a close friend, he explained that they (Lutherans), don't keep the Sabbath as they try to live as close as they can to the early church. When I asked him if he could show me where the early church substituted Sunday for the Sabbath, the discussion was over. They had fallen into the trap of substituting a tradition of man over a commandment of God (Mark 7). But, he was right in his premise that we should live as close as we can to the early church.

I have and will use the line of "substituting a tradition of man over a commandment of God" many times in this book. Why? Because Jesus told you that modern religion will do it in an "unholy" way. They will teach their tradition in such a way that you can believe it is what God wants you to do, and yet, it is in direct conflict with His commandments. What should be more important to a real Christian, God's word, or man's tradition?

Read Matthew 15, verses 1 through 20. It is a story of Jesus being asked by the church leaders why His disciples didn't wash their hands before they ate bread. This hand washing was a tradition passed down by the elders. Jesus rebuts them by asking them why their traditions allow their congregation to leave everything to the church, so that the member can enjoy it all for himself, but then left the remainder of the wealth to the church after his death.

You may think this was a good tradition, and it was an excellent source of church revenue. But Jesus points out that this tradition was a way for the congregation to keep all that they had during their life, and not take care of their aging parents who might be in need of help. After all, they couldn't give it to their parents if it wasn't their's to give. Taking care of your parents is a commandment of God! This tradition was in direct violation of God's Law. Jesus was referring to honor thy Father and mother.

Picking and choosing what commandments you want to follow by substituting tradition over God's commandments isn't true Christianity. It is almost like explaining that you don't follow the Law because some commandments were of the Levitical law, or the cultural law, or of the law of governance. Look, they were all the Law and God expects you to keep it.

When asked if He came to destroy the Law, Jesus stated that he did not come to destroy the law, but to fulfill the law. He also stated that not one yot or tittle (Hebrew punctuation) would be removed from the Law until all be fulfilled (Matthew 5:18).

Look closely at the entire passage, He explains that first the heavens will be rolled up before this would happen. When you look at the stars at night, are they still there? It is true that Jesus fulfilled some of the law, but not all the law. There is a lot of prophecy yet to be completed before all is fulfilled.

If you don't believe this, read your Bible from front to back and ask yourself, "Have all the prophecies been fulfilled?" We know that the sacrificial laws are completed in Jesus Christ. He is the payment for our sin if we accept Him. God the Father took away any semblance that the old form of payment-for-sin could be continued. Where is the temple? God the Father allowed it to be destroyed in about 70 AD.

How about the line that Jesus fulfilled the Law and now it is no longer important? Where do you find that in scripture? All New Testament writers point out how using the Law as a yardstick against our actions can identify sin to us. Why all the concern over the Law and commandments when we are talking about sin? Do you understand how the early church looked at sin?

There is not one New Testament writer that stated that you could now sin as you are under Grace. When Paul writes to explain about "grace," he usually explains that we use the Law to show us what sin is. He also explains when he is testifying before Festus in the Book of Acts, Chapter 25, that he never broke the Law (Jewish or Roman). Why? Because that would have been sinning. Let's look at what the early leaders of the church used to identify sin.

Many Bible writers: Paul, James, John, and Peter have stated that anything that is contrary to the Law is sin, and that sin is not in those that are saved. Many softer and gentler Christians state that the only commandments they need are "love God and love your neighbor." Proof texts showing that you are not under the Law are found in Romans and Ephesians when they state that you are "not under the Law." But what did Paul mean when we read we are not under the Law? Only, that the Law can not save you.

Paul rarely quotes the commandments of God and even less the Ten Commandments. Does this mean that he felt they were null and void? Of course not, you just have to read what he wrote. Look at Ephesians Chapter 6. Paul refers to the Ten Commandments when he states to the youth to "honor your father and mother as this is the first commandment that comes with a promise." What promise, and where is this commandment found?

The promise was that your days would be long on this earth. Oh yeah, that is from the Ten Commandments of the Torah (Hebrew for the first five books of the Old Testament). Why would he be referencing the Ten Commandments for his authority if it had no significance in their lives?

The only thing the Law does, is show us sin. It can not save us. So, if you are saved will you follow the Law? Yes. Does this contradict statements in Galatians Chapter 3, such as, "you are not under the Law you are under grace?" Not at all. It just explains that the commandments of the Old Testament show us what sin is and although we will still stumble, God hates us committing them. Paul tells you that the Law was your schoolmaster. It teaches you what sin is. After you have "faith," you are no longer under the schoolmaster. But James in the Book of James told us how to test if your faith is real: "you will have works."

So, can I continue to sin if I am saved? Paul tells you at the end of Romans Chapter 5 and continuing into Chapter 6, that if we are dead to sin, that we can no longer live unto it. Look at Hebrews Chapter 6. The writer of Hebrews feels it is impossible for those who were once enlightened and partakers of the Holy Ghost, if they fall away, to be renewed again unto repentance.

John states in 1 John Chapter 3 that "whosoever abideth in Him sinneth not: whosoever sinneth hath not seen Him, neither known Him." Earlier in the same chapter he states that "whosoever committeth sin transgresseth the Law; for sin is the transgression of the Law." This chapter and Chapter 5 are packed with John's belief that we will not continue to sin, and that sinning has already been defined by God in the Law. No, the Law does not save you; Grace through Faith saves you, but if you are living in Him you will not sin.

Peter states in 1 Peter Chapter 4, that we will "cease from sin; that he no longer should live the rest of his time in the flesh to the lusts of man, but to the will of God."

Let's look at sin in our lives and the consequences of it. If I am under Grace, doesn't that pay for the sin in my life? Ezekiel Chapter 18 talks about the soul that sinneth. Read it for yourself, and you will see it all depends on how you end your life. All sinners will get stripes. More to the one that knows he is sinning and fewer to the one that is sinning in ignorance, but they all get stripes. And as for life after death, if you are righteous and turn wicked, then you will loose it! Doesn't that really step on once-saved-always-saved? It looks really clear that there is no such thing.

But what about all those verses from Paul that we like to recite? Open your Bible and read any complete epistle by Paul in one sitting. If you find a word that you don't understand, get out your concordance. They are all easy reading books once you get over the Greek to English translation. There is no reference made by Paul that a saved person can knowingly break the Law of God in good conscience.

Paul didn't have any hidden meaning that he was waiting 2,000 years to be discovered. He was sending his letters to a church full of common people like you and me. Paul and all New Testament writers believed that you had to accept the free gift of Grace. Once you had, your life would change from one of "the world" to one of "the spirit." A life of the world was one that sinned. A life in the spirit lived counter to that of the world.

Most of Paul's theological discussions in his letters go like this: Man sinned and continued to sin more. The Law was given to show man his sin. Man needed payment for the sins he had committed and God the Father provided the answer. The Father sent His son to live a sin free life and die on a cross for us. When we accept this gift for our <u>past</u> sins (Romans 3:25), our lives change. We repent from our sinful ways and start living for God. This is Faith in Grace. Although my sins are future to the death of Christ and He died for them, there is no reference that He died for the sins that I will knowingly commit after I understand what sin is.

The hippies thought they understood love in the 1960's, but polluted it into selfishness and lewdness. That is why God spells out to you all the commandments, in the Law and the prophets. There are even dietetic laws. These limit the eating of some flesh like pork and shellfish. The Jews made traditions to help them keep the Law even better, but this only turned into legalism. The MEC tries to tell you that the Mosaic Laws have no place in a modern Christian's life, but I have found no scriptural text that shows that any New Testament writer ever broke one of the Ten Commandments or one of the other Old Testament Laws.

But, if you doggedly stick to the fact that if you have said a few words and believe that you are a Christian, that all things will be OK for you after death, why not look at the words of Jesus Christ Himself? Are you so fixated on the out-of-context words by Paul that you will ignore what the creator of the universe has told you? Read Luke Chapter 12. When you come to verse 47-48 it goes like this: "and that servant, which knew his lord's will, and prepared not, neither did according to his will, shall be beaten with many. But he that knew not, and did commit things worthy of stripes, shall be beaten with few."

Jesus has just validated what Ezekiel has quoted in the Old Testament. This one statement alone wipes out any modern teaching that all your sins will be wiped away by just saying a few words. I do believe that your sins will be forgiven you if you ask for forgiveness and repent. But, that means that you have to purposefully look for sin in your life and stop committing it. This is obedience!

So what is living in sin? Modern vocabulary has blurred too many old sayings and words into new meanings. Living in sin is simply doing the same sin over and over without repentance from that sin. It could be petty theft, cheating on your time card, or fornication and adultery.

Can a Christian live in sin? You have already learned that Paul tells you "no" in many places! Even the writer of the Book of Hebrews tells you that, "For if we sin willfully after that we have received the knowledge of the truth, there remains no more sacrifice for sins, but certain fearful looking for of judgment and fiery indignation, which shall devour the adversaries (Hebrews 10: 26-27)." Doesn't that send chills down your spine? It should! But before we discuss your life style choices you need to know what sin is.

The Old Testament clearly taught what sin was, and the penalty for doing it. Some sins "were unto death." Some weren't. Adultery was a great example of a sin unto death. Both the man and woman caught in the act were stoned to death immediately. Some sins, like stealing had a lesser penalty. If you were caught stealing, you had to repay the theft and then add additional "like and kind" to it. Read Leviticus.

The MEC have discounted the Old Testament, as Christ is our payment for sin. This is true. Jesus Christ died and put an end to our need to perform a sacrifice for the payment of sins. But does this give us a license to continue to sin? How about the same sin over and over (living in sin)? Some MECs go as far as saying that if you are trying to live a life without sin, you are committing blasphemy, as Jesus Christ is all we need. That is utterly ridiculous and had to be the brainchild of a perverted mind!

Look at the New Testament. Where can you find an example of an early church member being caught in adultery? The closest example to this is located in the Book of John Chapter 8 when Jesus took the adulterous woman that had been presented to Him and, after all her accusers had left, told her "go and sin no more." The example is clear. Stop sinning (repent) and sin no more (the works of repentance). But, the adulterous woman mentioned is not even of the early church. She was just another Jew of the day.

Look for someone in the New Testament who is saved and find them living in any type of "Old Testament" sin. You will not find it. Sure, there are many stories of the different Mary's being this or that, but it can't be found in the writings anywhere. It is all a stretch of someone's sick imagination.

The problem for the MEC explaining that you should not live in sin is that sinning is so convenient. How can an earthly father tell his son not to get a girlfriend pregnant, when he himself is seeing another woman on the side? He has no credibility. Living within God's framework will put limitations on the way we live and the lusts we have.

It would be easy for the MEC to say, "stop sinning," and most do, but fall short of what they say sin is. They can't! Because most MECs already break the fourth commandment (Sabbath). They all say it is OK to break the food laws, or add extra ones such as vegetarianism. Some accept homosexuality. In the New and Old Testament this was called sodomy and was plainly not acceptable.

Some have women preaching in the pulpits. This one sounds strange. Why is it wrong for a woman to be a preacher or church leader? Paul stated in 1 Timothy Chapter 2, that the serpent deceived the woman, showing that she is led by emotion and should keep silent in church. Some churches make no bones about two people living together as long as they attend church and are planning to get married. Hey, that is called fornication. The list goes on and on. If the MEC was to limit membership to those that at least tried to remove sin from their lives, their membership would be low and hence, no income!

Your lifestyle might be acceptable to the church you attend, but is it acceptable to the Lord? If the early church did not do it, what makes you believe that the Lord will accept it? The MEC would not have such high membership if they placed on you the limitations in your lifestyle that the Lord has on it. Don't blame me, it's in your Bible.

How do you know if you are living in sin? Read your Bible from front-to-back, and then do it again. Pray about it, and ask the Lord for understanding. Then, when you find an area of your life that is not pleasing to the Lord, do something about it. Don't allow someone to lead you astray using Paul's writings (out-of-context). Paul kept the Law, as he explained that it was the schoolmaster teaching us what sin is.

Does living in sin really matter? Besides the fact that Paul stated that you can't sin if you are Christ's, don't forget to look back at prophecy. Read Ezekiel Chapter 18 again; he is prophesying "The word of the Lord came unto me again, saying…" Why not look at the words of Jesus again in Luke Chapter 12? I do believe that your sins will be forgiven you if you ask for forgiveness and repent. But, that means you have to purposefully look for sin in your life and stop committing it. Once again, it is obedience!

So, if you profess to be a Christian, will you believe what your MEC pastor is telling you? Or, will you go back and read the Bible for yourself and live as the early church taught? What was it that our Lord told us? **"If you love me, keep My commandments."**

Christian Worship

Up until now I have talked about the Bible and its origin. We have covered the importance of understanding the entire Bible, not just the New Testament. You should understand that sin is unacceptable to God and a Christian will consciously try to avoid it. Grace is the gift from God that will bring us into His plan for our future lives in eternal life.

But, who is God? Was Jesus Christ God living among us? Let's take a quick snap-shot of Jesus. Jesus Christ is the First Begotten of the Father. He lived a sin-free life on earth. He died on the cross for all our sins. He did not deserve to die, yet it was predestined to happen.

Without His sacrificial death, there would have been no payment for the sins you and I have committed. The payment for sin is death. Without Jesus Christ, we were all doomed. This is what Grace is.

A Christian must accept Jesus Christ's pain and death on the cross as your payment for the sins you have committed. If you have faith that Jesus died for your sins, it will be imputed unto you for righteousness. Although you are deserving of death, His righteousness and righteous act of death on the cross will wash you clean for the Father.

Although Jesus Christ is the most important being to the Father, he is not God. God is the Father. When you read the first four of the Ten Commandments, they are about the Father. Do you know them? They are located in Exodus Chapter 20 and others. They go something like this:

1st Commandment: Don't have any other Gods other than me.
2nd Commandment: Don't make any images that you think represent me
3rd Commandment: Don't take My Name in vain
4th Commandment: Keep My Sabbath Holy; do no work

These are obviously paraphrased, but if you are a Christian, don't you think that these should be important to you, especially when you know by now that the early church followed the Old Testament?

Is God any less of a God today than He was when He delivered the Children of Israel? Which brings us to the 1st Commandment. Is Jesus Christ God? Has Christianity blurred the lines between the Father and the Son? The New Testament is very clear as to His position.

Do you believe in the trinity? I believe that there is the Father, the Son and the Holy Ghost, but are they entwined in anyway? Are they the same being? The scripture states that They are no more entwined than the family unit is suppose to be here on earth.

Sometimes Christians or leaders can't put a concept together and so they build a story to help them with the facts. How did they have the one God concept of the Old Testament and then have Jesus on earth who they wanted to worship as God?

Is Jesus Christ God? Where is your scripture? There are plenty of texts that show that He isn't. He is a Holy being, the most important being to God the Father, and your redemption, but He is not God.

What about the 4th Commandment? Do you really love God to the point of death? Jesus did. He lived unto death, for the Father. But will you give the time He has set aside each week? You may say you do. But do you really? Is it just too inconvenient for you to do it in modern society?

In the following chapters you will learn the relationship the Father has with the Son and the one we are to have with Them both. You will see that man, through tradition, has thrown out the 4th commandment of God. Have most so-called Christians picked another time that they feel is appropriate, although totally non-scriptural?

Most denominations have substituted various hours on Sunday for the Sabbath of God (Friday sundown to Saturday sundown). The tradition is so deep that even though there is no reasonable argument to keep Sunday as a day of worship, they still do out of the inconvenience to change. Do you think that God will accept this feeble excuse?

Was Jesus Christ crucified on Easter, or on any Friday for that matter? Did He rise on Sunday morning? Not if Jesus Christ is to be believed. Do you believe Jesus Christ? If you don't believe in Him then you have much larger Christianity problems. How could Jesus Christ state, He will be in the belly of the earth for three days and three nights if He is crucified on Friday and then is risen by Sunday morning. Do the math. There are only two nights maximum.

How can you call what you do "worship," when you refuse to do what your God has demanded?

What is the Trinity?

Before we start to discuss what the trinity is, where does the word come from? It's not in your Bible in any form. Could it be just another man- made tradition? The earlier chapters have helped you understand what are real "Bible" truths as opposed to what man would like you to believe. Now take the time to examine your Bible to learn more of the word "trinity."

Is Jesus Christ God? Could a question like this be blasphemy? Only if the answer wasn't directly out of scripture. This chapter will contain all of the relevant scripture that talks about the subject, pulled into a tidy package, for you to decide. Remember, it is either scriptural, or it is a fairy tale we want to believe in. Don't you want to know for certain what the scriptures state about this subject, or don't you really care?

I really don't want to offend anyone here, and I won't downplay or denigrate our Lord Jesus Christ's holy position. This chapter is directly out of scripture and should help you understand who Jesus Christ is, and more importantly, who He isn't. It is only through Jesus Christ that we are saved. He is the most loved by the Father. But, who is God? It was the fact that the word "God" was used to explain several Holy entities that early Roman Catholic church clergy wrestled with Jesus Christ's position and chose the one that modern Christians still cling to today. But was this decision scriptural?

If you just want to say that a supernatural being is God, because he is more than human, then Jesus could be God by that definition. But, then that would open the gates for every other supernatural being to be called God also. How about Satan? This is utterly ridiculous. Go back and read the Ten Commandments. There is only one God and that is the Father.

Is Jesus Christ God? Was Jesus Christ God before He came to earth? What is God, and are there various levels to being a god, or is it just that Jesus Christ is Holy? This is the most basic fundamental of not only the Modern Evangelical Church (MEC), but also most Christian denominations. Plainly, it is not biblical to say that Jesus Christ is God. But, to be a Christian, you better understand who Jesus Christ is!

Saying Jesus Christ is God, as in God the Father, is not found in the scriptures. The root of this misunderstanding goes back to the concern in the Old Testament scriptures that God was monotheistic. In other words, He was a single God. What made this important was that there were many polytheistic religions, which believed in many gods. Elevating Jesus Christ to the level of God the Father, or worse stating that they are the same being is just proof that so-called

Christians just won't read or believe their Bibles. The answer is plainly printed in the New Testament if you would read it in its entirety.

The problem has always been that it looks like there are several different beings that are in the Law that are interchangeably called God. So, does this make them all the same "God?" Is this why we have the "trinity" in so many church doctrines? What do we mean when we call Them the trinity? Most, if not all church doctrines agree that God is in the form of the trinity, or a single being that is able to be three separate forms at the same time. But is this scriptural? This explanation did help early Roman Catholics explain the Old Testament scriptures.

But is there another, better understanding that has been overlooked? Unfortunately, even when the scriptures are screaming at most so-called Christians, they choose to stay with the traditions they already have. Read the book of Exodus. You will see the word "God" used to explain at least three different Holy beings.

You have the "I AM" of the burning bush who is Jesus. You have the God that the elders and Moses ate with, but obviously not God the Father. You have the angel that went before them, that was just an angel, and yet he is referred to them as God from time to time. And then you have "God the Father," of whom Moses was only permitted to see His passing presence. During this encounter, Moses' face glowed for days. Which one of these is God?

If God is ever-knowing, never changing, always the same, how can he repent from an action or thought? He can only be ever-knowing if He is outside time as we understand it today. It appears that He is able to go forward in time and backward at will. This is because he is at "all-times" at the same time. Jesus explained that only the Father knows the future. Only the Father can do this. Only the Father is "God."

Someone who is ever-knowing can't be wrong. Read Exodus Chapter 32 and then ask yourself, how can "God" repent? It is simple. Throw out the trinity, and understand that just because the Old Testament referred to them as "God" or "Lord," those titles were given to the supernatural beings that went before them, and were not meant to be referring to a single holy being.

We are continually bombarded with Christian doctrine and even Christian music that refers to God coming down from heaven and living among us. Does this mean that the God that the Ten Commandments referred to in commandments 1 through 4 (Thou shalt have no other Gods before me), came down in the form of Jesus? Of course not! God is "God the Father." He is the only ever-knowing, never-changing, always-the-same Holy being.

The scriptures show clearly that the Son was present as the Son before he came to earth. Read the Psalms. Take Psalms 2. It states clearly that "The Lord hath said unto me, Thou art my Son; This day have I begotten thee." At the close of the chapter you read "Kiss the Son, lest he be angry, and ye perish from the way, when His wrath is kindled but a little. Blessed are they that put their trust in Him."

Look up the word Son in the concordance. You will find references to Jesus as the Son of God all over the Old Testament. One of my favorite passages is in Proverbs and I will discuss it at the close of this chapter.

Why not read Isaiah Chapter 49? There is a thought that is formed from verses 5 through 12. It is very clear that God, is talking about, and to, a lesser deity. That deity is clearly Jesus Christ. But He is referred to as Lord. There are several of these conversations in the Old Testament between God the Father and Jesus Christ our Savior if you want to look for them.

But, most so-called Christians won't look for them, because it would challenge their values. If they did, they may have to look at God and Jesus differently. Their new observations may not be accepted by their peers. This new-found knowledge has always been there, yet ignored because it is not convenient.

A case can easily be made that when the "Holy One of Israel" is used, that this refers to Jesus Christ. But this does not make Him God, just Holy. Read Isaiah Chapter 55. It is very apparent that "the Holy One of Israel" isn't God. But a Chapter that all Christians should be familiar with is Isaiah Chapter 53.

This is the chapter that starts like this: "Who hath believed our report? And to whom is the arm of the Lord revealed? For he shall grow up before Him as a tender plant, and as a root out of the dry ground: he hath no form nor comeliness, and when we shall see Him, there is no beauty that we should desire Him. For He was despised and rejected of men…"

Who is this chapter talking about? If you can't say without a doubt it is Jesus Christ, then you can't find Jesus anywhere in the Old Testament. Read the whole chapter and then come back to verse 4. There are two focal entities. One, is the one that is going to be punished for "our" sins, and the other one is God. The one that is to be punished is "Smitten of God."

It does not say that God smote Himself for our sins. There is nowhere in the Bible where God states that He will come down on earth and live among humans and then die for us! It is a prefabricated lie by the Roman Catholic Church to help them understand the "man" Jesus Christ.

Probably the strongest argument from the scriptures that Jesus is God comes from Book of John Chapter 10, where He states "I and the Father are one." You have to read the entire chapter to understand it. First, Jesus makes that statement, and then the Jews get ready to stone Him. Next, Jesus sets out His defense by quoting Psalm 82 (John 10:34-35). He quoted this passage to explain what He meant when He stated "I and the Father are One." He isn't elevating himself to the level of the Father, only to a "Son of God." If you look at Psalm 82, His defense was to elevate Himself to the level of a "god," as to say He is a Child of the Most High (Psalm 82:6).

Paul even tells you that <u>we</u> will be Sons of God. But, there is still only one God Almighty and that is the Father. If you read the Gospels over and over you will never find a time when Jesus claims to be God the Father. In fact, He always makes the distinction, "I do the works of my Father"…or…. "No one knows me accept those given me by my Father"…or… "No one can know the Father if they don't believe in me." If you want to stand on the statement found in John Chapter 10, verse 30 (I and the Father are one), you must read the rest of John Chapter 10 to hear Jesus' reasoning to that claim. You must look up Psalm 82 and understand what Jesus is referring too in His defense of saying "I and the Father are one." Once you have, your claim that Jesus called himself God is false.

But let's take the line "I and the Father are <u>one</u>." It is also found in a similar passage in 1 John Chapter 5, verse : " for there are three that bear record in heaven, the Father, the Word, and the Holy Ghost: and the three are <u>one</u>." Doesn't this sound like a good case for the trinity? But the original Greek text doesn't say that the three are "common" in the form of unity. How can this be? It is because the word "one" in both of these passages is the Greek word "heis." It has been translated into 25 different English words, so which translation of 'heis" is it?

Remember, Greek is a much more precise language than English. Heis has been translated into whatever they want it to say to frame a sentence. If you can't nail down the true meaning for the Greek word "heis", how conclusive can that statement be? You really can't because the word "heis" is too vague.

Go back and look it up in an interlinear scripture analyzer. Better yet, research the various compilations of the Greek scriptures and see for yourself. The statements about Jesus and the Father being one are too inconclusive from the Greek text to ensure that it stated that they were "one" in any fashion.

What makes this passage even worse, is that most of that statement about the trinity isn't found in any of the early Greek translations. Those words were added. In the early Greek manuscripts this verse and the following verse actually read, "(1 John 5:7) For there are three witnesses: (1

John 5:8) the spirit, the water, and the blood; and all three give the same testimony." There is no reference to the Father, the Son or the Holy Ghost, let alone the Three in heaven!

To put it bluntly, if you whip out a Westcott and Hort compilation of the scriptures, you will see that words were added! It is only in the Textus Receptus, because it was in the Latin of the day. But it can't be found in any of the old Greek manuscripts. This passage was never there!

How about in John Chapter 8, verse 58 when Jesus claimed, "Verily, verily, I say unto you, before Abraham was, I am." Does that sound like Jesus was claiming to be God? No, but it does infer that Jesus was claiming to be the voice of the burning bush. Does that make Him God? Are you sure? Do you remember our first Christian martyr?

Read who Stephen said was the voice of the burning bush in Acts Chapter 7, verse 30. Stephen states that the "I AM" of the burning bush was the "Angel of the Lord." In fact, if you read all of Acts Chapter 7, you will have in a nutshell an understanding of who Jesus Christ is. I believe that Stephen, who could do miracles and was with Jesus from the beginning (although not one of the twelve), had a closer understanding of Jesus and His relationship to the Father, than any so-called modern-day Bible scholar.

What about when Jesus was asked in the Gospels (Mark 12:28 and many others), which is the first commandment of them all? Jesus responded and conversed with the scribes and it progressed into a conversation of who God was… "for there is one God." Jesus doesn't refute this, he agrees with this. He doesn't add, "yes, we are a trinity." Because the trinity is a man-made idea to help early (AD 300+) church leaders cope with "the man" (as stated everywhere in the New Testament) Jesus Christ.

It is easy to line up all the scriptures that talk about Jesus, including the passages from the Old Testament into one position. There is the Father, who is God. Then there is His Son, Jesus, who is Holy, but not God Almighty. In the Old Testament when He appeared before Moses and Joshua, He stated: "take off your shoes, you are on Holy ground." But He does not say He is God the Father, just that the ground they were on was Holy. The best I can make out from the word Christ, it means the "anointed," and Messiah means "the sent one."

In fact, the Father tells you who Jesus is on several occasions in the New Testament. The Father testifies that Jesus is His son. The Father doesn't state from Heaven to those on earth, "This is Me up here, living down there with you, so listen to me." No, He states, "This is my Son, listen to Him (Mountain of Transfiguration)." Where do these churches come up with doctrine like, "Jesus was God Almighty living among us?" Who is it then, that Jesus refers to as the Father that talks to Jesus from Heaven? When Jesus is on the cross, who is He talking to when he cries, "My God, my God, why hast Thou forsaken me?"

We appear to understand that there is God, the angels, demons, and the devil. Why is it so hard to understand that there is the Father, the Son and the Holy Ghost (who is also Holy, but not the Father)? The most noteworthy statement in the New Testament about Jesus Christ and His position comes from the only prophetic book in the New Testament, Revelation. The first several verses tell it all… "The revelation of Jesus Christ, which God gave unto Him, to show unto His servants…" It doesn't begin with, "The revelation of Jesus Christ, given to Him, by Himself."

If you read Revelation you will understand that Jesus Christ is not God Almighty (the Father), but He is the most important "Holy being" to the Father. Read Revelation again and you will see all of them in Heaven with a few more Holy individuals. Where does Jesus get His power? If you read Revelation you will learn that His power comes from the Father.

The writer of the Book of Hebrews shows in the first several verses the position of Jesus in the Supernatural world. The first four verses can be condensed into: God hath spoken to us through His Son, whom He hath made heir of all things and being made so much better than the angels. But once again, it doesn't say that Jesus Himself had done those things, only that God (the Father) had spoken through His Son (Jesus).

Read the entire Book of Hebrews. You may have to do it several times, but you will conclude that its author was just trying to explain that Jesus Christ is the second highest deity in the universe. Only God the Father is greater. The Book of Hebrews compares all things that man, at that time, considered holy in relationship to Jesus. He concludes that there is none better than Jesus, except the Father.

In the New Testament the devils testify that Jesus is Holy, but sent by the Father (Mark 1:24). And again the unclean spirits testify "thou art the Son of God." (Mark 3:11). Read all the Gospels. There are at least a dozen of these statements by devils. I find it funny that we have supernatural beings testifying who Jesus is and His position, yet we dig in our heels and follow the handed down, non-biblical, tradition of man.

Obviously there was plenty of confusion with having only one God as it states in the Ten Commandments, and then having Jesus hanging around. If He isn't God, how do we answer the "No other Gods before me" part? There is plenty of documentation showing when the Roman Catholic Church Bishops got together to decide Church doctrine.

One such meeting was the Council of Nicea (300 bishops and 1 pope). Two main issues were blundered at this meeting. One was over the replacing of the Sabbath with Sunday worship and the other was over Jesus Christ's divinity. Ever since their decision, we have lived with it. Peruse the Internet for yourself and you decide. Did these leaders have a divine link to God Almighty that has been denied to you? I don't think so!

Some contradictions occur even in the Gospels, but they all agree about who we pray to. Take the Lord's prayer. The disciples have asked Jesus to teach them how to pray. Read the prayer. It starts out, "Our Father, which art in heaven…" Who does Jesus instruct them to pray to? Just the Father. He adds later, that if you ask your prayer in His (Jesus') name, He will intercede on your behalf. He still never instructs them to pray to him. He never explained that they could begin praying to Him once He got to heaven. Do you pray to Jesus? Why? What scriptural reference are you using? Pray to the Father in "Jesus" name. Why? Because that is what Jesus told you to do!

Let's look at the Bible again. It should be your guide for all spiritual questions. Don't take a few pet (out of context) phrases by the MEC. Look at the whole thing! To start with, we know that Jesus Christ was the Son of God. What God? The Lord God Almighty. All of the books of the New Testament were written by Spirit-filled men, but these were not prophetic (except for Revelation); most were letters of encouragement and council. Each writer will make the distinction between Jesus Christ the Son, and God Almighty the Father.

The book of James starts: "James, a servant of God and the Lord Jesus Christ." The Apostle Peter in the Book of 1 Peter Chapter 1, verses 1-2 states, "Peter an apostle of Jesus Christ… according to the fore knowledge of God the Father..." The Apostle John in 1 John Chapter 1, verse 3 "…and truly our fellowship with the Father and with His Son Jesus Christ." The same is found in Jude!

Did all these New Testament authors get it wrong? Did mankind need to wait 2,000 years for modern day Bible scholars to interpret what they really meant? Was there some kind of hidden meaning behind their writings that they themselves didn't even understand?

Paul, is my favorite New Testament author. He gives you insight into Jesus Christ's position in relationship to the Father in most of his correspondence. Read each of his epistles. They usually start off with some type of greeting coming from "God the Father and our Lord Jesus Christ." He never refers to Jesus as God, only his and our Lord. Even medieval Europeans understood the difference when they set up titles among those of an empire. A lord is mighty, but not the top dog.

It is very important to note that each of these writers have made a distinction between Jesus Christ and God the Father. None of these writers have even blurred the two deities. There is the Father and the Son in each of these letters. How can the case be made that they are one God?

For a real definitive set of proof texts that states that Jesus Christ is not God, read 2 Thessalonians Chapter 1, verse 1-8. You can read on, but in the close of those verses Paul explains that Jesus Christ will come with His angels and will take vengeance on those that know not God. Paul doesn't say that Jesus Christ will take vengeance on those that don't know Him, just that Jesus will take vengeance on those that know not God.

To make it more blunt, read 1 Timothy Chapter 2. The whole chapter is good, but in verse 5 he states: "For there is one God, and one mediator between God and men, the <u>man</u> Christ Jesus." Paul doesn't say "one man that is also God." No, Paul refers to Jesus Christ with many titles, but never God. Why? Because Jesus is the first begotten of the Father. He is the Son!

And again, Paul tells you the same thing in 1 Corinthians Chapter 8. He is explaining that the gentiles have many gods that they offer sacrifices to, but Christians know that they are not really gods. Then, in verse 6 he states: " But to us there is but one God, the Father, of whom all things, and we in Him; and one Lord Jesus Christ, by whom are all things and we in Him." Paul never calls Jesus God, just Lord.

I've written on the name Emmanuel before in this book, but was Jesus Christ, Emmanuel? You know, the child born of a virgin, foretold in Isaiah Chapter 7, verse 14: "Therefore the Lord Himself will give you a sign; Behold a virgin shall conceive, and bear a son, and shall call his name Immanuel." In that prophecy it stated that the virgin would conceive a son and his <u>NAME</u> would be called "Immanuel." When the angel appeared to Joseph and Mary, the angel told them to name the baby "<u>Jesus</u>," not Immanuel. So, was Emmanuel supposed to be Jesus? Matthew appears to be telling you that Emmanuel of Isaiah's prophecy is Jesus, but there is no other mention of it in the New Testament. Would that make him God? No!

They named children as a sign of the times. Take Hosea. He was instructed to name one of his children, "You are not my people," and another child, "you are my people." So, was the second child in this scenario the "People of God?" No. It was a sign of things to come. Get a grip. Read your Bible and you may start to understand what He wants from you.

Go back and read your gospels again. You will find that the religious leaders of the day asked Jesus several times to tell them "plainly" if He was the Christ. Each time He would say something in the order of, "Let my signs and wonders attest that I am sent by my Father." But, He never said "I am the Christ," or "I am the messiah," or worse "I am God!"

Was He the Christ or the Messiah? Is Jesus worthy of worship? Of course! Read Revelation again. The Father expects all to worship Him. All except the Father. Does Jesus ever rise to the power and authority of the Father? No, He only grows to the authority that the Father gives to Him.

Take it from Jesus Christ's own words about His relationship to the Father in Revelation Chapter 3, verse 12. He is talking to John about believers that live in Philadelphia. "Him that overcometh will I make a pillar in the temple of <u>my God</u>, and he shall go no more out: and I will write upon him the name of <u>my God</u>, and the name of the city of <u>my God</u>, new Jerusalem, which cometh down out of heaven from <u>my God</u>, and My new name." There can't be a more definitive description as to the relationship between the Father and the Son now that He is in heaven. The Father is God to the Son.

I really don't like to look deep into the scriptures. You know, try to suggest they say something that they don't, but early on in my Christian life I came to Proverbs Chapter 8. It talks of wisdom. No church leader to date that I have discussed this with has refuted my understanding of this passage. If you read the wording, it can't be about what you and I call wisdom. It is about someone that was with the Father since the beginning. It is a physical being, not an understanding of knowledge. Read the chapter.

The second half of the chapter is obviously pointing to Jesus Christ. If you draw the same conclusion, you have to note that in verses 22-23 you will see that the Lord possessed Him from the beginning and set Him up to everlasting. This would denote that Jesus was created first, hence the First Begotten, yet created.

Who do you worship? Do you worship Jesus equally to God? Why not read Revelation again? Over and over it expresses that Jesus will lead us, but that we will worship "God." Remember when John fell down to worship the angel two times in Revelation? What did the angel state? "I am a fellow servant, and have the testimony of Jesus, worship God." He did not say worship Jesus Christ, only God! (Rev 19:10; 22:8-9)

So let's add up the biblical facts: Jesus never stated that He was God, only the Son of God. He instructed His disciples to pray to God, not to Him. God the Father tells you that Jesus is His Son several times in the New Testament. All the New Testament writers tell you that He is the Son and also show His relationship to the Father. The only verses that appear to support a "trinity" have been added to most Bibles. Even the devils in the presence of Jesus testify that He is the Son of God.

If you still believe that Jesus Christ is God, what weird twisting of the scriptures are you using to follow a tradition started by the Roman Catholic Church? The trinity is a man-made tradition that has no biblical support!

When was Jesus Christ Crucified?

Most Christian churches celebrate the crucifixion of Jesus Christ on Easter. Is that when Jesus Christ was crucified, and does it matter? It only really matters if you have placed traditionalism over truth.

To answer when Jesus Christ was crucified, you really need to ask yourself three questions. Was He crucified anytime near what we call Easter? Was it on a Friday? From these, can we work out what day He rose? Scripture can answer all these questions.

Any Christian who has done a little studying on Christian holidays should understand that Easter is rooted in paganism, not Christianity. Think about the tradition of Easter itself. People celebrate an egg-laying rabbit. What did those symbols represent? Fertility! Somehow many Christian leaders today still try to pull some type of relationship to show that it is OK to celebrate Easter egg hunts and chocolate rabbits.

It's too bad. As a young child these are some of my favorite memories. I still enjoy looking back at video of my sons having the same pleasure. But, if given the knowledge that I have today I believe I could have had just as much fun with my children, while teaching them the truth of the traditions. What's wrong with children coloring eggs and then finding them? Nothing if they understand that it has nothing to do with our religious beliefs!

I really don't mind the tradition of Palm Sunday or an early morning service trying to bring Christ back into one's life, but did Jesus Christ's death have anything to do with Easter? How did we get Easter into Christianity anyway?

Easter is mentioned only once in early English translations of the Bible, this includes the King James Version. If your Bible has it, it will be in Acts Chapter 12, verse 4. As mentioned earlier in this book, you find that the Greek word in this verse is "pascha" or Passover.

The true word in the scripture, Passover, was replaced by the word Easter to bolster the blending of this tradition into new Christian values, maybe as far back as the 3rd century. Newer translations of the Bible show clearly that the word Easter was never there, and they correctly use the word "Passover." You should look it up for yourself if it is in your Bible.

So, was Christ crucified on, or around the celebration of Easter? We know depending on which gospel account you read that He was arrested either the day of, or sometime around Passover.

We will cover it more thoroughly later in this chapter. To understand approximately what season of the year Jesus Christ was crucified, all you have to understand is when Passover <u>was</u> celebrated each year.

If you look on the Internet you will find that the Jewish calendar celebrates the Passover on or around the Christian Easter celebration. I believe, and scripture will prove, that this is many months off. Why would the Jewish calendar be changed? I really don't know. Maybe the Jews in times past found it to be a little more expedient to celebrate Passover along with the Christians' celebration of Easter.

Just as we have no original Christian letters, they too have no original calendars. There are sects in the Jewish community that believe that the days of the year have increased and so the calendar moves. As it is very clear when Passover was celebrated from the scriptures, you will see that they celebrate it at an incorrect time of the year as ordained by God. Jews have given way to tradition over the Commandment of God. I have heard it stated that they now try to line up their calendar with lunar events. Why not just follow God's ordained time frames?

Look, the Jews know when the month of Abib begins. It is the first month in the Jewish calendar. The Passover was to be celebrated on the 14th day of Abib. So, 14 days after the Jewish New Year is the date God gave Moses to hold the Passover. Do you know what Rosh Hashana is? It is the Jewish New Year celebration. When is that held? In 2008 it began at sundown on the 28th of September. What do you know? If you use your Bible you will see that even the Jews would celebrate Passover on the correct date if they would read the books of Exodus and Leviticus. But religions don't exactly do what God wants, if it is inconvenient.

Passover was celebrated for the first time in Egypt. Read Exodus 12. It explains what, when and how the Passover would be celebrated for all times. Read the preceding chapters. They explain what has been happening in Egypt before this event. The Lord has wiped out all their crops. How many crops grow prior to April? None!

Passover is the 14th day of the Hebrew month Abib. Abib is the first month of the Hebrew calendar. Abib was the month the Children of Israel left Egypt. It was a time of the harvest. Look up the word Passover in your concordance and you will find that fall time references abound. Do we harvest in the spring, or the Summer, and or Fall? It was to be held at the same time each year. So, just from this one fact, we know that Jesus Christ was crucified sometime around the harvest or in the late Summer or Fall.

We also know that the celebration of the Passover today has been moved to accommodate the Jews in a more modern society. When was it moved? Who knows? It was a long time ago, but you do know if you read Exodus again, that it was originally during the harvest.

There really isn't too much in the Gospels that helps you nail down the time of year, except for the fig tree. In Matthew Chapter 21, verse 17 and again in Mark Chapter 11, verse 12 we have the story of Jesus just days before the crucifixion. He goes over to a fig tree because He is hungry. Finding no fruit on the tree, He curses the tree and it withers. Why would He curse a tree for not having fruit, if it was not the time for the tree to be fruitful? Mark does state that is was not yet time for figs, but then, Mark's Gospel is filled with a lot of added material that is in error.

It would be like planting tomato seeds in an evening and cursing the plant the next morning for not bearing fruit. The story is clear in Matthew, the only first-hand witness to this event, that Jesus came to the tree for food and found none. I lived in the Mediterranean for 2 years. Fig trees don't put on any fruit until summer, and then it is there for several months.

So, when was Jesus Christ crucified? We now know it was during the harvest, not on some Friday in April. But can we be more accurate? Was it a Friday? Two thoughts will sum it all up if you trust your scriptures. First, what was the Passover? Second, what and when was the Last Supper? Understanding these two different celebrations has everything to do with understanding what day of the week Jesus Christ was crucified.

How was the Passover celebrated? It was celebrated in conjunction with the Feast of Unleavened Bread. To see what you do and the order of events, read Exodus Chapter 12. Read the chapter at least twice. Remember to think Levitically, days begin at sundown and go on through the next daylight period and then end at sundown. You will conclude from verses 8-10, that they were to eat the Passover beginning in the evening, but finishing before the the morning. This shows that the passover started at the end of a "day," and it happens to be the 14th day of Abib. It concluded at night which is the beginning of the 15th day of Abib. That day is a memorial and kept as a feast (Exodus 12:14). This isn't to say that the two days are drawn together. It just happens that the Passover concludes before the Feast of Unleavened Bread begins.

To see the specific dates, read Leviticus Chapter 23. Moses has made it perfectly clear that the two celebrations are not the same. In Leviticus it gives the exact date of the Passover as the 14th day of Abib. It also makes it clear that the Feast of Unleavened Bread begins on the 15th day of Abib and was to last seven days. It is very important to understand that Passover is not part of the celebration of the Feast of Unleavened Bread, it proceeds it by one day!

To help solidify these two dates, look at Numbers Chapter 28, verses 16 and 17. Here again, Moses is telling you the date of Passover is the 14th day of Abib and The First day of the Feast of Unleavened Bread is the 15th day of the month of Abib. It is too solid and indisputable that Passover proceeds the Feast of Unleavened bread by one day!

In Exodus Chapter 13, it again shows the Feast of Unleavened Bread being a seven day feast signifying the coming out of Egypt by the Israelites. So there was the Passover, held by God's chosen people. Then the angel killed all the first born of man and beast in Egypt not "covered" by the Passover. This is followed by the Children of Israel being cast out of Egypt by Pharaoh. This casting out, or deliverance by God, is a celebration called the Feast of Unleavened Bread. It follows the Passover. Leviticus Chapter 23 tells you it is the following day.

Leviticus Chapter 23 lists all the Holy convocations. These are days when a Jew would perform no work. It starts with listing the weekly Sabbaths. Next it lists the Passover, followed by the Feast of Unleavened Bread. The first and last days of this feast are Holy convocations, where no work will be performed. So, the Jews didn't need to improve their calendar to place these days on a weekly Sabbath. God gave them additional High Sabbaths, no matter what day of the week they fell on. Back in Exodus Chapter 16, verse 16, it explains that they can perform work to prepare the meals, but that's it!

A real condensed version of these two celebrations goes something like this. You take a lamb of the first year without blemish, and bring it into your home on the 10th day of Abib. On the evening of the 14th day of Abib you slaughter it, and roast it without breaking a single bone in its body. The family eats the entire "sacrifice." The next seven days are a celebration. So the Passover, and the first and last day of the Feast of Unleavened Bread are all Holy convocations where NO ONE is allowed to perform any WORK. They are High Sabbaths. Go back and read the Law. It is covered several times. This gives you two Holy convocation days in a row, the Passover and the first day of the Feast of Unleavened Bread. And, if the weekly Sabbath just happened to fall on the preceding or following day, it would be a three day weekend with no work other than preparing meals allowed.

I really don't care if Jews today follow some different ritual that they call Passover. It is too clear from the scriptures that Passover and the first day of the Feast of Unleavened Bread are two different days, and they are both High Sabbaths. It's also clear that Passover was held on the 14th day of Abib and that just happens to be in the Fall.

Forty-three years later, after the first Passover, we see the 10th day of Abib referenced again. Read Joshua Chapters 3-4. It is the story of the Children of Israel crossing into the Promised Land. We read that the Children of Israel came up out of the river on the 10th day of the first month (Abib) in Joshua Chapter 4, verse 19. Strange, this is also the same day they are to take their lamb (sacrifice) into their home. Joshua had the congregation cleanse themselves in preparation for the Passover. Four days later they celebrated the Passover. In Joshua Chapter 3, verse 15, it is clear that this is the time of <u>harvest</u>. It is clear here, that God's ordained celebration was not in the spring.

It is profound to understand that the 10th day of Abib was the day the Lord had them prepare the Lamb for the Passover so the angel of death passed over the Children of Israel, while they were in Egypt. It is also the day the Children of Israel began to possess the land of Israel by passing over the Jordan to enter into the Promised Land. It is only fitting that this is the day our Savior prepared to pay the price for us, so we could pass into a life with the Lord God Almighty, His Father.

This last thought is the real gift we should focus on when we think of the Passover and His crucifixion, but we tend to forget the true meaning and power of these gifts and focus on religious externalism which gains us nothing. Hiding behind a set of religious beliefs and traditions will gain you nothing when you meet your Maker. Study to show yourself worthy of the reward. Let's do a little thinking here.

Any real Christian wanting to learn the truths of the Bible, to be closer to God the Father and His Son Jesus Christ, has to agree that Jesus was not crucified in April. But, could Jesus Christ be crucified on a Friday and rise on a Sunday, as the Christian tradition declares?

If you believe that Jesus rose from the grave on Sunday morning you have a problem, unless you let go of the notion that He was crucified on a Friday. It's very important that you look at the Lord's own words on how many days He would be in the earth. "Just as Jonah, the Son of Man will be in the belly of the earth for three days and <u>three nights</u> (Matthew 12:40 paraphrased)." How does He do this if He is crucified on a Friday and is risen by Sunday morning? What happened to the three nights?

The time frame is spelled out for you in the Gospel of John. Yes, I understand that the other Gospels tell it differently, but then who do you believe, John the guy that stood by the Lord at the Cross, or another "witness" that is telling a different story? Besides, Jesus already gave you the time frame He would be in the "belly of the earth." It just happens to coincide with John's account.

It is very important to show why you need to believe John's account, because John's account is very different than the other three Gospels. John's account actually chronicles the events with the days before the Passover. His chronicle of these events is in direct contradiction to the other

Gospels. You can trust only one time frame. Remember, Mark and Luke were not there. So, it is either Matthew's account or John's. Don't forget, John wrote the only New Testament book of prophecy, Revelation. God spoke directly to him!

But to help you set aside the other accounts, go back and recall the error potential of these witnesses. Only Matthew was another of the "twelve" with John who would have been at the Last Supper. Look closely at Matthew's translated account. There is a very big discrepancy in the translation, and or, the oldest copies of his letter. Read Matthew Chapter 26, verse 17. "Now the first day of the Feast of Unleavened Bread the disciples came to Jesus, saying unto Him, Where wilt thou that we prepare for thee to eat the Passover?"

Remember the real reason to read your Bible is to get closer to the truth and the love of God. It isn't to find loopholes to support your traditions. It appears that the translation of the Book of Matthew has made it clear that the meal they are about to eat is the Passover. What's wrong with this account? From Leviticus, it is clear that the Passover is the <u>day before</u> the seven day period they called the Feast of Unleavened Bread.

They could not have the Passover on the first day of the Feast of Unleavened Bread, it would have already happened. So we know that this account is polluted at least by this much. This is a good time to take out the Interlinear scripture analyzer and look at the words. It is vague at best, what is being translated!

It's not that the other Gospels should be totally discounted, it just shows that there are errors, so why not look at the more accurate account? Besides, later in Matthew, you will see that this meal is obviously not referring to the Passover.

As you know that the Bible is not error free, or written by the Holy Spirit, you have to ask yourself; what is the error potential of this account? Take the other two Gospels. Mark was a youth at the time, maybe not even born yet, as you learn his youthful age years later when working with Paul in the Book of Acts. Luke was not supposed to even be a Jew, and the Book of Luke is probably a legal document that was sent in defense of Paul when he was on trial in Rome. Isn't it odd that during all Roman encounters in the Book of Luke the Romans are the good guys?

The last supper account has many discrepancies, even though Mark and Luke have many sentences that read word-for-word. Does this make them witnesses? No, they were just stories that have been told the same and then written down. Want proof? Find where Jesus tells Peter he will betray Him in these two Gospels. In one it is while they are in the upper room. In the other, it is after they left. If they are not exact, then they are polluted.

This is why I like John's time frames more. They are accurate to the Levitical Law. Look, who was at the cross when Jesus was crucified anyway? John, Mary the mother of Christ, her sister, and two other Marys are the only ones mentioned in any of the gospel accounts. Since John was there, I would give his account more credibility, as we know the Bible is not inerrant. Remember, Mark and Luke were not even Apostles. Their accounts are only hearsay from others.

So, was the Last Supper a Passover? Did Jesus eat the Passover with the disciples? Of course not. He was our Passover, our sacrifice, our Lamb, our payment for sin and was in the grave over this festival. Read John Chapters 13-17. It is a lengthy story of the Last Supper. Do you read anything about a roasted lamb? Is it even mentioned in the other Gospels? More importantly, it was important to have the lamb live with you for the four days prior. Where is the Lamb in this story, or in any of the other gospels for that matter? Jesus Christ was the Lamb!

Now read John Chapter 18. After Christ had eaten His last meal with the disciples, He goes out to the Mount of Olives. It is late at night, He is arrested, He goes before the Jewish council, and then He is taken to Pilate. And after all these things, it is the next day. So Jesus' last supper is the day before His conviction.

Then in John Chapter 18, verse 28, we find the Jews leading Jesus into the judgment hall. But, the Jews would not enter, as it would make them unclean. It was the day of preparation for the PASSOVER. It's in all your Bibles. Jesus is in the judgment hall before the Passover! How could the Last supper be the Passover if it hasn't happened yet?

Read the verse for yourself! It is too clear! Had they entered, they would have been defiled and could not have partaken of this festive occasion. That same day they crucified the Lord. But, they had to get it over with quickly, as it would soon be sundown. All days in the Jewish calendar begin at sundown (The evening and morning were the first day, Genesis.).

But wait, am I sure that it wasn't a mistranslation? John mentions two more times that the Passover hasn't happened yet. In the same chapter, verse 39, you see that Pilate tells the Jewish masses that it is custom to release a prisoner at Passover. He is giving them one last chance to change their minds. But more direct, in John Chapter 19, verse 14 it states: "And it was the preparation of the passover, and about the sixth hour..."

So, John, a first-hand witness, has made it perfectly clear that we have not had the Passover yet. Could the Last Supper be the Passover? No! Remember, think as a Jew, when does a day start? At evening, so this has to be the daytime of the 13th day of Abib. Even Jews today celebrate

Rosh Hashana beginning at the evening. Sabbath is still celebrated beginning in the evening of a day. That is because a day is a 24-hour period of time ordained to begin at evening by God.

When is Passover? Passover is the 14th day of Abib. When does a day begin? For a Jew, and God, it is the evening and the morning. Jesus was slain on the daytime of the 13th of Abib. That evening is the start of the 14th day of Abib, when they would hold the Passover. They had to slay Him before the evening or they would have been Levitically unclean and could not take part in the Passover.

Remember Matthew, the other first-hand witness? Read Matthew Chapters 26 and 27. It takes you through the crucifixion and the burial by Joseph of Arimathaea. But what does Matthew Chapter 26, verse 62 say? Remember this is after Jesus has been laid to rest in the tomb.

Matthew Chapter 26, verse 62: "Now the next day, that followed the day of preparation, the chief priests and Pharisees came together unto Pilate..." So, this is the following day after they have crucified the Lord. It also happens to be the day after the day of preparation that John explained was when the Lord was crucified! So the fact that modern Christians would like the wording of Matthew's letter to state that Jesus ate the Passover with His disciples, is refuted here.

The other two Gospels do state in such a way that the Passover was the Last Supper, but their error potential is high. This would also make their accounts in conflict with Levitical Law. Their errors could be explained by the fact that Luke may not have understood and Mark was too young when the event happened. Either way, they both would have written this down many years later after they traveled with Paul.

So Jesus was crucified around the time of harvest. He also had His Last Supper with the disciples the day prior to Passover. But was He crucified on a Friday?

The evening after Jesus' crucifixion was Passover. That makes it a High Sabbath, not the weekly Sabbath, and it is written that way in John Chapter 19, verse 31. He tells you it is a High Sabbath to ensure two things. First, to explain why they wanted to take His body down from the cross before an evening of a non-weekly Sabbath day; and second to ensure you don't think the day He was crucified was on a Friday. If it was a Friday, he would have just stated the next day was a Sabbath. But he doesn't. He tells you the next day was a High Sabbath.

To make it crystal clear, for those who are entrenched in the Friday crucifixion theory, ask yourself this: If a High Sabbath falls on a weekly Sabbath, is it a Sabbath? Yes. If a High Sabbath falls on another day of the week is it still a Sabbath? Yes. So, any day of the week on which a High Sabbath falls, is a Sabbath.

If it were Friday, would the next day be a Sabbath or a High Sabbath? It's a Sabbath either way. A High Sabbath can be called a Sabbath, so you wouldn't make any differentiation if it was a weekly Sabbath "Saturday."

But if it were any other time frame than Friday sundown to Saturday sundown, you would have to explain that it was a High Sabbath or your Jewish reader (who it was written to) would not understand why the haste to remove the body from the cross. More clearly, John had to state that it was a High Sabbath to show it was not a regular weekly Sabbath.

The other less accurate gospels state that it was a Sabbath. They do not differentiate whether it was a High Sabbath or not, but that just makes John's lengthy account more accurate. They do not oppose John's account if you take into consideration that they could have been referring to it as a Sabbath when it was actually more accurately a High Sabbath.

So we know that He died before the celebration of the Passover. It was also not on a Friday or John would not have stated that He was crucified the day before a High Sabbath.

Jesus entered as a King on the 9th day of Abib (John 12:12). He also showed us that he was to be our Lamb. He lived His last few days with His family (the disciples). He was slaughtered before Passover and then rested in the earth for three days and three nights. Did He rise on Sunday? It all goes back to what the Greek words "Heis sabbaton" mean.

In the Gospels it states that Mary went to the tomb on the "first day of the week." If you look at it literally in the Greek it states that she went there on "one Sabbath." But if you want to say that it was the first day after a Sabbath, it might be. Does this mean that it was a Sunday?

What was the day following the Crucifixion? It was a High Sabbath. So Mary could have gone to the tomb after a High Sabbath and it wouldn't have been a Sunday. But that doesn't take into account the three nights.

So, He was crucified and buried before the Passover, on the 13th of Abib. He was in the grave across the Passover, the 14th of Abib. He rested on the High Sabbath, the 15th of Abib (1st day of the Feast of Unleavened Bread), and then arose the following morning. That would be three days and three nights and no need for a weekly Sabbath. This is why the Book of John is so important. It tells you the complete sequence.

After all, what Gospel account tells you they (the women) prepared spices and came to anoint His body? Only Mark and Luke. The two first-hand witnesses (Matthew and John) only state that

Mary and or Mary and another woman came to the sepulchre. The body had already been anointed before it was laid in the tomb by Joseph and Nicodemus.

Note: Only two men were righteous enough to allow themselves to be made "unclean" by quickly anointing and wrapping His body and placing it in the sepulchre. These were Joseph of Arimathaea and Nicodemus. This act was not forbidden by Jewish Law, it only made them unclean to partake of the feast to come, the Passover.

All Gospel accounts tell you that "they"came on "heis Sabbaton." Before we go any further, please look up the the phrase "first day of the week" in your concordance. It comes from two Greek words "heis" and "Sabbaton." These two words are literally translated almost exclusively into the English words "one" and "sabbath." Only in the nine times that they want to translate these two words into "the first day of the week" are they mistranslated in this fashion. We will cover this translation in depth in the next chapter , but for now you must have at least a little knowledge of the translated phrase.

Was it breaking the Law to visit the grave on a Sabbath? No. If Jesus died on the 13th of Abib before evening, He was our Passover. We know from John's passage that it was the day before a High Sabbath. That day is followed by another High Sabbath, the 1st day of the Feast of Unleavened Bread, the 15th of Abib. Mary finds the tomb open on "heis Sabbaton." Why is it so hard to believe that she found the tomb open on the "first Sabbath" or one Sabbath after the event?

After all, in the phrase "first day of the week" the Greek word for "day,"which is "hemera," is missing. To get the phrase you have to say that "heis" is translated into the English word "first," although it usually is translated into "one." And finally, you have to change the Greek word for Sabbath into the English word "week," where it only appears in these few occasions. But to reference Sabbath, it would have been a day after the Sabbath, so "meta" would have been used, as when Jesus' words where quoted ... <u>after</u> three days in (Matthew 27:63).

If the Gospels really wanted to say Sunday, it would have been a better translation if they had used "protos hemera meta sabbaton." Better yet, why not use the word "morrow." It means the day after. If you want to talk about Sunday, it was in the Old Testament: it was the morrow of the Sabbath. Morrow is used in the New Testament. But not in morrow of the Sabbath, because nothing recorded of any importance happened on Sunday in the New Testament.

Still, for you die hards that want to believe the other Gospels, let's use them to show their own faults. Using Luke's story found in Luke Chapters 22 and 23 you learn that supposedly Jesus had the Passover (22:8). Then He is arrested at evening and taken before Pilate the next day (23:1).

They hold three trials (Jews, Pilate, Herod and back to Pilate) all across town, yet are still able to crucify Him (32:33) by noon of that day.

Then in Luke Chapter 23, verse 56 you read, "And they (the women) returned, and prepared spices and ointments; and rested the Sabbath day according to the commandment." This account is what the Friday crucifixion story hangs on. According to this story they have to prepare the ointments and quickly, as the Sabbath is approaching.

Did you forget your Jewish Law so quickly so that you can grasp firmly to this tradition? Just for argument sake, let's say that Jesus ate the Passover with His disciples (which He didn't). That would be the 14th day of Abib. That night they arrested Him, as the Passover was a celebration into the night. This means that they crucify Him in the daytime on the 15th day of Abib. If this is so, the women would have had to prepare the ointments on either the 14th or the 15th day of Abib. But, these are both HIGH SABBATHS. Jews are forbidden to do any work on these holy days to include an execution. These days have the same non-work rules as a weekly Sabbath! Go back and re-read Leviticus Chapter 23

How do you explain that? You can't. That is because the entire storyline is off. Matthew, Mark and Luke follow the same story line, but only Luke gives you the info you need to drive home the Friday crucifixion. And if you want to rely on this witness (that wasn't there), go back and read *The Books of Luke*.

What makes it worse, Luke throws you a curve ball. Luke Chapter 24, Mark Chapter 16 and Matthew Chapter 28 tell the story of Mary going to the sepulchre after the Sabbath had ended. Luke and Mark tell you it is very early, but Matthew tells you it happened "As it began to dawn." Remember Sabbath ends at sundown Saturday night. Was the Lord in the Tomb on Sunday in the "daytime?" Not if you believe these witnesses.

Here is the curve ball. Remember the story of Jesus walking with the two believers on the road to Emmaus in Luke Chapter 24? How many days had they said the Lord was in the tomb? Verse 21 reads like this, "But we trusted that it had been He which should have redeemed Israel: and besides all this, to-day is the third day since these things were done."

Even the author of the Book of Luke knew that He had to be in the ground for three days and nights. Even if you count Sunday, although He was risen before Sunday daytime, in all three accounts, count backwards with Luke. Even Luke is telling you that the Lord was crucified on or before Thursday. The Greek translation is a stretch to say that He rose on a Sunday. Why not look at a better view of what really happened?

So, John makes it clear, and I will repeat it here. Passover is the evening starting a High Sabbath. The following day after the Passover is the first day in the holy week called the Feast of Unleavened Bread. On the first and the last day of the festival of Unleavened Bread there was to be a sabbatical from work. They are both High Sabbaths. So, do the math with the Apostle John, as none of the Gospels line up with each other.

Christ died before Passover (preparation day). He was in the ground on Passover and in the ground the first day of the Festival of Unleavened Bread, which are both High Sabbaths. What if Passover was on Wednesday that year? What if Mary came to the sepulchre on the first Sabbath after the crucifixion? These are the three days and three nights. Then He is risen. This shows that He wasn't necessarily in the grave over the weekly Sabbath (Saturday), and risen on a Sunday. It fits the Greek if you would test it. But what if He was risen on a Sunday? What day of the week was Jesus crucified? If you refuse to believe the disciple that Jesus "loved" more than any other, do you also refuse to believe Jesus? If you don't believe Jesus, then you have bigger problems than to figure out what day of the week He was crucified!

It had to be Thursday if you believe He rose on a Sunday. Jesus predicted that He would be in the ground for three days and nights. If Mary arrived at the grave early Sunday morning (before sun rise), count backwards.

They were strictly prohibited to touch a dead body and then partake in the Passover. Read the Old Testament. God stated that if they were unclean, then they had to wait a month and then they could have a mini-Passover, but they would have missed this big feast. And of course, they wouldn't work on a Sabbath or a High Sabbath.

Do the math for yourself. Could Jesus have risen on a Sunday and died on a Friday? Is there any way a reasonable person can believe that harvest time and a crispy spring morning are the same time of year? Should a true Christian be celebrating an egg-laying-rabbit tradition?

Because of the High Sabbath issue with the Passover and first day of the Feast of Unleavened Bread, and the fact that the translation of heis Sabbaton is really unknown, there is no way to know what actual day of the week Jesus Christ was crucified. What is for sure, He couldn't be crucified on a Friday and then rise on a Sunday, because He told you He would be in the grave for three days and three nights..

If you take into account the two High Sabbaths, Jesus could go into the grave on any day of the week, stay there over the two High Sabbaths and rise before dawn of the following day and that would be in the belly of the earth for three days and three nights. If He goes into the grave on

Wednesday afternoon and rises on Saturday before dawn, He meets all His own criteria and is totally explainable with the Heis Sabbaton translation in ALL of the Gospels.

The day of crucifixion and resurrection are the source of false traditions used by man for years to hold celebrations and worship other than what God has ordained. Sunday worship is supposed to be linked to the resurrection of Jesus. But if you want to celebrate the resurrection of Jesus on Sunday, it would have to be before the sun comes up.

One last thought, Jesus set and predicted the days that He was to be in the grave. If He did rise on Sunday, "He" provided Himself a rest over His Sabbath. If He died on a Friday, then He arose on a Monday, and He again gave Himself a rest on His Sabbath. Why not rest with Him on His Sabbaths?

What is the Sabbath and Does It Matter?

Attending church is a tradition. Not all traditions are bad. But if the tradition is one where you are linking the tradition to your Christian walk, don't you think it should be scriptural? Let's say your tradition states that you can't eat meat on Friday. Where is that in the scriptures? Most Protestant Christians would explain that this was a Catholic tradition that Protestants have ignored. Why would you ignore it? Because although it had been followed by most of the civilized world for over a thousand years, it just isn't scriptural.

Why then do Christians resist the thought of a Holy Sabbath unto God? What is the excuse real Christians use to explain that following the Sabbath, as God has ordained, is some form of externalism that can be ignored? Why have we substituted a tradition of man, also from the Catholic Church, for a commandment from God?

If you skipped the previous chapter called, *When was Jesus Christ Crucified*, and want to link your Sunday worship to His resurrection, you must go back and have an understanding of what day He was crucified. More importantly, you will not be able to conclude that He rose on Sunday morning. With that said, why wouldn't you worship God when He ordained it?

Go back and read Matthew Chapter 15. Jesus condemned the substitution of a man-made tradition over a commandment of God. After this chapter you will see that there is no biblical way to explain Sunday worship of God. With that said, how can you support your Sunday church in spreading a tradition of man over the Commandment of God?

Face it, in today's society, keeping the Sabbath is inconvenient. There really aren't any scriptural churches that keep it. And, with the so-called Lord's day worship on Sunday, all you have to do is attend one of these churches and say a few words and you have met the minimum standard to be saved. At least, that is what you have chosen to accept with your so-called Christian friends.

Is a Christian really a Jew to God? Are all Jews chosen vessels of God? When Jesus spoke to John in the Book of Revelation, was the message intended for what we call the "Christians" of that day? You have to say yes, but also to the Christians of today. What is meant when Jesus refers to Jews in the Book of Revelation? It is always in reference to those "saved" in the churches that He is talking about. Look at the verbiage in Revelation Chapters 2 and 3. Some of the peoples in those churches are obviously "unsaved." They are referred to as "not Jews at all," in the letters to Smyrna and Philadelphia. These 2 chapters state that those that are saved in those churches are "true Jews."

Why does Paul explain that we (Gentile Christians) are part of the Holy Olive Tree in Romans Chapter 11? He explains that a Jew of Israel through unbelief is cut out of the tree and that we Gentiles can be grafted in. He also explains that we can be removed, if we "do not continue in goodness." Read it again and again and you will have to see that we, the saved of God, are of one family to Him.

Why are the Christians in the New Testament referred to as Jews too many times to be ignored? Look it up for yourself. We that are "saved," are referred to as "inward Jews" over and over throughout the New Testament scriptures. What does this have to do with the Sabbath? Any promise that is given to the Nation of Israel was also given to an inward Jew! Sabbath was a gift from God. Yes, it does limit the work you will perform on the Sabbath, but it is really a gift, a limiting of work, a rest in your work week.

I began my REAL Christian belief and understanding somewhere about 1994 (mid-life). Of course, I was raised in a Christian home and attended church during my youth. Of course, I was baptized when I was in my early teens. And like most people, it was not based on any real understanding and hence, I fell away. But my real understanding of God and my love for Him began in 1994.

My Christian growth was during a time that the only church I could attend was one of many Sunday keeping churches. I really didn't think it mattered for years. As I aged, I read my Bible daily and the truths in the scriptures began to question my values. At this time in my life I was closely associated with the Calvary Chapel.

I had given them thousands of dollars each year and I was an usher. When I started to ask why the scriptures teach one way, but we Christians believe another, I got no answers. No one wanted to know. Do you know that you will be held accountable for what you teach? God will hold me accountable for what I put in this book. Let's just take a basic look at what the Bible states about the Sabbath.

Whose Sabbath is it anyway? I'm so tired of hearing, "It is the Jews' Sabbath." Do you know what the Sabbath is? The Sabbath is a 24-hour period of time each week. God ordained it and called it "His Sabbath," not the Jews' Sabbath, not the Christian's Sabbath, but "My Sabbath." Yes, in Exodus, God does state that when the Jews keep it, it will be a sign of the covenant between Him and them. But He never states that it is "their" Sabbath, just His Sabbath. In the Old and New Testament it is called Holy, or His Sabbath, or Holy unto the Lord, and He even blessed the Sabbath day. Have you read anywhere in the Bible that there was a holy "thing" that then became unholy?

I will not argue about this topic, it is too clear from scripture. Either you are a Christian, you are playing Christian, or you are a professed non-Christian. If you are a Christian you will be looking for God's will in your life. What does He state about the Sabbath? Let's start with the Ten Commandments. The first four are about love and honoring God. The last six are about love and honoring man. The fourth commandment is showing reverence to "His" Sabbath. It can't be any clearer. Go back and read the Commandments. It is called "His" Sabbath.

Before you take the advice of a Sunday-keeping church leader about the Sabbath, why not read Ezekiel on this matter. In Ezekiel Chapter 20, God is explaining why He is allowing Jerusalem to fall into the hands of the heathen. Read the whole chapter, but in verse 12, God explains that He gave "His Sabbaths" to them and later in the chapter He explains that they polluted them. Then again in verse 20, He explains the relationship between the Jews keeping His Sabbaths and their covenant with Him.

God explains that if they hallowed His Sabbaths it will be a sign that they know that He is the Lord God (Exodus 31:13). So, keeping the Sabbath was a sign from the Jew (or you), showing that they knew that the Lord was God. Does this sound like a Jewish thing? No! In fact, the land was to keep a Sabbath also (Leviticus 25:2). Is the land Jewish, Christian, or pagan? None of the above, its just dirt, but meant to keep a Sabbath..

The Sabbath starts at sundown on Friday night and ends at sundown on Saturday night. It is a time that He rests and expects all others to rest too. Has this time ever changed, or hinted as being changeable in the Bible? No where! So, who are we as mere men to change a holy time given by God, to a time we feel is more appropriate? I can see it now when you are judged about the many sins you may have committed. Do you think you will start explaining to the Lord, "Well God, I felt you were mistaken when you told us......"

Read Genesis Chapter 1. It is the creation story. Genesis Chapter 2 starts with "Thus the heavens and the earth were finished, and all the host of them. And on the seventh day God ended His work which He had made; and He rested on the seventh day from all His work which He had made. And God blessed the seventh day, and sanctified it: because that in it He had rested from all His work which God created and made."

Now jump forward to Exodus Chapter 16. This was the deliverance of the Children of Israel in the wilderness with manna. They were instructed to gather extra on Friday, as there would be none on Sabbath. This way they would rest on the Sabbath. And, it directly states in verse 25, that it is the "Sabbath unto the Lord."

If you look at what is stated in Chapter 16 exactly, God, who sends manna, still rested on the Sabbath, by not having to give manna to the Israelites on the Sabbath. Read the chapter carefully. Verse 28 specifically shows that God was expecting them to keep His Commandments and Laws already at that time. This was before the Ten Commandments in tablet form were given. This shows that God expected them to be keeping the Law already. Could God's Law already have been known? Read it again, you will have to decide for yourself, but I believe this is the case. Otherwise, why would He have been displeased when they didn't obey it?

As the Sabbath is part of the Law of God, it is actually indirectly mentioned much earlier. God states in Genesis Chapter 26, that Abraham obeyed His voice, kept His charge, kept His commandments, kept His statues, and His Law. Moses wrote Genesis. The same Moses that wrote in detail the Law of God in the Book of Exodus.

Since Moses wrote both books wouldn't you think that Moses would have known what God's Commandment's were? From this passage you can easily make the case that Abraham probably kept the Sabbath and all of God's Law for that matter. Read your Bible through or use a concordance and you will not find any mention of Abraham doing anything that would be considered breaking the Mosaic Law.

In Exodus Chapter 20 we see the Ten Commandments. You know, the nine we believe in keeping and the Sabbath one that we don't. Exodus Chapter 20, verse 8: "Remember the Sabbath day to keep it Holy. Six days wilt thou labor, and do all thy work: But the seventh day is the Sabbath of the Lord thy God: thou shalt not do any work, thou, nor thy son, nor thy daughter, thy manservant, nor thy maidservant, nor thy cattle, nor thy stranger that is within thy gates: for in six days the Lord made the heavens and the earth, the sea, and all that in them is, and rested on the seventh day: wherefore the Lord blessed the Sabbath and hallowed it."

You can see from this passage that the seventh-day Sabbath is linked all the way back to the creation. There is no wiggle room for not keeping the Sabbath. Even if you want to attend church on Sunday, you have an obligation to God to keep "His" Sabbath.

Take the word "Sabbath." It is obvious when you read it anywhere in the Bible, that they are talking about a specific time period from Friday sundown to Saturday sundown. It is the Greek word "Sabbaton." But, did you know that every time you find the phrase "first day of the week" in the New Testament, it is actually formed by two Greek words? They are the Greek words "heis" and "sabbaton." It is a poor argument to say that these two words can come to mean Sunday when translated into "the first day of the week."

Heis has been translated into the words: one, several, another, every, only, one-by-one. In fact, the original translators translated "heis" into 25 different English words. Which one is it? Then, only on the occasions that suited the translators, for whatever reason they chose to translate the word "Sabbaton" (which is the word Sabbath) into the English word "week" to be used in the "first day of the week" references in the New Testament! In all other locations in the New Testament where the word Sabbaton is found they correctly translated it into "Sabbath." Somehow they have translated a certain Sabbath day into Sunday. Why would they do that?

Let's kill the idea that the "First day of the week" translation could have anything to do with Sunday, or a new day of worship for that matter. Take out your Strong's Concordance and look up the word "week." It is used only in the "first day of the week" translations of "heis Sabbaton."

Before we look at each of these translated passages, look back at any of the "first day of the week" sentences using either the concordance or an interlinear scripture analyzer. The word "first" originates from "heis." Out of the over 340 times heis is used, only 8 times is it translated into the word "first," and for all of these it is the "first day of the week" phrase. Usually, some 289 times, it is translated into the word "one."

Next, look up the word "first" in your concordance and you will find it used hundreds of times, but it isn't the word "heis." It is either the words "proton" or "protos." Heis will appear the sum of eight times where they want to use the phrase "first day of the week." You really don't have to be too bright to understand that "heis" is not a good translation for the English word "first." You just have to be pig-headed if you want to believe it.

Now, look back at the concordance at any of the "first day of the week" translations and you will see the word "day" is italicized. For those that don't understand what that means, it shows you that the word is added. So are the words "of" and "the." Yes, they aren't in the scripture at all. And we already know that Sabbaton is the word Sabbath. The scripture really states that on "one Sabbath" these things happened.

This translation is used a total of eight times in the New Testament, six of which are used in the Gospels covering the day the Lord was found risen from the dead. First, ask yourself what day did Jesus enter the grave? It never tells you a day, so it isn't conclusive. But, John makes it perfectly clear that Jesus was crucified on the preparation day for the Passover (John 18:28)!

Yes, Passover is the evening starting a High Sabbath. So the next day is the first day in the Holy Week of Unleavened Bread. On Passover and the first and last day of the Festival of Unleavened Bread, there was to be a sabbatical from work. They are all High Sabbaths.

When the other gospels talk of the crucifixion or the resurrection before or after a Sabbath, you don't know if it was the seventh-day Sabbath or the High Sabbath. John makes it perfectly clear that it was a High Sabbath (John 19:31). So, was He crucified on a Friday? No, but we looked at this in depth in the chapter titled, *When was Jesus Christ Crucified*.

Other than the Gospel event of Jesus' resurrection, the next account of the "First day of the week" translation of "heis Sabbaton" is found in Acts Chapter 20, verse 7. So when they met on Heis Sabbaton, they were meeting on "one" Sabbath, maybe after the days of the Feast of Unleavened Bread. It is only hard to understand this when you doggedly want to continue to follow a tradition of man, set up by the Roman Catholic Church. But also remember from your understanding of the accuracy of Luke's books, they can be a little false.

Is it so odd to think that if Paul came to town, they would gather together and listen to him? Is it so strange to think that if they went into the night talking that they would want to break bread together? Does this account show a new weekly tradition? No, just that Paul was on a tight schedule and they all got together and listened to him over dinner.

The last time "first day of the week" is used is in 1 Corinthians Chapter 16, verse 2. Read it and ask yourself, could he be calling for a once a year pooling of the resources? It really isn't clear. You can substitute almost any time or day into this sentence. It could be the first Sabbath after the Passover. It could be the first Sabbath of each month. But remember, the word heis didn't have to mean "first" and usually didn't. It could mean almost anything, but probably meant "every Sabbath!"

This is a great time to use the interlinear scripture analyzer and look back at who was the first-hand witness in the Gospels. There was no Jewish law that stated that Mary could not go to the sepulchre on a Sabbath. Only that she could not do any work. Sure, her distance of travel was limited, but it was easily within a Sabbath's day journey. John and Matthew are the only two first-hand witnesses that wrote one of the Gospels and they don't tell you that she is going to anoint the body; after all, she is alone or with another woman in their accounts. How would she have moved the stone away?

Think about the facts, the body had already been anointed by Joseph and Nicodemus. If you look at the only two first-hand witnesses that wrote Gospels, they just state that Mary was visiting the sepulchre and found it opened. Use your interlinear scripture analyzer and look these passages up and the ones found in the Acts of the Apostles. It is very clear that the authors were writing of "a Sabbath day event."

Looking closely at the verbiage in Acts Chapter 20, verse 7, where you read the "first day of the week" phrase in your Bible. Replace the phrase to read "first" or the word "a" or "one Sabbath" as it is written in the Greek and you see that it fits comfortably, without any added words. Why? Because this is what the scripture is talking about, a Sabbath day event.

If you have been reading your Bible diligently and come to this spot in Acts you have to ask yourself, where and when has Paul been preaching? There is only Sabbath day preaching and sometimes continual preaching, but never "Sunday" preaching unless you try to add words or change the Greek word for Sabbath into the English word "week." Remember, changing the Greek word for Sabbath into the English word "week," is only used during these poorly translated passages. I feel sad for you, if you can't get over this bad translation. You obviously don't want to get over it no matter how obvious it is!

While you are looking at translated words, why not look up the word "morrow" in the concordance. Why? Because by this time, if you have been reading your Bible, you will have become familiar with the fact that days and events are placed in referenced to the Sabbath. If you want to talk about Sunday it is the "morrow after the Sabbath."

Were the Bible authors Jews? All but Luke. Did they speak in Hebrew or Greek? What language did Paul speak to the people in, when he was arrested in Acts Chapter 21, verse 40? It is Hebrew. Go back and read all of Leviticus Chapter 23. Sunday is mentioned several times because some Sundays were important celebrations and "Sabbaths" for the Jews. It is referred to as "the morrow after the Sabbath."

The word morrow is used 23 times in the New Testament. So it's not that they didn't use it. In fact they used it 4 times more often than the heis Sabbaton translation into Sunday. Why didn't they just say morrow after the Sabbath? Because nothing worth taking about was recorded that happened on Sunday in the New Testament.

Ask yourself: If heis Sabbaton is supposed to be the first day of the week, why wouldn't they just say the morrow after the Sabbath, as they already have that "known" and understood way of referring to Sunday? This isn't rocket science. It's just a bad translation that helps to keep an instituted non-God-ordained tradition alive.

The first real translation of the Bible into English was commissioned by King James. He was the monarch over England and was also the head of the Church of England. He was obviously following Sunday worship, as was the whole world at that time. Does that make it OK to continue to follow the practice today just because the whole world is doing it wrong? Take out your concordance and look the words up for yourself. There is no Sunday worship in the Bible!

Don't trust your Sunday worshiping friends or church leadership. Don't even trust me, just buy a concordance, download a free interlinear scripture analyzer, and look it up for yourself!

Just for argument's sake, lets say that Heis Sabbaton could mean Sunday. How would those passages where you find Heis Sabbaton or "first day of the week," change the Sabbath Law of God? In the Gospels they aren't worshiping, they are hiding!

Later in life when I was attending another Sunday-keeping non-denominational church the pastor actually stated that we would discuss a certain matter next Sabbath. Obviously, he did not know that Sabbath was not Sunday. God has ordained the Sabbath as Friday sundown to Saturday sundown. That 24-hour period is non-negotiable. Call Sunday worship anything you like, but don't call it Sabbath.

While I attended there I took some heat because the members would do church clean-up on Saturdays. I would have to decline, as I would show them the passages forbidding to "work" on the Sabbath. Once again, no one really wanted to know, as that would not be convenient for their lives.

It isn't a Jewish thing; it is a rest that God gave to all mankind from the beginning of creation. This is what Jesus meant when he stated that man was not made for the Sabbath. The Sabbath was made for man. It was a present from God to you, a 24-hour period of rest each week. As all the days in Genesis Chapter 1 and 2 are listed, it begins at sundown on Friday night and ends at sundown Saturday night. So, how did this rest period change from Sabbath (24 hrs) to Sunday (12 or so hours)? If Sabbath worship was the norm for the early Church, where did Sunday worship come from? Let's look at your Christian values and you decide.

Catholicism: The early Christian church became an underground church in the Roman culture. Even though it was persecuted, it became larger than its pagan rivals. Not wanting to loose power over the society, Caesar, the Roman ruler in the early 300s AD merged the two religious beliefs and made himself Pope (which makes the fable of Peter as the first Pope ridiculous).

He combined the God of the Christians with the holy days and festivals of the pagans. Why do you think Catholics worship on "sun"day? It was because they took the pagan day of worship, but substituted the "sun" god with the Christian's God. Everyone knows about the god of fertility, played by an egg-laying rabbit. Somehow this celebration has come to represent the death of our Savior (Easter). The winter solstice and its yule log burning ritual became our Savior's birth (Christmas). Remember what Paul stated about the wolves corrupting the church (Acts 20:29)? Just look at your Christian Holidays!

Once this merger happened, the leadership of the Roman Catholic Church would gather together to revise and explain doctrine with the Pope. One such meeting was the Council of Nicea (300 or more bishops). Two main issues were blundered at this meeting. One was over the Sabbath and the other was over Jesus Christ's divinity. Ever since then, we have lived with their bad decisions.

If you think I am stretching it a little, why not do your own research? Peruse the Internet for yourself and you decide. Just look up "Council of Nicea" on any good search engine. There is too much documentation to refute it. Did these leaders have a divine link that God Almighty has denied to you? I don't think so!

Or better yet, why not read from Catholic books on the matter. The following is from Catholic printed material I found on the internet. [Catholics observe Sunday instead of Saturday because the Catholic Church transferred the solemnity from Sabbath to Sunday. At this same council the following edict was passed: "Christians must not Judahize by resting on the Sabbath." The penalty for disobedience was death!] -Peter Gerermann, "The Convert's Catechism of Catholic Doctrine," 2nd ed., p. 50, 1910.

It is obvious that the Roman Catholic Church felt they had the right to enforce changing Sabbath worship to Sunday worship, and as they were the only Church in town, the world went along with it. There are too many well-documented examples of how the Roman Catholic Church felt they had the authority to change the commandments of God. After all, they actually felt the Pope was "god" on earth. Who can argue with "god?" We would not be so persuaded today, but in times past, no one could read, so how would they know any different? But, you can read, and you should read the Bible for yourself. Did the Pope have the authority to change the direct word of God?

Sunday Observing Protestants: This is one of my favorite controversial discussions. It is the one that took me out of the Calvary Chapel (CC) church movement. First, the CC we attended had the best praise music of any church we had ever attended. Unfortunately, they didn't encourage group study of the Bible, unless they guided it. We covered Deuteronomy in a line-by-line study of the Bible in church. When we got to the Ten Commandments, and number 4 to be exact, the pastor stated something like this: "We don't believe it; it is not relevant, so I will pass over it and you can read it at home if you wish to." It left me wondering. If we don't believe in it, what other parts of the Bible don't we believe in at the CC?

I prayed about this and every time I turned on Christian radio for the next two days I heard another CC pastor talking down the Sabbath to the point where one stated that: "if you were trying to keep the Sabbath you are sinning." Sorry, that isn't scriptural. I had to find a better place to worship.

Oh, but you say that the Modern Evangelical Church (MEC) explains that this was only for the Jew; we worship on the Lord's Day. What is the Lord's Day? It is only mentioned once in the New Testament, Revelation Chapter 1, verse 10. Many would like you to believe this is referencing Sunday, but there is no proof of that. It doesn't even state that it is "Heis Sabbaton." Even if it was, there is no other referencing in the Bible to worshiping on this day or any day other than Sabbath.

In fact, there are many references to the "day of the Lord" in the Old Testament. It is the end times scenario. Funny (Hum, not ha ha), the whole Book of Revelation is the leading up to, and including what we know from the Old Testament as the end times. Could John have been stating he was in vision about the end-times scenario? That only makes sense. First, he tells you he is in vision about the end-times scenario, and then, he is!

So, where did the Protestant churches get their Sunday worship? The Roman Catholic Church of course. The Protestant movement came from the Reformation in the 1600s. They broke off from the Roman Catholic Church in protest of bad doctrine. But, so many people had worshiped for so long that the leaders of the movement were too afraid of what the masses would do if they changed the day of the week for worship.

In fact, the Catholics stemmed the tide of the mass exodus from Catholicism in Europe by pointing to the authority the Pope had over mankind by changing Sabbath to the Lord's day worship. After all, the Pope had the authority to change it for Catholics, but the Protestants had no authority to worship on Sunday, as there was no scriptural reference for the practice. Look it up on the Internet. There are too many historical books on the subject.

So, if you believe in Jesus Christ as the Son of God, and the only way to the Father, are you keeping His 4th commandment? Why not? Let's look at the reasons a Christian will keep the Sabbath.

Sabbath keeping Christians: First, let's not forget who we are worshiping and whose Sabbath it is. Jesus stated in Matthew Chapter 12, verse 8; Mark Chapter 2, verse 8; and Luke Chapter 6, verse 5: "the Son of Man is Lord of the Sabbath." He didn't say, I'm the Lord of the Sabbath, but we will be changing it soon!

I have not found a Sabbath keeping organization that follows the rest of the Bible, so I am not stating that just because a church may keep the Sabbath, they are more scriptural than "some"

Sunday worshiping church. I am stating that Sabbath keeping, i.e., the limiting of work efforts or personal gain on the Sabbath, is scriptural.

I have been told that the only Commandment not mentioned in the New Testament is the 4th commandment. The most frequent citing of this is when Jesus is talking to the rich young ruler. He asks him if he had broken commandments numbered 5-10. If this is your proof that Sabbath is not required, then I guess that you don't need commandments 1-3 either. 1-4 are all about honoring and loving God.

All New Testament writers kept the Sabbath. Read your Bible from front to back. The only areas that you can find verses that appear to be referencing "not giving Sabbath its due," are in Paul's writings. These are taken out of context along with many other themes in Paul's writings. Most of Paul's Sabbath issues will be discussed below.

If Paul wrote that Sabbath can be ignored or changed, do you think Paul broke the Sabbath? Paul never broke a Roman or Jewish law. Read the story of Paul in chains before Festus in Acts Chapter 25. After you read the account, not only could the Jews not show him breaking any Jewish Law, but Paul himself testifies that he has not broken a Jewish law. By the way, breaking the Sabbath was a law unto death, and that is what they wanted: to kill him!

Paul is quoted as saying that we treat all days the same in Colossians Chapter 2. First, you don't know the question that leads to his answer. It talks about meat, drink, new moons, and Sabbaths. If Paul was telling you that you don't need a seventh-day Sabbath because all days of the week are the same, then I guess that all days could be the Sabbath. If so, then you would be forbidden to work at all, as Sabbath was and is a day of rest.

Paul is the one that stated that if there is one among you that does not work, he will not eat. (Actually, the English translation of Colossians Chapter 2, verse 16, doesn't follow the Greek text). Over half of the sentence is added. Look up each word of the verse in the concordance and you will see that it is followed by NIG. That means that the word was not found in the Greek Text. Better yet, view the verse on an interlinear scripture analyzer to better understand what Paul stated.

Every letter of Paul's that talks about his work and travels demonstrates his preaching in the synagogues on the Sabbath. Sometimes he is not permitted into the synagogue and so he preaches to the Gentiles in another place, but it is still on the Sabbath. In a couple of places it does appear that they came together on the "first day of the week." But, remember from above in this chapter, this translation from "heis Sabbaton" is a very poor translation. Look up the word "week" in the concordance again.

Yes, it is the same Greek word that Jesus used when he stated "The Son of Man is Lord of the Sabbath." Does it sound like you can make that day Sunday? It is used 57 times in the New Testament for Sabbath. There is no other Greek word for Sabbath, but Sabbaton.

If there is nothing in the New Testament to show that you are to worship on Sunday, why do Christians still do it? It is definitely not in the Old Testament. In fact, there are plenty of Old Testament prophecies about end times and after. In most of these, Sabbath worship is mentioned. Every MEC loves to talk about Ezekiel Chapters 38 and 39: the battle of Armageddon. This is when Jesus comes back to the Earth to rule and a Great War between good and evil occurs. But that is followed by Chapters 40–46. These are the chapters of life after Armageddon, where God has a temple where we all come and worship. Read it and in Chapter 46 you will find that we will be worshiping on the Sabbath.

Out of all the scholars and Bible authors, who do you trust most? How about out of the lips of Jesus Christ? If He told you directly to keep the Sabbath, would you? He does. Read Matthew Chapter 24. It is Jesus' explanation of three events. They ask Him to (1) explain when the temple will be destroyed, (2) the signs of His Second Coming and (3) the signs of the end of the world. First, as you read through verse 16, is He talking to believers or nonbelievers? It is obvious that He is talking to those that love and worship Him.

As He explains about the end of time on earth He warns that they should... "pray that your flight be not in the winter, neither on the Sabbath day." If the Sabbath had no significance to believers today, don't you think He would have understood that? Does anyone have a better idea of the end times than Jesus?

Off topic, but up through verse 13 you see persecution and many will fall away, but those that endure shall be saved. What about those that thought they were saved and said those few magic words, and went up the saw dust path at a revival or church? It is clear from this passage that if they fall away they are not saved, hence once-saved-always-saved is a stretch.

I know, you will say that the Books of Mark and Luke also have this story and they don't mention the Sabbath in their account. Were they there during this event? No, but John was. If John had told this story it would be the most credible, but he didn't. But Matthew, as one of the 12, was there as a first-hand witness. So, who is the most credible? Matthew's account must carry more weight.

How could it be that Sabbath was observed at creation; probably observed by Abraham; observed in the exodus from Egypt; observed by Jesus when He was on the earth; was observed by all in the early church; will be observed after Jesus comes back at the second coming; and yet we don't think it is necessary for us to observe it today? There is no question as to if it is a commandment of God.

But we have substituted a tradition of man for a commandment of God. Jesus warned you about this kind of substitution in Mark Chapter 7. Read what Jesus states. Then ask yourself, am I knowingly living in sin? Can a Christian knowingly live in sin? If this is troubling for you, don't blame me, it is in your Bible.

By the way, what was a Sabbath rest and what do you do? There are plenty of references for what you would not do on the Sabbath. It was anything that created physical labor for you or the creation of gain (i.e., making monetary gain). But it is really a heart issue. Isaiah Chapter 58, verses 13–14 explains it best as "a delight within ones self to honor Him in what we do on His day." It's funny how someone can make up rules around these passages to prove they can do whatever they want. Just ask yourself, Is this what He would want me to do today? If you are a bit hesitant, it's wrong. Paul stated, if you doubt, then it is sinful.

Are you willing to rest your salvation on a MEC decision when so many Old Testament prophecies show the importance of the Sabbath? To me there is an easy way to find out what type of Christian you are. You are either a true Christian, trying to live the life your God wants you to live, or you are "playing" Christian, an outward display your peers agree with. Your acceptance of early Christian doctrine will be tested in your desire to keep the Sabbath. Are you willing to accept this "God Ordained" time that He has stated that you will observe? If not, do you really love Him, or is it just too inconvenient?

If you are a traditionalist and believe that Jesus rose from the grave on Sunday, then you have to ask yourself: why did Christ rise on Sunday (if you really believe it)? Think about it, even He rested on the Sabbath.

Additional Notes by the Author:

I was given a pamphlet that was written by a Christian group trying to explain why modern Christians don't keep the Sabbath. One pamphlet is as good as another, so I thought I would break down their arguments for you. The first argument is that the word "Sabbath" isn't mentioned in the Bible until the Children of Israel left Egypt, so that is where many Christians explain Sabbath keeping began.

How stupid! The word "love" isn't mentioned until Genesis Chapter 27, verse 4, when Isaac is old. Does that mean that there was no "love" in the world before that time? We do not know when Sabbath keeping began, but we do know that God had a seven-day week from the beginning and on the seventh day He rested. Later in Exodus, we learn that it is called the Sabbath and linked back to creation (Exodus 20:8-11).

Remember, in Genesis Chapter 26, we learned that Abraham kept God's Law and Commandments. How can you say that Abraham didn't keep the Sabbath? It was one of His laws, and the Children of Israel were expected to understand it before the Ten Commandments were put in stone.

Later in Deuteronomy Chapter 5, we learn that the 4th commandment is expanded to include that Israel should remember their deliverance from Egypt when keeping the Sabbath. But in both of the deliveries of the Ten Commandments recorded in the Bible, the Sabbath covers "all" people to keep the Sabbath. Even the stranger in your gates was to keep it. Why does it mention your oxen? Think about it, your oxen were your work implements. How could your oxen work if you didn't?

It is suggested that the stoning of the man that gathered sticks on the Sabbath in Numbers Chapter 15, showed there were benefits to be obtained from keeping the Sabbath. No, in fact this showed there was a great penalty for not keeping it!

Many like to point out that Jesus broke the Sabbath laws. Did He? He did break the commandments (traditions) that man had added to the Sabbath law. The Jews over the years had made laws that explained what they could and couldn't do. But, did He break God's Law? Jesus explained it Himself. "Is it lawful to do good on the Sabbath, or evil?" Then He healed the withered hand.

Jesus explained that anyone can do good or acts of kindness on the Sabbath. Where do you see Jesus doing "work" or making "gain" on the Sabbath? You don't! By the way, did Jesus heal on the Sabbath or did He do the works of His Father? Wasn't it really power from the Father working through Him? Doesn't He instruct the disciples to pray to the Father in His name for "things?"

All such pamphlets point out the "first day of the week" phrases. As I have already pointed out, that isn't in the Greek text. Besides, even if it were an accurate translation (disputable), there are only a couple of times where it is mentioned. So! Go back and read each of those references. Most don't include any worship.

There are dozens of times that we see the disciples in the synagogue on the Sabbath teaching with both Jews and Gentiles, and these worship occasions are non-disputable. I would have hoped that the disciples broke bread together on every day of the week, why would it be so special? Does the breaking of bread mentioned, constitute a newer, better Sabbath. Sorry, that is not scripturally sound.

Lastly, it is always pointed out that in Hebrews Chapters 3-4 there is a rest that most have not obtained. Modern Sunday keeping Christians try to link the Sabbath as this "rest" that was not obtained. These two chapters are talking about Jesus Christ being our rest. Up to this point in the Book of Hebrews, Jesus has been shown to be better than the angels, and now it is showing that He can give us rest that those who have come out of Egypt never obtained. The writer of the Book of Hebrews explains in those chapters that the Israelites that left Egypt never had the faith required and died in the wilderness. Read it several times. There is no way you can draw the conclusion that through Jesus we have no need for "God's rest."

Although the word "Sabbath" is not mentioned in these chapters in the Book of Hebrews, let's say it is implied. Please read Hebrews Chapter 4, verse 2 closely. It states that the rest did not profit them as it was not "mixed with faith." Actually, this is probably the strongest argument for keeping the Sabbath, if this is the rest the author is writing about. If our Sabbath rest is mixed with "faith" then the Sabbath rest becomes relevant! Read Hebrews Chapter 3-4 again focusing on this verse and it will become apparent that the author believed that you must have faith or it isn't relevant, whatever the rest was that the author was writing about.

There is no way a real Christian who wants to be close to the Lord can deny the Sabbath. Even if you are a non-Christian with the above mentioned Sabbath information; there is no way any intelligent person who is a real Christian can ignore the Sabbath. Why is it then, that most Christians will read this, and then press on with their lives as if they had never read the facts?

Just go back to the words in John Chapter 13, verse 42-43, "Nevertheless among the chief rulers also many believed on Him; but because of the Pharisees they did not confess Him, lest they should be put out of the synagogue: For they loved the praise of men more than the the praise of God."

Following God is not accepted by our peers if it goes against a modern tradition of man that they find more convenient to keep! Unfortunately for most, being accepted by those around you now, is more of a reward than the one you will receive later.

Christian Myths

Do you believe that there is a guy out there holding up the world? I am referring to Atlas. Does he or has he ever existed as the Greek myth portrays him? Of course not. But the Greeks believed it. They truly believed it. They could not understand how the world was held up in the universe and so we got Atlas. Atlas is a myth. Myths sound great, but are not factual.

Many religions believe that they are founded on a Prophet of God. If you are a Christian, you believe that God is, was, and always will be. He is never changing. So, could a prophet come along in the mid-7th century or even the 20th century, telling of what God wants from His people, be contradictory to what is in the Bible? If so, God wouldn't be the same, yesterday, today, and tomorrow. You would have to say that this new "god" is a myth.

Can a Christian denomination say that something is "sin" if you don't have scripture to back it up? If so, and it happens all the time, where are your facts? What if scripture is screaming to the contrary? That really makes that "sin" a myth.

Take drinking alcohol. How many Christians think that it is a sin to drink alcohol? If drinking alcohol isn't a sin, why would you look down on a Christian that drinks? I don't drink alcohol, but that is a choice I made, not a Christian conviction. Paul tells you that the excess of alcohol is a sin. Paul accepted responsible drinking. Is there anyone that Paul stated that could not drink alcohol? Yes.

Paul stated very clearly in Titus Chapters 1-2 and 1 Timothy Chapter 3, that some are allowed to drink, but that one member in the congregation was not. The only male not allowed to drink was the leader of the Church. I can only surmise that it is to ensure that this leader always had a clear head. Others in the congregation are limited, but not forbidden, even deacons are allowed a little. So, why do we have this myth?

Christians have added rules to rules to ensure that they stay "holy." Does it make them more holy? No, I believe it sometimes makes them miserable. Sometimes they make rules that help them feel good about themselves.

Do you believe in once-saved-always-saved? Where do you find this concept in the Bible? It isn't there, unless you add a couple of words from one verse to several of some more verses (you know, pick and choose). The Bible is clear. There is no once-saved-always-saved concept anywhere in the Bible. It is a myth.

How about the Sabbath? Christians rationalize that they have the authority to worship on whatever day they believe is OK with them. I believe that you can worship on any and all days, but do you have the right to perform work on God's Sabbath? Is Sunday worship in the New Testament? No, it is just another myth.

Does the New Testament give you freedom to eat anything you want? You may say yes, but does it give you the "right" to eat blood? If you correctly stated "No, a Christian can't eat blood" then what text tells you you can eat anything? The same text that sounds like you can eat anything doesn't state "except blood," so that text must be out of context. It's a myth.

Are you a pre-tribulation Christian? You know, we don't want to go through the tribulation that is going to happen on the earth just before Jesus comes back. So to help weaker people we make up an idea that we will not have to go through it, by leaving just before it happens. Where is your scripture? There is no scripture that backs up pre-trib. You can make a scriptural point that you are mid-trib or post-trib, but not pre-trib. It is a warm fuzzy Christianity, but it is a myth.

Do you believe that Christians are the bride of Christ? Why? It is specifically stated in Revelation that the bride of the Lamb is the physical structure of New Jerusalem. You will be a Son of God. How can a son be a bride? It is a myth.

The following chapters all cover these myths and others in detail. Why should you care? Because if you can't discern Christian myths, then you can't discern between the Commandments of God and the Traditions of man.

Are You Really Saved? Can You Loose It? What About Once-Saved-Always-Saved?

This chapter's subject is probably the most misunderstood myth in this book. I believe that far to quickly Christians say they are saved. The odd verse or proof text is quoted without using the rest of the Bible for your factual basis. It's bad enough when Christians throw out the Old Testament on this topic, but you have to throw out most of the New Testament also if you want to claim those odd proof texts. Much of the material in this chapter has been covered in earlier chapters, but it needs to be developed here.

To know if you are saved, you must have a heart for God. If you have a heart for God, will it change your life? Can you still live as you did before you were saved once you have changed your life? Can you really accept sin into your life if you are saved? Do you understand why it was so important to first learn why you need the Old Testament to understand sin?

Before we go any further, many would like to discount the Book of James, and the other letters in the New Testament when they appear to disagree with what we want Paul to say. Why? Was Paul closer to God than the others? Paul is usually taken out of context with his run-on sentences, but did he have a closer link to the Father? There is no scriptural proof. Paul did have an amazing vision on the road to Damascus. But, if his was the more perfect way, why did he have to come to Jerusalem to get the blessing from the council?

If you read the Book of Acts you will find that the council sent him to Tarsus to cool off. The council put their "hands on him" before he started his "real" ministry. Who was the Council? Peter and John walked with Jesus and were in the council, but they were not in charge. It was James. When Paul wanted to clarify how he believed a Christian should live, he came to James. Who wrote the Book of Revelation? That was John. Yes, Paul wrote a lot of inspired work, but he was just one of many.

The most abused verse taken out of context is found in Ephesians Chapter 2, verses 8-9. I have heard it over and over in church. It is used whenever a Christian is struggling with passages that reference payment for sin, as if these verses will wipe away every consequence of sin we have done and will do in the future. Why do they reference it? Because, according to church leaders, you have to do nothing. And as long as you hold onto a "feeling," you're saved, no matter what.

But as with my constant reminder to you, it is taken out of context. They stop where they want in the scriptures and ignore the "effort" or works on your part that is about to be required. Why not read the "whole" thought that Paul was presenting? Then, look at how the other New Testament authors write about this most important topic.

Read Ephesians Chapter 2, verses 8-10. "For by grace are ye saved through faith; and that not of yourselves: it is the gift of God. Not of works lest any man should boast. For we are His workmanship created in Christ Jesus unto good works, which God hath before ordained that we should walk in them."

This is an amazing statement about our walk towards everlasting life. There are many passages in the New and Old Testament that testify to this statement. Jesus, John, and Peter all remark about what Paul has stated. Let's look at the above statement before we look at your salvation. Ye are saved through FAITH. Did you have it in the first place? To receive this Grace the passage testifies that you <u>must</u> have the Faith. It then goes on to state that God has ordained that the "saved" will walk in good works.

James, the leader of the early church states in the Book of James "if you have faith without works, it is dead, being alone (James 2:17)." He goes on, but it is very clear to James that if you do not have works, you do not have faith. Paul stated in the above passage (Ephesians 2:10) that we were created to do good works and God ordained that we should walk in them. So, to claim the promise of Ephesians Chapter 2, verses 8-9 you must walk in your good works as referred to in verse 10.

Many Christians would say that I am suggesting to "work" your way to heaven. Hey, don't disagree with me, its in your Bible.

By the way, the above passage is way too over used in Christian circles. Too many churches have built doctrine around verses 8 and 9. I do believe we are saved by grace, but Paul also teaches in Romans Chapter 8, verse 24 that you are "saved" by Hope. I don't believe that anyone who has studied the scriptures would say that the letter to the Ephesians was any more important than the letter to the Romans. On the contrary, most believe the letter to the Romans was Paul's most complete work.

Saved by Grace is a catchy phrase, but go back and read Romans Chapter 8. Are you saved by Grace or Hope? That is the whole point of my book. It really is a heart issue between you and God the Father. They are both pretty much the same. That is why you have to have an understanding of the entire Bible so that these odd verses do not send you down a dead-end road. Read the Bible a couple of times and you will see the bigger picture.

Have you ever had your salvation questioned? You know, when you are asked to answer…are you saved? Do you really know if you are saved? If you sin a little sin before you die will you still go on to eternal life? How about a big sin? How do you know you are really saved? Or, how about, once-saved-always-saved?

You know, say the words in Romans Chapter 10, verse 9, "if thou shalt confess with thy mouth the Lord Jesus, and shalt believe in thine heart that God hath raised Him up from the dead, thou shalt be saved." To the modern evangelical church (MEC) that's all you have to do. They say it is a gift. There is nothing you can do to add to it. Christ did it all. If you try to add to it, it is blasphemy.

Wow, what an easy Christianity. Everyone can be saved, just say a few words and know it in your mind, and presto, you are saved. And with a few more passages like John Chapter 10 "no man can take you out of the Father's hand." Or the closing of Romans Chapter 9, where Paul states that… "For I am persuaded, that neither death, nor life, nor angles, nor principalities, nor powers, nor things present, nor things to come, nor height, nor depth, nor any other creature, shall be able to separate us from the love of God, which is in Christ Jesus our Lord."

This is the problem with quoting a verse here and there to make doctrine. Even if that is what Paul really meant, and I don't believe so, Paul could make that statement, but can you? He had conversations with the Lord. Have you? He lived a life that was zealous for the Lord. He lived for God and not for himself. If you are truly saved, you will live a life that is focused on the Lord Jesus and the Father. Your life and desires will take second place, always striving to bring Glory to God. Does that sound like a tall order? Paul lived it!

Lets look at the facts whether just being a so-called Christian and saying "those words" will get you to everlasting life. The US Center for World Missions stated that in the year 2000 the active world population for Christians was 33% of the entire world's population. So if they stated those few words (from the above paragraph), they are all saved according to the MEC. The Bible tells you, this is wrong. Jesus Christ tells you, this is wrong. The Gospels point out that Jesus Christ stated that the path to eternal life is narrow and few will find it! Do you question Christ's prediction? But the New Testament sounds so much easier. Does It?

Out of all the worldly scholars and or Bible authors, who do you trust most? How about out of the lips of Jesus Christ? If He told you directly about the walk of a saved man and the loss of a soul, would you believe Him? Read Matthew Chapter 24. It is Jesus' explanation of three events. The disciples ask Him to explain when the temple will be destroyed, the signs of His Second Coming and the signs of the end of the world.

First, as you read through the chapter, is He talking to believers or unbelievers? It is obvious that He is talking to those that love and worship Him. Read Matthew Chapter 24, verses 1-13 again. He is teaching them, and us, of the persecution during this time and that many will fall away, "but those that endure shall be saved." What about those that thought they were saved and said those few magic words, and went up the saw dust path at a revival or their church? It is clear from this passage (and identical passages in the other Gospels), straight from His lips, that if they "fall away" they are <u>not</u> saved, hence once-saved-always-saved is wrong.

Does anyone have a better idea of the end times than Jesus? Off topic, but in verse 20 you see a warning to true believers. He explains about the end of time on earth. He warns that they should… "pray that your flight be not in the winter, neither on the Sabbath day." If the Sabbath had no significance to believers during the end times, don't you think He would have understood that? Do you keep His Sabbath?

In the New Testament there are four stories about Jesus Christ's life, one on the early church after His death, a prophecy, and then some letters. Paul writes most of these letters. These are what get quoted usually to justify a Christian's selfish lifestyle. By selfish lifestyle, I am referring to verses that sound like Jesus saved you as you are, so there is no need to change your life to a more righteous way of life. Many of these letters are answering questions asked of him. You know, they sent him word that their church was struggling with a problem or issue and Paul answered them.

Do you know the questions the church asked? No! Is he always speaking from enlightened thoughts? No! How do I know? Don't forget, he even clarified that he is speaking to them as a man in Romans Chapter 3, verse 5. You just don't know all the facts surrounding these letters.

So, are you saved? The Bible makes it clear that it is a heart issue. Some would like to call it a "mind" issue as the heart is a biological muscle, but the Bible uses the heart as a metaphor and I will to. Can you know your heart? In 1 Kings Chapter 8, and 1 Chronicles Chapter 6, it states that "ONLY" God knows our heart. Let's look at scripture and find out if you are really saved.

To accept the gift of salvation you must take it. I mean really take it. A prisoner can be pardoned for his crime, but if he does not take the pardon given (this is a committed act), he will still pay the price for his transgression. I look at it as a great prize.

Did you ever ride a carousel? On some there is a ring that appears on the outside, that, as you go around, you try to grab it. If you are successful you win a prize. This is a committed act of trying to achieve a desire. You have to desire eternal life and then "go for it." The whole Bible is your "God supplied" manual, and it shows you how to "go for it" through the experiences of others.

The Bible gives us a lot of great examples of living a righteous life. The Father has given you a life on earth to interact with His creation, so you can learn of Him and His Son.

I really hate the statement "I'm saved and I can't add anything to it or I will be committing a works trip." Easy Christianity states it is a gift, you can choose to do nothing and you are in. I state to you that the Bible teaches that you are saved by Grace through faith, and it is a gift. But it also states that you are either of the world (fleshly lusts) or of the Spirit. Can you be saved and be of the world? Galatians Chapter 5 teaches in a nutshell the fruits of the Spirit are love, joy, peace, long suffering, gentleness, goodness, faith, meekness and temperance.

I put to you that if you are saved, truly saved, that you Love God. Your life will be God centered, as was Paul's. That means that you will, out of desire not duty, do the things that are pleasing to God. This is how you know that you are saved.

Do you trust Him? Then you will release everything to Him. What He likes, you like. What He hates, you will hate. I believe that you will believe something like this: "I am saved and I love Him, and so I want to please Him." How can you please Him? How about living the lifestyle that He has stated to you. God hates sin.

Paul stated in the Book of Acts when he was before Agrippa (Acts 24- 25), that he wished all men could live as he (Paul) does, repent and do the works of repentance. Plainly stated that means, stop sinning, ask for forgiveness for your past sins and then live the life that is sin free. Can I choose what I feel is sin? No. God has already done it for you in the Law.

As stated earlier, Paul, James, John and Peter have all stated that anything that is contrary to the Law is sin, and that sin is not in those that are saved. Proof texts showing that you are not under the law are found in Romans and Ephesians, but look at the end of Ephesians where Paul refers to the Ten Commandments when he states to the youth to "honor your father and mother as this is the first commandment that comes with a promise."

This obvious reference to the Ten Commandments shows that Paul felt that they were still current in his day. Doesn't that make it current today?

Does this contradict Paul's letter to the Galatians where he obviously wants to teach that Christians are not under the Law, they are under Grace? Not at all. It just shows us that the commandments of the Old Testament show us what sin is, and although we will still stumble, God hates us committing sin. How can you imagine yourself sinning and being saved?

Again, Paul tells you that the Law was your schoolmaster and it taught you what sin was. After you have "real" faith, you are no longer under the schoolmaster. But remember how James explained real faith? You will have works.

So, can you continue to sin if you are saved? Paul tells you at the end of Romans Chapter 5 and continuing into Chapter 6, that if we are dead to sin, we can no longer live unto it. And again, Hebrews Chapter 6 shows that "it is impossible for those who were once enlightened and partakers of the Holy Ghost, if they fall away, to be renewed again unto repentance." Boy, that is strong. It is actually scary. It is telling you that if you are truly saved unto God and choose to live in sin, there is no way to pay for your new choices.

Look back at the other early Christian leaders thoughts on this matter. Although covered in the chapter defining sin, it is more important to note it here. John states in 1 John Chapter 3 that "whosoever abideth in Him sinneth not: whosoever sinneth hath not seen Him, neither known Him." Earlier in the same chapter of 1 John, he states that "whosoever committeth sin transgresseth the Law; for sin is the transgression of the Law."

Chapter 3 and Chapter 5 are packed with John's belief that we will not continue to sin if we are saved. No, you are not saved by the Law, you are saved by Grace through Faith, but if you are living in Him, you will not sin. How much plainer can it be? If you are continuing to sin, then how can you say you are saved?

Peter states in 1 Peter Chapter 4, that Christians will "cease from sin; that he no longer should live the rest of his time in the flesh to the lusts of man, but to the will of God." What are lusts? They are selfish desires that you covet that are contrary to the Law.

It is pretty clear that we are saved by Grace. But if we have truly taken that gift, our love for Him will be apparent in our lifestyle. We will want, desire, and be driven to, (through our love) live a sin-free life. What sins will we want to avoid? All of them! But what if some of them are not convenient to my present lifestyle? Do you really love Him? Have you really been saved? If you have, you will desire to change for Him. As Paul stated in many of his letters, "Once you were thieves and fornicators and the like, but now you are not." Paul is pointing to the change in your life.

Remember Jesus stated that the path is narrow. "Many will say I cast out devils in your name and Jesus will say 'I knew you not'." Do you grasp the severity of that last quote? The Creator of the universe has just told you that some will even have the power of His name to cast out devils and they are doomed for destruction.

How is it that we have so many different Christian walks of life? It stems from inner selfishness. Let's take the homosexual lifestyle. Is it a sin? The Bible makes it clear that it is sin and an unacceptable lifestyle for a Christian. How about a non-married heterosexual relationship? How about taking pens and pencils from work? Do you cheat on your Federal Income taxes? Which one is worse? Are you saved?

Can a saved person live under these circumstances? The Bible makes it clear that when you choose for yourself what is sin, you are living for yourself and not God. The Israelites did as they felt was right in their own eyes. That was stated at the end of the Book of Judges and it was meant as a slam. Any so-called Christian that is living a life that is contrary to the Bible, one where you choose what you feel is sin and not one where you accept what God has told you what is sin, is not focused on God. Hence, I would have to question whether they are truly saved? Once you are saved there is no backsliding. If you are backsliding, you have never made the commitment.

It comes back to Grace or the Law. It's not either or, it is salvation is by Grace through Faith that is evident by their works. And if you have accepted the gift, you will follow the Law, as it is the schoolmaster that shows you what sin is. Avoiding sin will show others your love for God. If you knowingly choose to commit sin, then I have to ask you, are you really saved?

The absolute authority on this matter as to who is saved comes from God in a vision given to Ezekiel. Read Ezekiel Chapter 18. Your eternal life choice boils down to what type of lifestyle you choose during your time on earth. Ezekiel explains that you can choose to live wickedly or righteously. But, if you end your life in a wicked lifestyle, you will die. No matter how righteous you once were, if you conclude your life wickedly, you will die! Those who conclude in a righteous lifestyle will live, even if they had been very wicked before.

There is no New Testament teaching that contradicts this vision. How could there be? If God gives a vision and then changes His requirements later, He would not be the same today, tomorrow, and everlasting. You would never know what He would require for salvation later. So, the notion of once-saved-always-saved is a nice thought that brings peace to those that prefer a little sin in their lives, but it is not scriptural.

But you say, that was Old Testament. Don't you remember, I am still sticking to the fact that I am a New Testament Christian? It's funny how the MEC tries to glide over passages they don't like in the New Testament. Paul, in the Book of Romans says the same thing beginning in Romans Chapter 11, verse 16 with the story of the Holy Olive Tree. If you read from this point through verse 24, you will see that you, a "saved" Gentile, can be grafted into the tree. But in verse 22 you will learn that you can be cut out once you were grafted in, if you don't continue in

God's goodness. Does that sound like once-saved-always-saved? No, it is in complete disagreement.

OK, you say that is the gospel according to Paul, I need another witness. How about Jesus? Yes, Jesus Himself tells you the same thing beginning in Luke Chapter 13, verse 20. He is asked if there will be only a few saved. Jesus explains that many will seek to enter, but few will be saved. He talks of the things the "want-to-be-saved" state they have done for or with Him, but He states that He "knows them not." Who does He "know not?" "Those that are workers of iniquity." Are you a worker of iniquity? It is an old English word that was used to translate a Greek word that meant, "breaking the Law." Look up the word iniquity in your concordance. Do you follow God's Law? It can't save you, but it is a pointer of those that are saved!

Christ even went a little further by adding a parable about this very subject. If you can't get it from this parable, you never will. In that case, you are one of those that will "see and not perceive" (What Jesus stated about why some do not understand).

We all know the story of Jesus Christ before the multitudes explaining many parables. The parable of the sower is my favorite. It blows holes in the way modern Evangelical Churches like to use the term "once-saved-always-saved." I do believe in once-saved-always-saved, but not in the framework that the MEC will use it. They teach (and will be held accountable for it) that when you have an emotional acceptance to the Lord and say "you believe" out loud, then you are "saved." Now that you have the "saved" status you can plan on eternal life. That is bunk.

Once you are saved, you have already started eternal life. But a saved person has a life change. You put away earthly lusts and live a life that is of the Spirit. You no longer live a life that is sinful and of earthly lusts and values. All the verses quoted by the MEC are found in Paul's writings. I believe those writings, but I believe that you have to read the entire letter by Paul in one sitting. In each letter Paul explains that your life has changed <u>IF</u> you are saved.

Now for those that walk down the sawdust path they enter into one of four paths. That is what the parable of the sower teaches. Read the account in Mark Chapter 4. They all receive the message with <u>Joy</u>. It doesn't sound like someone walked down in front and crossed their fingers when they said those special words. No, all of them made the commitment when they said the words.

Don't believe my interpretation to this parable, listen to Jesus Christ's. Do you believe Jesus? If not, you have bigger problems than once-saved-always-saved. He tells you that the "the word was sown" into these four types of people.

At this point the MEC would have you believe that they are all saved. Since they made this choice and accepted this gift they can't loose it. But Jesus felt differently.

The first group had the word sown, but when they had heard, Satan immediately comes and takes the word that was sown in their hearts. So, they had it, and it was taken away quickly. Does it sound like they are still saved?

The second group immediately received the word with gladness, but have no root but endure for a short time. Without an understanding their belief is based on nothing. Being a believing Christian takes effort on your part. Study your Bible so that you can KEEP your salvation. Jesus goes on to teach that these individuals when they are faced with persecution for the Lord's sake fall away. Are they still saved? Jesus didn't think so!

The third group gets tired of the limits put on a real Christian's life. They begin to focus on the lusts and riches of the world and loose sight of the real goal in life, a meaningful relationship with God the Father and our Lord Jesus Christ. As a consequence, they are lost too!

Then there are the truly "once-saved-always-saved" group. These heard the word and became fruitful. These really are "once-saved-always-saved" but their lives changed. It isn't saying a few words and feeling a "feeling." It is a "new" lifestyle. It is a love. It is a giving of your life over to God the Father. It is reading your Bible daily and encouraging others. It is a giving of yourself, and happily changing when you find that the text convicts you of sin in your life.

Yes, once you are "really" saved, you are "always" saved, but for those that continue to sin, were they ever saved in the first place? All four categories thought they were at the time of their emotional experience, but Jesus taught that three of the four groups were not saved at all!

But, if you doggedly stick to the fact that if you have said a few words and believe that you are a Christian, that all things will be OK for you after death, why not look at the words of Jesus Himself again? Are you so fixated on the words of Paul that you will ignore what the Creator of the universe has told you? Read Luke Chapter 12. When you come to verse 47-48 it goes like this: "and that servant, which knew his lord's will, and prepared not, neither did according to his will, shall be beaten with many. But he that knew not, and did commit things worthy of stripes, shall be beaten with few."

Jesus has just validated Ezekiel's vision in the Old Testament. This one statement alone has wiped out any modern thought that all your sins will be wiped away by just saying a few words. I do believe that your sins will be forgiven you if you ask for forgiveness and repent. But, that means that you have to purposefully look for sin in your life and stop committing it. Once again, it is obedience! Something few will do.

One last quick thought that shows once-saved-always-saved is just not biblical. Read 1 Timothy Chapter 5. Paul is instructing on the caring for the church's elderly women. He states that some have already given themselves over to Satan. Do they sound like they are still saved?

You can't separate your life's walk from your saved status. Remember, salvation is a great prize, "To those that have been given much, much will be expected." I could go on and on, but if there isn't enough scripture here to show you that you really need to read your Bible and follow God's Law out of love and obedience, it really doesn't matter how much more I show you, you will never accept it.

For those that feel the scriptures I have shown are not important to your walk, there is a great parable by Jesus for you starting at Luke Chapter 16, verse 19. It concludes at the end of the chapter with the words, "If they hear not Moses and the Prophets, neither will they be persuaded, though one rose from the dead." Why does this apply to you? The Bible is very clear if you read it. But, if you stubbornly stay with your Church Club and play Christian, you will never change your ways.

Am I Pre-, Mid- or Post-Tribulation?

This chapter can easily be skipped if you are only concerned about the loving relationship you are trying to develop with your Lord. But, I had to write it because of all the hammering modern churches place on the rapture. To improve their position and to keep you in their flocks, they have invented a position that states, "before the great testing, or, if you will, before the tribulation comes, we will all be 'snatched' away to be with Jesus."

I guess if I had a choice of going through the great tribulation, I would skip it too. But you don't. It will be a great testing of your faith, and Jesus Christ actually talks about it. Let's test your position.

Well, do you believe you are Pre, Mid, or Post Tribulation. We are all the same if we are "saved." Your peace of mind depends on whether you have read your Bible. You can pick at a verse or two for a long time to feel good about going to heaven before the world collapses around you, but your position won't change when and where you will be going to meet the Lord.

First, I have to offend most of you that are Pre-trib. Get a grip. What does the Bible say? It's real simple. The Modern Evangelical Church (MEC) tries to give you a feel-good pill that goes something like this. We are all Pre-trib and we know it because John is called up to heaven in Revelation Chapter 4, verse 1, and they (MEC) say, "This is proof positive that "we" are called to heaven before the tribulation.

Look at the verse for yourself, and then ask, was John in vision? Of course he was. God had called John up to heaven to see what was to be in the future. You know, those things that God has ordained will happen to the earth when it is finished. It doesn't say come join "us saved" up here and watch what is about to happen to the rest of the inhabitants on earth. No, that's because Revelation Chapter 4, verse 1, has nothing to do with where Christians are at the time. Let's look at what John does tell us in Revelation.

All of end-times and eternal life is spelled out in the Book of Revelation. John tells you he is in vision. Do you know that your Bible states "in" the "Lord's Day," not "on" the Lord's Day. Go back to the Greek text. It actually states that John was in vision in the Lord's day in Revelation Chapter 1, verse 10. It doesn't say he was in vision on the Lord's day. This is just Sunday keeping Christians making themselves feel good for substituting a tradition of man for the 4th Commandment of God.

He is about to tell you what will happen on the Day of the Lord. Does that day sound familiar? It should if you are familiar with the Old Testament. That is the day the Old Testament tells you that the end times scenario will happen, and in Revelation it is about to happen.

So, what is the day of the Lord? It is when God will spill out His wrath on evil. Guess what, the Book of Revelation is all about God the Father punishing those who will not turn to Him and His beloved Son.

John goes to heaven when he is called "Come up hither"(Revelation 4:1). This is where the Pre-Trib position starts to break down. Look at who is in heaven in John's vision. In heaven there is the Father, Son, and Seven Spirits of God. There are also 4 creatures, 24 elders, and a whole lot of angels that like to sing really loud. The MEC would like you to believe that the 24 elders are the church, but that is a very poor argument. If it were true, then the Church is already there, as they were there before John arrived.

Do you mean to tell me you might believe that you will be part of one of those 24 elders? That isn't scriptural. We will be "Sons of God" (John 1:12; Romans 8:14; Galatians 4:5-6; Hebrews 12:7; 1 John 3:1) not "parts of an elder." That's the problem with taking a verse here and there and building doctrine from it. God the Father isn't looking for ornaments. He is looking for loving sons and daughters.

Later in the book there are two different sets of 12 used over and over. They are the 12 Children of Israel and the 12 apostles. I don't think you can make doctrine on it either, but these are the only two things that add up to 24 in the Book of Revelation. Besides, later in the book there are men from all nations and the elders are still there.

Next in the account by John in Revelation, we (through John's eyes) see the vials and bowls poured out. Somewhere in the process we see the souls of the slain under the altar of incense, but they are told to stay put, as it is not yet their time. Here is the great part. In Chapter 7, BAM (that's English for the French word "Voila"), John finds himself in the middle of thousands and thousands of people from all nations and tongues.

An elder tells John these are those that came out of the great tribulation. These are the **first** people that John sees. They are definitely mid-tribulation, as it isn't over yet. We don't know if they were slain or not from the passage, but we do know that they came out of the tribulation, hence they are mid-trib. I believe that they are the slain from the tribulation, but that cannot be proved from the scriptures here.

Am I Pre-, Mid- or Post-Tribulation?

I have to jump to one other book quickly. Turn to 1 Thessalonians Chapter 4. It is a chapter devoted by Paul to those that thought the resurrection had already occurred. He explains to them why they are wrong and what must happen before the great "snatching away" can occur. In 1 Thessalonians Chapter 4, verses 16-17, Paul tells you that **first** the dead in Christ will rise when He comes to the earth, and then those that are alive will be caught up to Him in the clouds. So, there will be a resurrection of the dead before all those remaining Christians are taken up to meet Jesus in the clouds.

Note to unschooled, unread Christians: Paul is telling you that Jesus will be back, but only after the dead in Jesus are resurrected! Remember this as it is needed to see when the saved will be "snatched away" in the Book of Revelation.

From what you have read in Revelation so far, the dead have not risen yet, and we are already 4 chapters past when the MEC try to say that their flocks will be with the Lord.

Now, back to Revelation Chapter 20, verses 4-5. Several more things have happened to the inhabitants of the earth. Jesus comes back to the earth and will reign for a thousand years. But, first the dead in Jesus are risen.

Paul and John have both written the same thing! And John states in Revelation Chapter 20, verses 4 and 5 that "This is the first resurrection." Don't believe me, just read your Bible. The first resurrection will occur when Jesus comes back and this is **after** the Great Tribulation.

Since most Christians like to trust Paul's slant on doctrine, why not take an uncut version for this topic. Even though it is very plain from the Book of Revelation, why not read 2 Thessalonians (about a five minute read). In Chapter 2, it gives the Thessalonians an exact recount of the things that will have to happen before Jesus comes back. It is obvious that they are concerned that there has been a "rapture" and they have been "left behind" (sounds like a great title for a fiction movie [also untrue]).

Paul is explaining that there will be "No" rapture, just a Second Coming. His explanation of the events reads just like Revelation with the son of perdition sitting on the throne and calling himself "God." Oh, but Paul doesn't leave anything to "dream" about, like "come up here." Coupled with the earlier passage in his first letter to the Thessalonians we know that this will also be the first resurrection of the dead.

So, for those of you that will blindly listen to what your non-biblical church is teaching you, believe what you want. But without getting too deep, Paul explains that first there will be a resurrection of the dead and then those living will meet Jesus in the air. He further explains that this is after the "son of perdition" "exalteth himself above all that is called God (2 Thessalonians 2)."

Can Paul be any more clear? Have we seen the son of perdition yet? No, that is because we haven't been in the Great Tribulation.

John explains that our meeting Jesus in the air is after the tribulation when Jesus comes to rule on the earth for a thousand years. Christians will not be going to heaven anyway, unless they go there during the time of the tribulation. There won't be a "snatching away" before the tribulation happens. If you die before the tribulation you will be "asleep" until he calls you after He comes back to the earth. Christians do not inhabit heaven anyway. That is God's habitation. We will live on the "New Earth."

Why is it so hard to understand? There is no scripture that will refute this order of events, because it is scriptural. It isn't hard to find the answers to any biblical question if you would read your Bible! This subject can easily be understood if you read 1 and 2 Thessalonians and then the Book of Revelation. Don't add anything you wish to read into the text. Just read what the author wrote!

But wait, there's more! Who are you wishing to meet in this rapture? Why not read what Jesus states on this issue. Read Matthew Chapter 24. Don't stop until you read at least past verse 31. Remember, Matthew was one of the two only first-hand witnesses in the Gospels.

In Matthew, Jesus has just criticized the scribes, Pharisees, and hypocrites. As He is leaving the temple His disciples come and ask Him to tell them of the future. Specifically, they want to know of the end times. Jesus then spells it out for all that want to learn the order of events. Don't you think that Jesus' own words should carry more wait that some "wishing" non-biblical account that has been thought up by some dreamer!

Read it for yourself. First many will come in His name (Matthew 24:5). Then there will be wars, famines, and pestilences (verses 6-8). Then Christians will be persecuted for Jesus' sake (verses 9-10). We will have false prophets teaching bad doctrine (verses 11-12).

In verses 13-14 Jesus tells you those: "That shall endure to the end shall be saved." He doesn't say, "those that have faith but fall away will be saved." No, it will be those that endure through the coming tribulation will be saved. And the gospel message will be taught to the whole world.

Here is where it gets really good if you want to believe your Bible over a Pre-Tribulation fairy tale. Jesus explains that there will be an abomination of desolation as spoken of by Daniel the prophet. Still in Matthew Chapter 24, verses 15-22 it explains what it will be like. The "saved" will be fleeing for their lives! That is why it is called the Great Tribulation.

But take note to verse 20. I have to re-emphasize it here. What is one of Jesus' concerns as to the day of fleeing? "Pray that your flight be not in the winter, neither on the Sabbath day." Why, if sabbath isn't important according to modern Christians, is it important to Jesus Christ, who is obviously telling you the future? It is because if you are a real Christian living for God the Father and His Son Jesus Christ, you will have become an obedient child of God.

Still, verses 23-28 tell of additional false prophets that will still arise, and a way to test if they are really Him. Most churches stop here, especially if they are pre-trib. Verses 29-30 explain the immediate time frame before and during the actual coming of Jesus. Is it over yet? No!

Has the tribulation taken place yet? Of course it has. Has He told you of the righteous being taken from the face of the earth yet? No. This is why I stated earlier in this chapter that I believe those that John meets in heaven are the slain of the tribulation. That verse in Revelation states that "These are they which came out of the great tribulation (Revelation 7:14)."

Read Jesus' account of what will happen next in Matthew Chapter 24 verse 31. "And He shall send His angels with a great sound of a trumpet, and they shall gather His elect from the four winds, from one end of heaven to the other."

For those that would like another witness to this account read Mark Chapter 13, verses 1-27. It is clearly the same account of the event. Jesus has told you that there will not be a pre-trib rapture.

When does Jesus clearly say that He will send His angels to gather us? If you have read Matthew Chapter 24 or Mark Chapter 13, you will have to say that it is after the tribulation. When does Paul tell you that we will be with Jesus? After Jesus comes back to the earth. When does John tell you specifically when the dead will rise and the rest of us will be taken up to meet our Savior in the clouds? After Jesus comes back, which John explains is after the Great Tribulation.

How simple can it be? Either you are living in a fantasy world and expect no trials in your life, or you are of the saved, and will be tested and tried your entire life. Just read your Bible.

Who is the Bride of Christ?

Although a very short chapter, this is one of those overused, non-researched Christian sayings that has No basis. I can't avoid talking about it. Who is the Bride of Christ? His Church, right? Wrong. Yes I know that this is what you have been taught. But, you will only believe that if you haven't read your Bible completely through a couple of times.

I was listening to Christian radio the other day and heard it again. I think it was someone from Calvary Chapel on the radio. It always goes something like this, "We see the church in Revelation until Chapter 4. And then it isn't mentioned again until we see it coming as the Bride of Christ."

I always want to talk back through the radio and ask; have you ever sat down and read Revelation in one sitting? First, the Bride of Christ is never stated anywhere in the New Testament, or Old Testament for that matter. Revelation teaches plainly, in easy to understand language that the bride of the Lamb is the city of New Jerusalem. It is clear when the angel guiding John around in the vision asks if he would like to see the bride, the Lamb's wife? The angel takes him to see "that great city, the Holy Jerusalem."

We are talking about a structure. It can't be the Church as we will be fellow heirs with Christ. Read Revelation Chapter 21 again, and focus from verse 9 on. The angel actually states in verse 9, "Come hither, I will show thee the bride, the Lamb's wife." Doesn't this sound plain? Could it be more clear? Does it leave anything up to your imagination? What is the angel about to show John?

If you read on, John talks about New Jerusalem. He covers the construction to include the gates, the size and the wall material, the foundations and more. It will be a fantastic building and city, but it is just that! There is nothing to infer here, it is not the Church!

Before we go any further, earn your Christian stripes. Look up bride or wife in the concordance. You will find no reference to the church or any of us being the bride of anyone. Yes, I know that you can show nuances that because we will be dressed in white robes and such, but there is no direct verbiage anywhere that the church will be "the bride." But there is a direct statement explaining the bride in Revelation Chapter 21.

Then, what will become of the church? Most New Testament authors will tell you, if you will just read it for yourself. What did Jesus say we would become? Read John Chapter 15, verse 15.

"Henceforth...I call you friends." What did Paul say you were? He states in many places that we will be "Sons of God," or "Fellow heirs with Jesus Christ!" A Son of God the Father can't be a "bride" to Jesus Christ, and Heirs were male unless there were no males to leave the inheritance to.

Paul never refers to anything other than a male to male relationship between God and "saved" man (or woman). Jesus explained that after the resurrection we would be as the angels and we would not be in marriage or given in marriage (Matthew 22). This leads you to understand that it will be a sex-neutral life.

Wake up Christian and read your Bible for yourself. Don't be lead around by a shepherd that isn't Jesus Christ. His word can be found if you read the whole Bible a few times and then pray for wisdom to understand what you have been reading.

The notion that Christians are the bride of Christ had to be started by a very emotional person with a longing for the love they felt a husband should have towards his wife, but it isn't even close to being scriptural. God gave us the family to learn of love, but the relationship of the married pair is not the one found in the Bible intended for Jesus and you.

Jesus explains who Christians are in relation to the "bride" and Himself, the Son of God. Go back and read Matthew Chapters 21 and 22. In these two chapters, Jesus explains how the Son of God will be treated. He explains in Chapter 21 starting at verse 33 how He will be rejected by the Jews, and the Gentiles will be meant for life eternal with Him. He has told several parables by this time and then follows with a parable about the marriage supper at the beginning of Chapter 22.

Jesus explains that the King (the Father) has arranged a marriage for His Son (Jesus). He sends for those (the Jews) that should come to the wedding, but they refuse to come for various reasons. Then in verse 9, He bids people to come that normally wouldn't be given such a chance. This is us! We are bidden to the marriage supper. What is our (the saved) position at this supper? Are we the new bride? No, we are to attend and celebrate in the supper.

In another parable about this relationship, He again testifies what the faithful servants will do when their Lord comes from His wedding. Aren't Christians supposed to be "good and faithful servants?" Read Luke Chapter 12. In verse 35 it states, "Let your loins be girded about, and your lights burning: And ye yourselves like unto men that wait for their Lord, when he will return from the wedding; that when he cometh and knocketh, they may open unto Him immediately. Blessed are those servants, whom the Lord when He cometh shall find watching: verily I say unto you, that He shall gird Himself, and make them to sit down to meat, and will come forth and serve them."

Did Jesus state that Christians are the bride in either of these parables? No. We are to attend the ceremony and celebrate with Him.

If you are a son of God, how can you be the bride of Christ? Once again, it is clear what the church will become. John Chapter 1, verse 12 reads "But as many as received Him, to them gave He power to become the sons of God, to them that believed on His name." In another of John's epistles he writes, "Behold what manner of Love the Father hath bestowed on us, that we should be called the sons of God." 1 John Chapter 3 is packed with this very issue!

Paul agrees in Romans Chapter 8, verse 14 "For as many as are led by the Spirit of God, they are the sons of God." Finally the author of the Book of Hebrews writes in Chapter 12, verse 7 "If ye endure chastening, God dealeth with you as with sons; for what son is he whom the Father chasteneth not?"

Don't just go back and read those verses, read the ones leading up to them and those following them. You will see that it was a point that the authors were developing. It is a position we will be filling, the sons of God.

These authors have other passages that carry the same message. Look up the word "son or sons" in the concordance and you will be there for hours. You can see that the authors that wrote most of the New Testament all felt that we would become sons of God in our resurrected bodies. Jesus tells you that we will become "friends." There is no passage that states the church will be the "Bride of Christ." Why do we have to constantly try to support bad doctrine instead of taking the simple explanations that are found plainly printed in the Bible?

Isn't this more of the relationship you would like to have with your Lord? Not only is it a more appropriate relationship, it is a scriptural one! Jesus doesn't teach any other way. Christian, read your Bible before you start trying to explain the relationship you want to have with Him! Make it one that He approves of.

Are the Dietary Laws of the Old Testament Current Today?

This is as close to a gray area as there is for a Christian that I know. Are Christians under the health/dietary laws from the Old Testament? After reading my Bible through many times, I still have to say I am positive that they are, but it still isn't totally conclusive. I will show that there is a weak argument that you can eat flesh that God stated is an abomination at the end of the chapter. Pay close attention to the main body and then you will have to ask yourself, should I do without those meats that God had previously identified as abominable in my diet?

We read that God-ordained dietary laws have been around since the beginning of mankind. Remember the Garden of Eden? There was only one thing that would be attributed to man as sin, and it was ironically a food law. Adam and Eve were forbidden to eat of the Tree of the Knowledge of Good and Evil. Man broke that food law and he was cast out of the garden forever.

Many would have you believe that eating flesh started with Noah, but this is probably incorrect. The first two sons of Adam and Eve were Cain and Able. Cain was a tiller of the ground while Able was a shepherd of sheep? Was Able a shepherd just because he enjoyed playing with sheep? I'm sure it was a food group for Able and Cain was a farmer. You have to say that Able was the first rancher.

The food/dietary laws are located in Leviticus Chapter 11 and in other places in the Old Testament. It is a very thorough list of laws that really leaves nothing in a gray area, at least for those that they were written. These foods are said to be an abomination by God. If they still apply, the main things it would limit for today's Christian is pig in any fashion and a lot of seafood. Any seafood that doesn't have fins and scales is unclean. This would include shrimp, lobster, scallops, shark, mahi mahi and catfish. There are other things that are a regional thing, like alligator or rattlesnake, but they really don't have much of an impact on normal life.

Why should it matter if I keep the health/dietary/food laws of the Old Testament? First, it is part of the Law. It is in a list of Laws given by God. A lot of people have stated that it was necessary for them back then, as there was so many diseases in those animals, so we don't have to worry about it today. That is true, but if you read Leviticus Chapter 11 you will read that they are "an abomination to you." How can it be an abomination to the chosen people of God and not an abomination for the New Testament Christian who has been grafted into the Holy Olive Tree?

Understand that unclean food was broken into two categories at the time when Jesus Christ and Paul were walking in Judah. Those that were unclean because they were unclean flesh to start with, as in Leviticus, and those that were considered unclean either due to cooking and or preparation laws that had been added by the Jewish leadership.

Do you know that the Jews at the time of Christ had made laws to the laws to ensure they kept them Holy? They were not allowed to eat until they had washed their hands in a certain way. They could not drink out of a cup or use a plate until it had been washed in a certain fashion. They were absolutely forbidden to eat with Gentiles. If you did any of these, the food was considered unclean. Jesus and many of the apostles spoke out against the adding-too of this Law and others, trying to correct this ridiculous tradition.

Paul is quoted for most of the freedom from the Law and the food laws in particular. Ask yourself, would he be a hypocrite if he did not partake in the freedom he is giving to Christians under Grace? Let's put it another way. Do you think Paul would eat a pork chop if a Gentile had offered it to him? There is a very simple answer as to whether Paul broke the Law, to include the health laws. The food laws were as much of the Law to a Jew of the day as was adultery.

Go back to the story of Paul in bondage before Festus (Acts 25). In his defense he stated that "Neither against the Law of the Jews, neither against the temple, nor yet against Caesar, have I offended anything at all." In this one statement you learn that Paul kept all of the Law. He doesn't state that he kept Jewish traditions that were added to the Law, but to the Law of God. By this time in Paul's ministry he has written most of what we have today. His book to the Romans has definitely been written as he will be in Rome soon and this book was written before he has ever been there.

Either he kept it all, or he was a liar! Many things that Paul stated can be taken out of context, but when he was being charged with offenses by the Jews, they could not produce one instance of a broken law, and he in his own defense stated that he had never broken the Jewish law! How can you read Paul's letters and make the case that Paul was telling Christians that they could eat unclean flesh? It's obvious that he didn't!

So, what grounds do you stand on that allow you to eat that pepperoni pizza? If it is a statement by Paul, the above proves that the verse(s) you are using is/are probably being taken out of context. Paul did justify eating unclean foods, but it had to be those that were not clean to the Jew for other than the Levitical Law of Leviticus Chapter 11. Read each of the times unclean food is mentioned and ask yourself two questions? Could he be referencing how, or who they were eating with? Could Paul boast of the above statement from Acts Chapter 25 if it was an unclean flesh he is about to eat? Do you think that Paul would lie to save his hide with Festus and Agrippa?

With the understanding that Paul didn't give himself the freedom to eat whatever he wanted, let's look at the texts used by Christians to justify eating anything unclean.

Acts Chapter 10. Peter is at Simon the Tanner's house. He receives a vision of a blanket lowering down all kinds of unclean beasts and the statement is told him "rise Peter: Kill and eat." Do you read your Bible? Then keep reading. In verse 28 he explains the meaning of the vision. "God hath showed me that I should not call any man common or unclean." You can see how the eating with a Gentile was unclean when in Acts Chapter 11, verse 3, the brethren confront Peter and state: "Thou wentest in to men uncircumcised, and didst eat with them."

Peter then has to explain the vision once again to show them that God is not a respecter of persons. He doesn't explain to the brethren that God has told them they can eat Levitically unclean food. No, he just explains that he has this vision and from it, he has learned that God is not a respecter of persons. No big revelation here if you read the complete story.

Galatians Chapter 2. Paul is explaining how he rebuked Peter when he withdrew from eating with the Gentiles when certain men came from Jerusalem. I've heard a pastor state that Peter was eating a pork chop, but stopped. Is this what it says? You can't make that argument. Paul rebukes Peter from withdrawing from the Gentile brethren during mealtime. Nothing more, nothing less. Remember, it was considered sinful to eat with a Gentile under Jewish tradition.

This whole argument over the food laws would have been easy to answer if the Bible just stated that …Paul and Barnabas were at a pig roast lapping it up…or Peter was eating some muscles at Joppa…but it doesn't. There are very clear guidelines stating that these foods are an abomination. And, we know that Paul never ate anything unclean from his statement to Agrippa.

Who do you rest your salvation in? Jesus Christ? He even states that it isn't what goes into a man's mouth that defiles a man, it is what comes out. It sounds very clear that He felt you could eat all things, or does it? Jesus, like Paul is misquoted by only giving you part of what He has stated. You have to take all the gospels and line up each story. None of them are complete, so lets look at the most complete gospel account that has this quote. Remember, Matthew is a first-hand witness to this message.

Read Matthew Chapter 15, verses 1-20. This is the story I have quoted so many times earlier to show how Jesus deplored the substituting of a tradition of man over a commandment of God. But this story also carries another message that is usually taken out of context by church leaders who enjoy their pork. They usually take you midway through verse 20 and then end as follows:

Matthew Chapter 15, verses 17-20 "Do ye not understand, that whatsoever entereth in at the mouth goeth into the belly, and is cast out into the draught? But those things that proceed out of the mouth come forth from the heart, and they defile a man. For out of the heart proceed evil thoughts, murders, adulteries, fornications, thefts, false witness, blasphemies: These are which defile a man..."

If you read from verse 1 through this part in verse 20 it would be clear that Jesus felt that any "food" could not defile a man. It is just our hearts that matter. And, although partly true, we are still under the obedience to God. Matthew makes it perfectly clear that Jesus was not talking about what was eaten, but how it was eaten at the end of verse 20.

The second half of verse 20 goes like this: "... But to eat with unwashed hands defileth not a man." So, how can you conclude that Jesus would have allowed eating unclean flesh? You can't, but He was against improved rules added by modern religious leadership. This statement by Jesus is almost identical to the one quoted by Paul, that pork loving church leaders like to use to say that they "can eat all things."

Do you believe in end-times-prophesies? Most come from the Old Testament, and some are very specific of the things and times to come. If you don't believe they are true, what makes you believe that there is everlasting life? Your faith needs to be built on facts. Read Isaiah Chapters 65-66. Shouldn't the condemnation for those in the last days, which eat boiled swine be taken at face value?

Many times to non-scripturally based Christians this is passed off as a Jewish thing. Remember that Paul stated that you (Gentile) are a wild olive branch grafted into the Holy Olive Tree. Are the end times about the Jew only? Don't you want to be with the saved at the end times?

You should believe that God is, was, and always will be. Does He change His mind? If He does, will He change the requirements for your entry into eternal life? The answer to all of these questions is No! Did they believe in Old Testament times that they must uphold the food laws? Of course they did. And there are too many examples to list. Once the Food laws are given in the Old Testament, there are no "examples" of eating unclean foods in the entire Bible except when showing disdain. (i.e. Samson eating the honey from the lion's carcass).

Here is the challenge. Find one reference anywhere in the Bible where a "saved" person is eating any unclean flesh, or were he is even caring (shepparding) for them. You can't. It just isn't there.

Yes I know, you like the taste. But so do many so-called Christians like committing adultery and it just can't be tolerated.

When you see the righteous in the Bible we see them with flocks of sheep, and cattle and even goats. But where are the pigs? If they are OK to eat, don't you think someone that we "know" was righteous would have kept them? After all, pigs are easy to care for, and they are a great converter of vegetation into protein. That is why they are raised today. Yes, the lack of this fact yells at you. We do see swine in the Bible, but only raised and eaten by the unsaved.

I believe that I am fair and balanced, so here are the gray areas. There are three areas in the Bible that show the possibility for eating unclean flesh. We all know the story of Noah and the Ark. God made a distinction between clean and unclean animals (Genesis 7). Of the clean, Moses was to take to thee by sevens, male and female, but of the unclean by twos, male and female.

The real distinction between clean and unclean animals comes after the ark had landed (Genesis 8). The clean animals and fowls were the only ones that could be sacrificed to God. But we learn that for Noah (Genesis 9) "Every moving thing that liveth shall be food for you; even as the green herb have I given you all things." Blood was forbidden in the same chapter. Why blood, because it is the "life" of the animal according to God.

So, Noah and his generations were allowed to eat everything that was on the earth, except blood. In the New Testament the eating of blood is also forbidden for Christians (Acts 15). There really wasn't anything else for Noah to eat, as the Lord had wiped out the face of the earth.

Colossians Chapter 2 has an excellent argument for the eating of whatever you want in verse 16: "Let no man therefore judge you in meat, or in drink, or in respect of an holy day, or of the new moon, or of the Sabbath...." It sounds, sound! That is why I don't believe in quoting a verse and then closing the Bible and making doctrine on it. Read the rest of the chapter.

In Colossians Chapter 2, verse 22, Paul wants you to be sure to understand that he is not talking about commandments of God as in the Sabbath or dietary laws. He is referring to extra commandments made by man to these laws. It reads "Which are all to perish with the using after the commandments and doctrines of men." If your Bible has used a question mark, ask yourself why? There was no punctuation in the original manuscripts. So although verse 16 sounds good, it has to be tamed by verse 22.

I Timothy Chapter 4 is the best chapter that fuels the fire to say you can eat what you want, "in the later times that some should depart from the faith, giving heed to seducing spirits and doctrines of devils; speaking lies and hypocrisy; having their conscience seared with a hot iron;

Forbidding to marry, to abstain from meats, which God hath created to be received with thanksgiving of them which believe and know the truth. For every creature of God is good, and nothing is to be refused, if it is received with thanksgiving: For it is sanctified by the word of God and prayer."

The case can be made that Paul is stating that every living "creature" can be eaten as in the time of Noah. But is that the case? The word translated for creature is the Greek word "ktisma". It is only used twice in the Bible, here and Revelation Chapter 5, verse13, where it is also translated into "creature." In Revelation it is used as follows: "Every creature that is in <u>heaven</u>, and on the earth, and under the earth, and such as are in the sea, and all that are in them, heard them I saying, Blessing, and honor, and glory, and power to Him that sits upon the throne, and unto the Lamb forever and ever.

With this second, and only other use of the word ktisma, it shows that this could then be referring to every living thing created by God. How about an angel? Doesn't this fit into the Revelation scenario of the Greek word "ktisma? Can you eat an angel? I'm sure that the original translation to this word is wrong.

We also know that Paul was giving direction to Timothy and answering a list of questions from the Ephesians. Are you sure you understand what they had asked him? What if the question was asked: "We have been told by the Pharisees that we will loose our salvation if we don't wash our cooking pots in a certain way before we cook our dinner? Or, "We have been told we cannot eat with our Gentile Christian friends." Is this a sin as the Jews have stated?"

Two things you do know from the passage, forbidding to marry and abstaining from some type of eating is not a scriptural requirement for salvation. This is the only scripture that you could hang your hat on to say that you can eat all things (i.e., unclean flesh), but only if it is <u>sanctified by the word of God and Prayer</u>.

One part about this is absolute. If you do take this one "translated" verse, it tells you that the food must be sanctified with prayer! When you go out in public for a big pork meal, do you ask a blessing at the table? Or, is the peer pressure too great and you just dive right in. Now, if you dove in without saying a blessing first, was that unclean-flesh covered by this scripture?

We also know that <u>this</u> scripture can't actually state that we can eat <u>ALL</u> things. Blood was, has, and always will be forbidden, even in the New Testament. It is the life of the animal (Genesis). The part about nothing is to be refused couldn't refer to Blood! (Acts 15:20; Acts 21:25) So even with prayer, eating blood is an abomination. So, it is a fact that Paul was not saying you could eat all things, because you can't.

With just this one fact that the verse can't mean ALL things, can you be certain that Paul wasn't just referring to how it was prepared, or who they were eating with, or how they had cleansed themselves before they were about to eat? You really can't be certain because it is either all or nothing. Either the translation stands and all things are clean to you, or it doesn't. And we know that we cannot eat blood!

Also, you have to remember who he was writing to. Paul wrote two letters to Timothy that we have today. Don't you think that Paul's writings would line up? How can you rest your hat on what he states in one letter if it is a direct contradiction to what he writes in another? What this tells you is that one of them is taken out of context. As you now know, Paul couldn't have meant all things, as he wouldn't have said you can eat blood.

In 2 Timothy, Paul is imprisoned and probably dying. Timothy is his closest associate and he even refers to him as his "son." He is telling Timothy how to live and lead the flock. Read the whole book. It will take about ten minutes, but in 2 Timothy Chapter 3, verses 15-17, it is very apparent that Paul is telling Timothy to live by the Old Testament scriptures. I won't take the time to help you understand that this is only the Old Testament here. Look back in *Is Paul Taken out of Context*.

How can Timothy live by the Old Testament and still break some of the Laws. He doesn't say, "Live by the Scripture that you like," or "Live by the Scriptures except the dietary laws and the Sabbath." No he states, "All scripture is given by inspiration of God, and is profitable for doctrine, for reproof, for correction, for instruction in righteousness: That a man of God may be perfect, thoroughly furnished unto all good works."

But are you sure when you read about the consuming of meats and other similar phrases that they were talking about eating these foods. Take the line found in Hebrews Chapter 13, verse 9, "Be not carried about with divers and strange doctrines. For it is a good thing that the heart be established with grace, not with meats, which have not profited them that have been occupied therein."

It sounds like some have started worrying about food over Grace, and this is true. But it has nothing to do with eating of food, it is the sacrificing of animals as a payment for sin over the accepting of Jesus' blood as our payment. How do I know? Keep reading the chapter.

"We have an alter, whereof they have no right to eat which serve the tabernacle. For the bodies of the beasts, whose blood is brought into the sanctuary by the High Priest for sin, are burned without the camp." So if you stopped reading in the chapter before you completed it, you may easily be led astray into believing that Grace could allow for you to eat unclean meats, which it is clearly not talking about.

Breaking the Law of God is sin. There is no clear reference in the New Testament that the unclean flesh foods in the Law were ever made clean! Definitely no reference to one being consumed by a member of the early church. In Isaiah, Ezekiel, and many other Old Testament prophesies you will find condemnation of those that eat swine (pig) during the end times.

I would rather abstain from these foods because I see a clear message that they were an abomination, at least at first. If I am wrong and God really doesn't care, what did I give up? Do you remember the Garden of Eden? What did the serpent state, "Go on, take a bite" (loosely translated)! Let's say it is sin, is a little sin in your life OK? How did Lot, Abraham's nephew start down his wayward path? He turned his tent toward Sodom. It happens a little at a time.

Are you totally satisfied with absolutely no doubt that it is OK? How can you be? There is no real scripture to back you up. If you have doubt and you eat it, the same guy (Paul) that you claim tells you its OK, states that if you have doubt, it is sin (Romans 14:23).

One side note is the notion of vegetarianism. There are some religions that believe that the food laws are expanded to include all flesh and/or their by-products. This is not only unscriptural, it is a sure case of a false religion. Any religion that has a prophet that explains that vegetarianism or veganism is a requirement for salvation goes directly against 1 Timothy Chapter 4. Jesus Christ, after his resurrection never met with his disciples without eating fish. Go figure, some religions try to make a distinction between a live living fish, live living cattle and a live living chicken. It was all classified as flesh in the Bible.

Who is Lucifer?

As I wrote in my first chapter, the name Lucifer is a great example of Christians listening to others and repeating it. The name Lucifer has nothing to do with Satan, and is mentioned only once in the Bible. Yet we here the names Lucifer and Satan used interchangeably in Christian theology and music.

Who is Lucifer? The name is found in Isaiah Chapter 14, verse 12, and it is referencing the King of Babylon. Yes, he really did think he was supernatural, at least Isaiah spoke of him in those terms. Just read Daniel (about an hour read). With that stated, why do Christians call Satan, Lucifer, when he already has the "God" given name of Satan. Let's look a little closer.

Read Isaiah Chapter 14. It is the story of Judah and Israel having triumph over Babylon. Judah and Israel will be free, becoming captors instead of captives. Then, in verse 4 you see a proverb or lament against the King of Babylon. Basically it goes something like this: You were great and I (God) have crushed thee and thy city!

There is an analogy used here with different trees. Hell is waiting for him (the King of Babylon). Other kings are there and are mocking him, now that he has no power. Then, in verse 12, it states: "How art thou fallen from heaven, O Lucifer, son of the morning! Art thou cut down to the ground, which didst weaken the nations!" Let's stop right there and look at the position of the "man" called Lucifer. Is it really being stated that he was a supernatural guy? No!

The last part of the phrase helps you to understand that we are talking about a human being "Art thou cut down to the ground, which didst weaken the nations." Just because it states that he is fallen from heaven doesn't mean that he is supernatural. It could be referencing that he has fallen from God's grace.

Did you read the Book of Daniel like I asked at the beginning of this chapter? In Daniel Chapter 8 there is a King in Greece after Alexander the Great that has waxed great to the host of heaven and cast down some stars to the ground and stomped them. Does this sound like a man? It is an analogy! It is the author's way to say that he is/was great.

Nebuchadnezzar was a tool of God. God tells the world that he is a tool for righteousness. God gives him victory after victory to wipe out those nations that are evil and sinful, and yet we see this God given power go to his head. He begins to see himself above mortal man. God warns him of this self importance in Daniel Chapter 4. This is the only chapter in the Bible written by a

Gentile king. Read it and you will find that God sends Nebuchadnezzar a dream. In verse 8, Daniel interprets the dream.

It starts with Nebuchadnezzar being portrayed as a great tree that grew unto heaven (sounds familiar), where all the earth is given rest. Then the tree is hewed down and bound, and the heart of it was changed from a man to a beast. Daniel explains the interpretation that the king has exhaulted himself too high and that he needs to understand that God gives and takes away power.

In verse 30, we see that the king is walking in his palace and states "Is not this great Babylon, that I have built for the house of the kingdom by the might of my power, and for the honor of my majesty." And then, Poof! God delivers His sentence on him and he eats grass like a cow for seven seasons. You will have to read the rest of the chapter for yourself.

Before we go any further with Isaiah Chapter 14, have you read anything like this anywhere else in the Bible? If you are well versed in your Bible you would have to say yes! Let's look at how God sees a few other kings and princes in the Book of Ezekiel.

Read Ezekiel Chapter 28. It actually starts in Chapter 27, but what you find in verses 1-10 is a lament against the Prince of Tyrus, and another lament against the King of Tyrus in verses 11-19. The lament against the prince starts with "because thine heart is lifted up, and thou hast said, I am a God, I sit in the seat of God, in the midst of the seas; yet thou art a man and not God, though thou set thine heart as a heart of God: Behold thou art wiser than Daniel."

Verses 8 and 9 show how he will be delivered to death and a question is asked, " Wilt thou yet say to him that slayeth thee, I am God? But thou shalt be a man, and no God..." It is clear that this guy who thinks he is a God is only a man.

Then it changes to the lament to the king of Tyrus. It could be the same guy, but it isn't clear as one is a prince and the other is a king. We see the mention of him being in "Eden the garden of God" and a covering of precious stones. He is even called the anointed cherub in verse 14, and thrown from the holy mountain. But, what does verse 19 state? "All they that know thee among the people shall be astonished at thee: thou shalt be a terror, and never thou be anymore.

This guy is to be destroyed and those people that knew him will see his destruction. I have news for you, Satan is immortal. It states in Revelation that he will burn forever. There is no end to his suffering. So can this king or prince be Satan? No, because they will die.

Jump to Ezekiel Chapter 31. It is a lament over the Pharaoh of Egypt. You will see that God made him great and the "great tree" analogy is used again. All beasts and birds find him (the great cedar) for rest. In verse 9 you read "I have made him fair by the multitude of his branches: so that all the trees of Eden, that were in the garden of God, envied him." Was Pharoah ever in Eden? No, that is how you know it is an analogy!

I could go on and on with Chapter 31 showing the similarities, but who is Ezekiel talking about? Pharoah, the King of Egypt. Once again God has delivered through Ezekiel an analogy explaining that God has given power to build a nation unlike any other to a king, and now He will destroy it, and it's leader.

Are we talking about Satan in any of Ezekiel's laments? No, but first you have to read the entire book of Ezekiel to see his writing style. He laments over and over to nations, and sure enough they are all destroyed. Is is too hard to believe that Isaiah would lament in the same way? After all, they are writing to the same audience at the same time in history.

So, let's go back to Isaiah Chapter 14 and see what is stated about the King of Babylon to see if he falls in line with these laments. In verse 13 it states that he will try to ascend to heaven. Satan was already in heaven, why would he try to ascend there? Then in verse 16, when he is on his way to hell it states, "Is this the man that made the earth to tremble. That did shake kingdoms..."

Did that last verse state he was a man? Of course it did, we are talking about a king on earth, not a supernatural power. The topping on this cake comes in verse 21, where you have a curse on his children. Now, does Satan have children?

I really don't know who Lucifer could be other than a King of Babylon. We know this if we take the Bible for face value. Isaiah Chapter 14 is a lament against a man and a nation state, nothing more, nothing less. Besides, why would God disguise a lament for Satan in a message that was to be delivered to some king on earth?

So, will you feel the same when you are in church and start singing a song that references Lucifer? I hope not. If you still want to call Satan Lucifer, then I guess you have to call him Pharoah, King of Tyrus, and the Prince of Tyrus and a ruler in Greece. After all, these laments have stronger ties to heaven than the one found in Isaiah.

What Should I Give as Tithes or Offerings, and to Whom?

This is why all churches through the ages have existed, to take your money! I have a hard time listening to Christian talk radio, and refuse to watch it on the television. First, it is incorrect doctrine, and second, they are always begging for money.

Tithing is found throughout the Bible. It, in its purest form is a homage, or thankful giving to God for what He has done for you. Look at when Abraham gave tithes to Malchizedek (Genesis 14). Or, when Jacob promised the Lord that if He would bring him back to Canaan safe, he would give Him 10% (Genesis 28). These were before the Children of Israel received doctrine from Moses and yet it was understood.

A better understanding of the loving heart that God wants you to have is the story of the widow's mite (Mark 12, Luke 21). Here we see it has nothing to do with any percentage at all. In fact, the guy in the story that gave the greatest out of his abundance, will receive nothing for it from God, as he had missed the heart issue God wants you to have.

Jesus warns you that tithing or any giving is low on God's concerns for your life. These are heart issues that you will do out of love for God and your fellow man. Read Matthew Chapter 23, an focus on verse 23. Jesus is explaining that if you give your tithes but neglect the more important weightier matters, such as the teachings of the Law, using just judgment, having mercy for others and faith, you are lost!

There are two different opposing doctrines on tithing. Some believe that we are under the literal tithe of the Old Testament. Many Churches teach that way, but they don't follow the Levitical Law if they are tithing your income from work. Others believe that we have a greater obligation from nuances found in the New Testament.

The Old Testament was under the tithe. It was a giving back of $1/10^{th}$ of what the land gave to you. You gave the tithe to the Levites (usually). If you never sinned you still gave $1/10^{th}$ of your increase from the land back to God. Why the Levite? They were the 1 tribe of Israel that was not given any land in Israel. They had all the functions of government on their shoulders, not just religious duties as churches today.

Please think about what God expected your tithe to cover. The Levites were responsible for the church, State and Federal Government, schools, and welfare for the widow, and the fatherless.

They had it all. Why do churches today expect you to pay them 10% as in the Old Testament? It isn't scriptural. Church was only part of what was covered.

It was a faith issue. God would provide for you, and you provided for the Levite. Sometimes the tithe was taken to the temple for a celebration and distribution, but once every three years <u>you</u> would give your annual tithe to the Levite, widow, orphan and stranger living within your gates directly (Deuteronomy 26:12). It is clear from this chapter that God didn't intend on you taking $1/10^{th}$ of your income and giving it to a church for their use, i.e. paying wages. You could look at it like God's welfare system. You didn't have federal and state tax, just a tithe.

Sacrifices were in addition to your tithing. They were either as a payment for sin, or voluntary. These could be avoided by not sinning or giving a vow you really didn't want to perform.

I have heard it stated many times in the modern evangelical church that if you add up all the tithes of the Old Testament it would be somewhere closer to 30% of your income. Why would they state this if it isn't true? They know that their sheep (you) do not read their Bibles, and if they state 30% you will be glad to give them 10%.

Unfortunately, they are wrong. If you read Genesis through Deuteronomy you will see that the tithe is mentioned many times but is limited to only a total of 10%. Please don't take my word on this, read it thoroughly for yourself. Giving of tithe was also a celebration. The giver takes part in eating at the celebration of giving the tithe (Deuteronomy 12:18). But once again, it was the <u>increase</u> from the land. How many of you farm, ranch and hunt for your livelihood? I have done some logging, so I would expect that this is a titheable income.

But remember, almost everywhere that the bible talks about tithe it is referred to as the "increase from the land." This was never your income from work. There were laborers and merchants back then. Where is it written, tithes from other than "increase from the land" income? There wasn't one! How do I know? Read Numbers Chapter 31. It is the story of how God delivered Israel's enemy, the Midianites, into their hand at battle. Wouldn't you think that if God did the work, He would be entitled to a larger share for His Levites? After all, it was an increase!

If you read Numbers Chapter 31, you will see that 12,000 Israelite men go to war against the nation of Midian. After they have utterly wiped out the nation, God instructs Moses to divide the spoils of women, beeves (cattle), asses and sheep into two halves. Half goes to the men that went to war and half is divided amongst the rest of the Nation of Israel.

Of the half that went to war, God levied 1/500 of their booty for the Levites. That is only $1/50^{th}$ of the rate of tithe! But the half that was to be delivered to the rest of the Children of Israel was given a different levy. As they did nothing for their half, wouldn't you think that they would give even a greater than "tithable," or to be more precise, greater than a $1/10^{th}$ share?

Adversely, God required less. It was Israel's duty to pay tribute from the spoils of war at a $1/50^{th}$ rate, even though those receiving it contributed nothing to the battle to obtain it! This is $1/5^{th}$ the rate of the increase from the land (tithe). So, there was a rate that you gave that came directly from the land and there was a different rate you gave that came from other incomes, like war gains. Once again, read your Bible from front to back and you will see that you are being duped by the MEC.

But read the chapter closely, this rate was only levied on the slaves and livestock that were taken. If you read carefully, you will see that the precious metals and jewels were not split or required a levy. But the men of war gave an "oblation" to the Lord in verse 50. It was totally voluntary.

What about the New Testament? Tithing really isn't mentioned other than as a teaching aid. It is used to show how they were doing a function rather than a loving gift back to their Creator. Take out your concordance and look up tithe, tithes, and tithing. Now, let's look at what was actually required. The new church at Jerusalem reminded Paul that among the Gentiles he was to remember the poor (Galatians 2). What was meant by this? The new church in Jerusalem had given all that they had to each other. They were persecuted and had nothing.

I believe it was a call for Paul to bring back a contribution to the Church from those where they were not persecuted. This example can be seen in many of Paul's letters such as in Romans Chapter 15, verse 26. It was called an "offering." I believe that a true Christian should understand that all things are given to them by God as a gift.

If you believe that, then you must believe that you are to lovingly give it away to His causes, as you are enlightened. I am not saying that He wants you to give everything away, just understand that your wealth is from Him and you should not be attached to it. God expects you to take care of your families. But He also expects you to understand that He is the provider through your hard work.

Once I learned of His love, I have always set aside at least 10% to His work. It is an acknowledgment that you believe that it is from Him. I don't believe that 10% is a requirement, but if you are selfishly holding on, even to 90%, then you have missed the boat. It is a heart issue.

Where do you give your offering? The money sent back to Jerusalem, by Paul, to the Church did not adorn a beautiful building, nor pay a handsome wage to Peter, James and John. It was for distribution to their needy. As in the Old Testament, these funds were used within the body of believers.

Paul talks about being a tent maker and not burdening others for his care, although he stated that it was his right. He did receive funding when he was imprisoned. It would have been pretty hard to make tents and sell them in prison. It is stated several times in his letters that he did receive money. But, more often than not, he mentions receiving contributions from the churches and taking them back to Jerusalem.

In 2 Thessalonians Chapter 3, Paul rebukes those that are not paying their own way, and who expect the brethren to support them. He reflects that while he was with them he didn't burden them in that way, so why are they contributing to this ridiculous giving. If you read it several times you will have to conclude that it was so-called "ministers" that he was talking about. Read it for yourself and then you decide. I am sure that Paul expected our Church Leadership to care for their own welfare, as he did.

Paul was not a farmer. He was a tent maker, we think. He made something that was sellable. Do you read of Paul sending back 10% of what he made by selling this commodity. No, but you do see him taking care of those working with him in the ministry by his trade. He is ministering to others and sharing the Word of God. The little that he makes is subsidized by various churches, but you don't see him sending back an offering to Jerusalem. He does take one back, but that is from other new believers.

What is not mentioned in either the Old Testament or New Testament is the notion that we should "buy" new members. You know, support the local community! Food/clothing drives for the poor. Trying to outreach our communities through giving them gifts. Look, that never happened in the Bible anywhere. You will be held accountable for the resources that are given to you. You can't buy a Gentile (or any lost soul) into Christianity.

Here in Spokane Washington they have a rice for Cambodia drive each year. They import tons of rice for villages. It sounds nice, but where do you see anything like this happening in the Bible anywhere? The analogy would be like this: Paul brings back money from a far, to Jerusalem. They in turn send some to Syria and say it is from the struggling Church in Jerusalem. Do you think that they would have saved souls?

No, that isn't how it works. You send Spirit-filled men to a lost nation to preach of Jesus Christ and the love that God has for them, if they turn to Him. In turn, they send back offerings of their meager abundance back to keep the mission trips moving forward. Yes, we have reversed the God ordained way that it works.

The other totally ridiculous way we waste God's money is on really non-productive missionary journeys. I was attending a church where they sent a half dozen members of the "favored leadership" from Idaho to Thailand to visit an orphanage to do some painting. Give me a break. Those expenses could have been used to paint the entire facility and probably half the village if they had utilized local painters. It was a ridiculous waste of money! But they did get a vacation at the congregation's expense.

What do I recommend you do with your gift to God? First you must understand that all you have is from Him and you are just showing how you acknowledge it. Then, whatever you believe is correct, send it to a worthy Christian cause. I would focus on Christian orphanages, Christian based abortion counseling, elderly Christians that are in real need, and true Christian missionary needs. This was the intention of tithing. Taking care of other "believers." Read all the references using a concordance. It won't take more than an evening to learn. By the way, the Levites weren't penniless. They were given cities and land for their livestock, just not a large "state" of their own. They lived amongst Israel.

I have given for years to a missionary group in Africa. For about $35 a month you can sponsor your own missionary. It is all the funding they need to survive. I have never visited with them, but may in the future. I am sure that they are not giving the message as I would, and I am sure that they may not have even read their Bible through. But, if they get the word out about Jesus, and have a Bible, maybe, just maybe, the Holy Spirit will work through them to save themselves and others.

Note: All the above recommendations are Christian focused. If you really want to be Bible focused, God states that He will bless those that bless you and curse those that curse you. Who was He speaking of? The Children of Israel. I can't think of a better cause than a Christian based cause in the heart of Israel.

What are the Present Day Gifts of the Holy Spirit?

I'm sure I will step on some toes here, but I don't see gifts given today. Yes, I know some churches say they believe you must have the gift of tongues and then everyone starts babbling in church. I don't know what the babbling is, but Paul stated that the Holy Spirit would work orderly in the congregation. I put it down to human desire to be the focus of attention. A gift has to give glory to God. If the gift glorifies God, and the person with the gift tells you it is from God, then give glory to God. But babbling doesn't glorify anyone, except the so-called babbler.

If you look at the New Testament, especially the Book of Acts, you will note that the gifts were heavily used and then fizzled out. Why? Christ taught you why, when he came back the second time to the disciples and met with Thomas, after His resurrection. Remember what He stated? Blessed are you Thomas, because you saw and believed. Blessed the more is he that doesn't see and believes (paraphrased).

The New Testament Christian had an uphill battle to prove that they were worshiping the Living God. They had a message and needed authority to prove who had sent them. The gifts gave them credibility. Once the message had spread, the need for the circus show was no longer required. Why? Living without the gifts requires a higher level of faith.

If I could raise the dead, how much faith would you need to believe me? Not much. But if I have only history and a loving message from my savior, it takes Faith. Fake Christian gifts are all around you. Take the Christian healing rooms. Are they Holy Spirit led? Look back in the Bible and find me a half-healed man. Or, how about someone that got better in a couple of weeks. No, that isn't how the Holy Spirit works. BAM, you're healed one hundred percent.

Read the Book of Acts in one sitting. You may note that an individual could be baptized and still the Holy Spirit hadn't filled him. Was that person saved? If he hadn't been filled, was he lost? Of course he wasn't lost. But, once baptized and if the apostles placed their hands on you, you could be filled with the Holy Spirit. This is referring to a gift given to that individual. Read Acts Chapter 8, verses 10–17. Sometimes they received the Holy Spirit and then they were baptized. But, as the book proceeds, and the number of believers increased, you will see a decline in the number filled with the Holy Spirit. I believe this is because what they referred to as a "filling," is the receiving of gifts, and the gifts became less needed to spread the word.

Does the Holy Spirit hear our prayers? Of course. The Father has answered many of my prayers. I have witnessed miraculous things in my day that can only come from God, but they weren't the gifts mentioned in early church time. As for now, I can only believe that they are no longer needed by God, and hence we don't see them.

Off Topic Note: Besides everlasting life, I believe God does give us the gifts of wisdom and discernment. Wisdom is the ability to understand knowledge and apply it to our lives. Discernment is the ability to tell the difference between correct and false facts and scripture. Pray for them.

What was the greatest gift from the Holy Spirit? Before you can answer this question you must ask yourself, "do I believe the words of Paul?" I do, but many of them are taken out of context. You have to read the entire epistle in one sitting before you will understand what he is saying. So, many times a verse here and there is quoted to mislead those that haven't really read their Bibles.

If you do believe Paul, he will tell you the greatest gift from the Holy Spirit is the gift of "prophecy." Read 1 Corinthians, and focus on Chapter 14. You may note that the English word "charity" as printed in older Bibles throughout Chapter 14 is the Greek word "agape" or God's Love. When you read the word charity throughout the New Testament, substitute "God's Love" and the sentence will make much more sense. So, the greatest gift from the Holy Spirit is to prophesy and to edify the church.

Why I bring this issue up is to ask you if you believe in modern day prophets. Many churches have them. Most are dead, but the "word" they have sown lives on. Were they really prophets from God Almighty? Set up a biblical test for yourself and then test them. Both Moses and Paul tell you how to test a prophet.

Moses tells you in the last half of Deuteronomy Chapter 18, that the test for a prophet is that everything that he or she says must come true. That means he has to be 100% accurate. So, let's take Nostradamus. Was he 100% accurate? No, so he was not a prophet of God Almighty. But he was great at guessing. There are many psychics, but none that are 100% accurate. They are either good con men or women, or they have a connection with someone other than God Almighty.

Read Galatians Chapter 1. Paul warns you of those that would deliver a gospel other than the one he is delivering. Why is this so important? He is telling you of false prophets. He states in verse 8: "But though we, or an angel from heaven, preach any other gospel unto you than that ye have received, let him be accursed." Now, read 2 Corinthians Chapter 11, verse 14. You will note that Satan can appear as an "angel of light." Why is this so important? Paul has told you how to test a prophet, and not to trust angels that teach contrary to his doctrine.

Moses has taught that the prophet of God must be 100% correct and Paul further explains that "the so-called prophet's teaching must not conflict with the Gospel of Jesus Christ that he (Paul) has taught. These make a very simple test for modern prophets.

Let me take a few. How about Ellen G White? She is the prophet for the Seventh Day Adventists (SDA). If the SDAs took all that they believed minus the added stuff from Ellen, they would be a very scriptural church. But they believe that her word is an extension to the scriptures. She prophesied about vegetarianism (not eating flesh). Some SDAs say you don't need to be, but she did say it. That is in direct conflict with 1 Timothy Chapter 4. Even Christ ate fish in His resurrected body!

She wrote from "vision" in her book The Great Controversy between Jesus and His Angels and Satan and his angels (not to be confused with her later work The Great Controversy). In Chapter 4 she is telling you the "true" story of Jesus' crucifixion. In print she states that the nail is thrust "THROUGH" His muscle and bone. She really didn't get the point that Jesus was our Passover. Not one bone was to be broken.

How about Ellen's expounded explanations of the Book of Revelation? Just the fact that she added to John's vision conflicts with the vision. Revelation Chapter 22 states, that if anyone is to add to or take away (as she is doing) from the vision they will be cursed and lose their part in the Book of Life (Rev 22:18-19). Even some of her later visions conflict with her early ones. So, by the test, she is thrown out as a real prophet.

If it will make you feel better, she never "actually" stated that she was a prophet. Their church has just "developed" her into one! Her exact words are this:

"Early in my youth I was asked several times, Are you a prophet? I have ever responded, I am the Lord's messenger. I know that many have called me a prophet, but I have made no claim to this title. My Saviour declared me to be his messenger. 'Your work,' he instructed me, 'is to bear my word. ... It is not you that speaketh: it is the Lord that giveth the messages of warning and reproof. Never deviate from the truth under any circumstances. Give the light I shall give you. The messages for these last days shall be written in books, and shall stand immortalized, to testify against those who have once rejoiced in the light, but who have been led to give it up because of the seductive influences of evil.' Why have I not claimed to be a prophet?--Because in these days many who boldly claim that they are prophets are a reproach to the cause of Christ; and because my work includes much more than the word prophet signifies." This quote can be found in the Review and Herald issue July 26, 1907.

So she is declaring herself as much more than a prophet. Notice how humble she is to explain that she is closer to God than all those humans in the Bible. Actually, if you use your concordance you will see that when the Bible refers to the Angel of God or the Angel of the seven last churches, it is the same word as "messenger."

I have not found one prophet that can pass the test. Look on the internet at any modern prophet and they have been picked to pieces with their own words. Why? Because God won't be mocked. Anyone that is attending a church with a modern day prophet is attending a cult. It's OK to belong to a cult, just don't call yourself a Christian.

Taking the same passage of 1 Timothy Chapter 4, we learn that the call to celibacy is also a sign of a false prophet/movement. So, in the past when the Pope declared himself god-on-earth and a link to God Almighty, it shows the flaw. If we are forbidding to marry, for any reason, it is a false religion. Does the Catholic Church allow their leadership to marry? No! Did Paul allow marriage within church leadership? Of course, but a church leader was to have only one wife. (Books of Timothy, Titus)

Has your prophet set up a way for you and your spouse to be coupled in the life hereafter? One such church is the "Church of Jesus Christ, the Latter Day Saints" (LDS), also known as the Mormons. There is a ritual that they have to seal your marriage. Why then does Jesus Christ (the guy they are supposed to be connected with, in their title) explain that they do not know their scriptures? Read Matthew Chapter 22, verses 23-30, Mark Chapter 12, verses 18-25, Luke Chapter 20, verses 27-36. Since LDS's like multiple witnesses, there are three different people recording the message from Jesus that states that there will be NO ONE married or given in marriage after the resurrection. We will live as the angels.

The angels aren't married. The only question here is, do you believe the words of Jesus? If you don't, you can't be a Christian! They also "elect" their prophet when the last one dies. Where in the scriptures did you ever read some group coming together and telling God the Father who will speak to them on His behalf?

On a side note, since the LDS's have the same divorce rate as the world around them, what will happen if they are "sealed" and then get a divorce? That is the problem with trying to add to the scriptures.

The list can go on and on. Do you have a prophet in your church? I haven't found one yet that can meet the test. Some churches say that their prophet is current so we have a more accurate understanding of what God wants. God left just enough scripture to survive to present day to help you understand if you are being misled.

Yes I know, they are a loving group of people that you enjoy to be around, or they have an excellent youth ministry. But, is the teaching scriptural? Does it conflict with the scriptures even a tiny bit? If it does, then you know that the altering/changing scripture that they have taught you are not from God.

All of the modern day "accepted" prophets state that they have been led by an angel. Remember, the angel that led those prophets around, and taught them so much, could be Satan himself (2 Corinthians 11:14). Now, that's scriptural!

Author's Thoughts

You are either a Christian searching for the love God has for you or you are just playing Christian. Take the time to reflect back on what you have learned.

Read these next few chapters and ask yourself, "Do I really want to live as God would have me live?" Read your Bible from cover to cover and you will have to agree that these next truths are hard to swallow.

Finally, why do you attend a church? Do you passively sit there while non-scriptural doctrine is being presented? It's bad enough when it is being fed to someone else, but what about your family? Vote with your feet if you are not strong enough to discuss bad doctrine openly.

Are you on Spiritual milk like those in Paul's first letter to the Corinthians? Judge your life for yourself. It is easy if you learn what type of love you have for the Father and His Son. Being a real Christian won't be popular. But, who are you trying to please, man, or God?

What are the Hard to Swallow Facts For Christians?

There are some pretty hard to swallow lifestyle choices that a real Christian will have to make. You are no longer ruled by modern society. You are lovingly following your Creator and the God of the Universe. Modern society can live as they please. Christians should respect there way of life as long as it is not forced upon a Christian's life, but a Christian has standards to live up to that society doesn't.

It is a real simple concept. Do you love God more than anything else? Then you have to live it. If you don't live it, then you really don't love God more than anything else.

Can a real Christian in all good conscience watch or read provocative TV, cinema or printed material? How about fantasy? Can a real Christian accept abortion? How about sex out of wedlock or homosexuality? Is the woman equal to the man, and can their roles be reversed? Who can lead a church? How should you vote, or should you vote? These are questions that should be easy to answer if you have read your Bible. Paul the Apostle has answered all these question plainly and will be quoted with other New Testament writers. Once again, these standards are not opposed to society, they are in addition to society norms.

Someone who serves in the United States Military falls under the jurisdiction of the Uniformed Code of Military Justice. They still must keep the laws of the land, but have additional ones to follow. Similarly, Christians must follow whatever laws govern the society that they live in, and a few more that are ordained by God. These are plainly found in the Bible.

I've heard it said that you are what you eat. More correctly, it isn't the physical input into your body that molds you, it is the emotional sensory that you allow into your life that truly molds you. Give me one good reason to watch a trashy show. Face it, if you enjoy watching raunchy shows or reading raunchy books you can't be of the spirit, you are of the world. It's OK to watch raunchy shows, if you don't care about your relationship with God the Father and His Son Jesus Christ. That is why if you "don't believe" it doesn't bother me if you watch them!

I had a young Christian lady once tell me that she watches those shows to see how the other side thinks. What a stupid idea, if she was telling the truth. No, most people watch those trashy shows and movies because they derive pleasure from watching them, and again that's OK as they are of the world, and not the Spirit.

Just read Romans Chapter 1. Paul states at the end of the chapter how man has darkened his heart. He lists many things that man has done to fall into this pit of unrighteousness. Finally, in

Romans Chapter 1, verse 32, he states: "Who knowing the judgment of God, that they that commit such things are worthy of death, not only do the same, but have please in them that do them."

It is clear that if you derive pleasure from watching these lewd or trashy shows, you are living them in your heart and are guilty of committing them. How can you call yourself a Christian if you don't put this lifestyle behind you? Christians must not watch any trash or filth or they are not of the Spirit, they are of the world.

It is that desire for something that is opposed to God's Law, that is condemning you. Just because God created it, doesn't mean that it is OK in your life. Take a beautiful flower. If you think upon it, is it sin? No, after all, it is a thing of beauty that God created. How about the woman's body? God created it, but dwelling upon a woman that is not entwined to you through marriage is a sin.

Does the world around you tell you that you shouldn't dwell on these thoughts? No, in fact lust is an acceptable part of life to the world we live in. How many shows on TV don't have some sort of lustful or lewd activity focused within them? Those types of shows ended with Andy of Mayberry or My Three Sons. I'm not trying to tell you that we need to change those of the world. You can't. I'm telling you that you can't participate in their activities and entertainment if you are of the Spirit.

In the same way, desiring to have supernatural powers is a sin. It is obvious that Satan worship is sinful. If we are dwelling on supernatural powers other than those by God, is it sin? To me it is obviously sinful. Anything that helps someone focus on a supernatural "power" or "force" other than one derived from God the Father is "anti" to Christ.

Fantasy is a real simple subject and yet, most people that call themselves Christians don't seem to have a problem with it. Is there anything in God's realm called white magic? No, it is either from God or power allowed by Him used by others for evil.

Take the Old Testament righteous man Job. Read the Book of Job. God gives Satan the power to do some pretty bad things to Job. Where else do you see "powers" in the Bible? The demons have powers, Satan and his angles have powers, even God's envoys have supernatural powers.

Here is the distinction between healthy reality and unhealthy fantasy. In reality, when God's envoys have "powers" and perform supernatural acts, they give the Glory to God! All of Satan's envoys don't have to give the glory for their magnificent acts to anyone.

So, what is white magic, you know, when the so-called good guy has powers to use against evil? How about Harry Potter? Is he a good guy? How about the Chronicles of Narnia? Are the good guys really good, or just less evil? This is what kills me about so-called Christians. I have heard it on talk-radio that the Chronicles of Narnia are really the God story in disguise. Where in the Chronicles of Narnia do we see the glory going to God? You don't! So why would they try to correlate some type of relationship with this book/movie to Him?

This is why fantasy is subtlety filtering evil into our lives. I remember when I was a very young man and went to see Star Wars. I really wanted "the force." Imagine the power to use a light saber and even levitate. I really wanted that "power." I guess that a so-called Christian could say that "the force" was God the Father. Yotta was Jesus. Luke Skywalker was a representation of one of his disciple. And the list could go on-and-on to prove that this fantasy is OK for a Christian.

Was my desire as a young man to possess "the force" healthy? Modern society says yes, but your Christian values should say, "Where is the glory to God?" It wasn't there. It is all about "me." It is self serving. Any fantasy in your life can only be self serving.

But you may ask, what about our children? It grows their minds. I agree that it does stretch their imagination. But does it grow them in a way that brings them closer to God or worldly values? There is fiction, nonfiction, fantasy, and filth. You can have healthy fiction without crossing the lines of supernatural powers.

Our children should be the main focus here. I read Cat in the Hat, Pooh bear, and you name it to my kids when they were young. But, I was not a Christian yet. How can a relationship for a child with a "living" stuffed animal be healthy? All these types of stories help children to believe that their desires for "what they want" to become "truth" is all that is required.

It is how we have turned black and white, good and evil, right and wrong, righteous and unrighteous, into "your truth is your truth and my truth is my truth."

Any way that you want to cut it, God's truth is the only truth. Any magical power, no matter how subtle, that doesn't bring Glory to God is wrong. It can only be evil. Kids should be taught that all power comes from God. They will be introduced to these, so you have to teach them that these powers are not "true" and never will be.

Can a real Christian believe that a woman has the right to choose life or death for the unborn child in her womb? Do you think that it is OK from God's perspective that we end the life of an unborn child? Only if you haven't read your Bible. First ask yourself, does God believe it is a life or just another appendage you can discard?

Yes, yes, I know that an unplanned child could become a burden on your life, but you made the choice! You had the sex! You took the moment of pleasure, and now you reap the consequences for your actions. But what about those unplanned events that may have been very hurtfully done to a woman?

God says it is a human life living within your womb. God doesn't make a differentiation between 1st, 2nd, or 3rd trimesters. Side note to this, but how can anyone think that killing a baby by dismembering it in the birthing channel (late term abortion) is anything other than murder? The child was fully formed and able to live on its own, if delivered.

If you don't believe me about God's view, it is time to take out your concordance and look up the word "womb." There are over 70 references to the womb and the knowledge that God has for those in them.

God not only knows that you are pregnant, he also knows what will happen with your child, and that child's child, while it is still in the womb. Read Genesis Chapter 25. It is the story of the birth of Issac and Rebekah's two children Jacob and Esau. Read verse 23. God tells Rebekah that the two children in her womb will be 2 nations.

He doesn't say, if you choose to have these two children they will become 2 nations. No, Rebekah didn't even have a choice as to what they would become. It was predestined. They are God's children, not your's.

Read about Samson in the Book of Judges, Chapter 13. Verse 5 states, "For lo, thou shalt conceive, and bear a son; and no razor shall come on his head: for the child shall be a nazarite unto God from the womb: and he shall begin to deliver Israel out of the hands of the Philistines." Samson was not only a nazarite during his life, he was a nazarite before his birth!

Read Job's understanding of who made each of us and when. It is found in Job Chapter 31. He is referencing why he does not despise his servants. In verse 15 he states; " Did not He that made me in the womb make him? And did not One fashion us in the womb?" It is clear to Job that God makes each of us, and allows for our position in life.

If you could be anyone in the Bible who would it have been? Whose throne will last forever? We know God's throne is from the beginning until forever, but for mankind, David's throne was the greatest. There are several good references to the womb, but read Psalm Chapter 139 and focus on verse 13. David states that God protected him while he was in the womb.

How about the prophets? Read Isaiah Chapter 44 where God states that he formed Jacob in the womb, or Isaiah Chapter 49 where Isaiah states that he was called from the womb.

Read Jeremiah Chapter 1 and in verse 5, God states that "Before I formed thee in the belly, I knew thee; and before thou camest out of the womb I sanctified thee, and I ordained thee a prophet unto the nations." So, you either believe your Bible or don't. God not only knew Jeremiah while he was in the womb, he knew him before he was formed in the womb. That is pre-fetus, even before the sexual act was committed.

Wasn't Jesus known before He was in the womb? Think of the Gospels. Mary is asked what she thinks of being the mother to the Saviour. If she had decided after a while, "I really don't like this idea," do you think it would have been OK for her to "choose" not to have Jesus?

How about those children out of wedlock that are not appreciated by the family. Should we get rid of them? Judah had three sons. The first wed Tamar, but died. The second was wed to her and died. Judah is tricked by her and becomes the father of her illegitimate child. Read Genesis Chapter 38. Before he knows that it is his child, he wants to have her burned with fire when he finds out that she is pregnant. Since the baby is his, he spares them both, but she would have been burned with fire if it had been anyone else's child.

That sounds like the ultimate birth control! But she and the baby are spared. Why is this story in the Bible? Turn to Matthew Chapter 1. It is the lineage of Jesus Christ. Which child does Jesus Christ descend through when you see Judah's offspring? It is the unwanted, almost executed before birth, son Pharez. God has a plan for every child in the world. Some for glory, some for destruction, but there is a God-ordained plan. Who are we to take the place of God and end a life?

There are too many references to us being known before we are born. I believe that it is clear that we are not the maker of that child within us and have no right to control it's unborn destiny. Find one reference in the Bible where you have the right to end the life within the womb. You can't find it!

It is your right at the present time to have an abortion under United States criminal law. But, does that make it right in the sight of God? I haven't seen a trial for adultery lately? Does that make it right? No, it is a sin to God, whether our government tells you it is OK or not.

But let's not kid ourselves. We are not directed to take physical measures to prevent abortions either. The trashing of abortion clinics, or worse, the threatening of those who do them isn't condoned anywhere in the Bible. Peaceful protests and education moving public policy is the correct way to remedy the appalling practice.

Which brings you to sexual misconduct. Can a real Christian accept or condone sexual promiscuity in their lives? This would cover sleeping around, any sex out of wedlock, adultery, or the gay (homosexual) lifestyle. The answer is clearly no! There are too many references to cover these lustful behaviors, but most can be summed up in Romans Chapter 1.

Paul explains that man has continued to pollute himself into a lower and lower state. He takes you through idolatry and ends with homosexuality. He calls them vile affects. In verse 26 he talks about female homosexuals and in verse 27 he talks about male homosexuals. These are explained to be of a reprobate mind.

The other heterosexual sins are found throughout the Bible, and really don't need to be covered, as we all know that they are not acceptable to God. If you want a few references, just look up the word "adultery" in the concordance. Where you find adultery, you will also find the other sexual sins listed.
It is spelled out quite clearly in the Law. Turn to Leviticus Chapter 20. This is a very thorough list of sexual sins and their punishments. It covers them all, but mentions in undeniable wording that homosexuality is a sin unto death, no more than adultery, but a sin unto death just the same. Leviticus Chapter 20, verse 13 reads: "If a man also lie with mankind, as he lieth with a woman, both them have committed an abomination: they shall surely be put to death;"

But you may say that a homosexual lifestyle is genetically predispositioned. How can God be displeased if He created a man or a woman that way? For those that believe that homosexuals have a DNA predisposition to that lifestyle, why not take biology? Only genes can be inherited, not behaviors. In the study of biology it states that if the target organism cannot reproduce with that gene, it will die out as a subspecies within one generation.

If you don't understand this, it can be stated a little simpler. If two gay people (either two men or two women) live together, they will have no children. Hence, if there was the possibility of a gay gene, the gene dies with them. No, a gay lifestyle is one of undeniable choice. A choice of lewd sex that God states is sin! It is a choice you make of the "world," and not of the Spirit.

Homosexuals can not reproduce, hence the notion that it is in their "genes" is bologna! It is not a reproducible gene, just a behavior. It is no more genetically predispositioned than a family where the father cheats on the mother and hence, his son must be a luster of woman also. Face it, lust is a behavior that is unacceptable to God, whether as a homosexual or as a heterosexual.

If you are a Christian then you accept that Jesus is the payment for sin. Do you believe Paul? If you don't believe Paul, then you don't have Christianity or "Saved by Grace." If you don't have Grace or Christianity, then what is your payment for sin?

Paul makes it perfectly clear in Romans Chapter 1 that society degrades itself down until we hit a reprobate mind. That point according to Romans Chapter 1 is homosexuality. You may ask yourself, how does that act hurt a Christian? It doesn't if we limit our relationship with those that are living that lifestyle. Paul tells you that it is a sexual immoral activity. When you live with or around someone that is committing any sinful act, it is natural that you begin to make excuses for that person, whom you are associating with.

Many would say that if they want to live that way, it is OK because they are both in agreement and hurting no one else. This would be a good time to reflect back on wife swapping. It was an acceptable practice in the past. After all, if all four individuals want to do it, what makes it wrong? It is the moral decline from God's values. God has told you to keep yourself from these people by commandment and example.

If not, you will grow into their values. I told my son when he had decided to marry a woman that did not fear God that if he did, he would loose his values and pick up hers. We argued the point to exhaustion. Only a year later he began to question whether it was OK for a Christian to be gay! It is obvious that his new friends that he has married into have different morals and they have begun to lower his standards.

With sexual sin you have to ask yourself, where do you draw the line? Pretty soon you are asking yourself, "is it OK to have sex with animals? You think that that question is far fetched? Where did AIDS come from? It is a well published fact that it was sex with monkeys. Then that same individual or individuals had sex with a woman or man.

A real Christian has to live in this world, but they don't have to be of this world. Your children have to be introduced to these lewd and worldly acceptable lifestyles, but it is your responsibility to explain to them why it is wrong in God's eyes.

So, when those friends or relatives want to come visit and stay the night, are they in a God-ordained relationship? If not, do you allow them to sleep together in the same room? If they are in a non-God-ordained relationship and you allow them to stay at your home, what type of message are you sending to your children?

I had the unfortunate experience of having to explain this to a member of my extended family. She was in a heterosexual relationship, but out of wedlock. Although I was much less versed in the Bible at the time, I understood that I wasn't to assist her in her lifestyle. I was out of favor with that side of the family for some time. But, why couldn't they accept my values? Why did they have to try to force their lifestyle in my home? They couldn't accept my values because they were and are of the world.

Is a man equal to a woman? Has "equal opportunity" grayed the lines between the "God-ordained" roles of man and woman. It's funny how the society norms have assisted in bringing worldly values into Christian life. Scientifically it is accepted that a man and woman are different. Study after study show that a woman has a brain where both sides talk to each other and a man's doesn't, at least not much. Doesn't this beg to ask why we try to call the two sexes equal? You could make the point that a woman's brain is superior.

They aren't equal, they are different. Each with their own strong points. It is my experience that women are more emotional than men, and men are more analytical than women. That is why little boys gravitate to playing war and little girls to playing house, dolls, and doctor. What is wrong with that? Nothing, unless you want a less God-focused society.

If you look at how God looks at the family and a woman's role you will understand why a woman was created more emotional, and hence better at her role than a man. Where does God see a woman's role in life?

It is obvious from the Old Testament where the hierarchy of the family rested. A woman was considered less than a man. She was considered the help mate to man. Take the temple. Women could not go as far as the men towards the two inner chambers. They had their own place to worship. They were forbidden from the priesthood.

But what about the New Testament, as we claim to be Christians? The one apostle quoted most about this is Paul, and usually out of context. Paul does state that we are equally the same, but that is in reference to our salvation. Let's see what Paul and others really state about the woman's role in relationship to the man.

First the family. Paul gives a crystal clear explanation of the man and woman's role to each other and their relationship with Jesus. Read 1 Corinthians Chapter 11. Verses 3 through 6 states, "But that I would have you know that the head of every man is Christ; and the head of the woman is the man; and the head of Christ is God." Then jump to verses 8 and 9, "For the man is not of the woman; but the woman of the man. Neither was the man created for the woman; but the woman for the man." Paul is reaffirming the Book of Genesis where you see God creating Eve for Adam.

Turn to Titus Chapter 2. It starts with the conduct of a man and then swings to the woman in verses 3through 5. "The aged women likewise that they be in behavior as becoming holiness, not false accusers, not given to much wine, teachers of good things; that they may teach the young women to be sober, to love their husbands, to love their children, to be discreet, chaste, keepers at home, good, obedient to their own husbands, that the word of God be not blasphemed."

Does this show a leadership position over their husbands, or over the home and children? Paul is very clear that a woman was to be a supporter of her husband, not a leader.

Look at the Proverbs Chapter 31 woman. This is an over achiever, but note who she gives the glory to!!! It is to her husband who is in the gates of the city. Why not go back to the beginning of mankind? What is said about Eve? Genesis Chapter 2, verse 18 tells you that she was Adam's "help meet." Is there any example of a righteous woman "ruling the roust?" On the contrary, there are many examples that "it is better to live on a corner of the roof than with a contentious woman" in both the New and Old Testament.

It is clear from every passage that you can find anywhere in the Bible about the relationship God has set up for man and woman. The man is the keeper of the family and the woman is to support him in his role. She is to take care of the home, providing the loving environment to bring up their family.

Does this mean that the Bible directly forbids women from having a career? No, in fact until she is married she is to be busy, not a busybody. But, once she is married, she has been given a role by God to care for the children that He provides for her. Find any passage that differs from that response. You can't. That is why it is a Christian fact that is hard to swallow by most.

Secondly, where is the woman's role mentioned where she is to lead men? There isn't one. Paul makes it perfectly clear that a woman, at least in relationship to God, has no business leading men. In fact, he tells them to be "silent" when at church. If they have anything to add, they are to talk with their husbands (or fathers) when they get back to the privacy of their home.

Look, if you don't like what I am pointing out, open your Bible and look it up for yourself. Don't take a line out of a verse here and there. Take a complete book at a time and read what is really being stated. God has defined roles for man and woman. Women leading any part of a church service is against God. Don't get mad at me, it is in your Bible. Take it up with God.

A direct reference for this is 1 Timothy Chapter 2, verses 11-15. Paul has explained why they keep quiet in church is because a woman is more easily deceived. "Let the woman learn in silence and with all subjection. But I suffer not a woman to teach, nor to usurp authority over the man, but to be in silence. For Adam was first formed, then Eve. And Adam was not deceived, but the woman being deceived was in the transgression. Not withstanding she shall be saved through childbearing, if they continue in faith and charity and holiness with sobriety."

Again, in 1 Corinthians Chapter 14 starting at verse 34, Paul is very clear that a woman is to keep silent in church. If she is to be silent, how is she to lead any part of the service? She isn't. The verse goes like this, "Let your women keep silent in the churches: for it is not permitted for them to speak; but to be under obedience, as also saith the Law. And if they will learn anything, let them ask their husbands at home: for it is a shame for a woman to speak in church."

There are several indirect, but straight-forward proofs to show how Paul felt about this "silence in the church." When Paul explains to Timothy and Titus how to pick a leader of a church, whether the minister or the deacon, he does not mention that it could be a woman. In fact for these positions, this male person has to have a wife with certain characteristics. A woman cannot have a wife unless they are in a homosexual relationship, and that is forbidden. Let's look at these texts.

The Book of Titus will take you less than 10 minutes to read. In Titus Chapter 1 you will find that the elders and bishops are "husbands."
1st Timothy is about a 15 minute read. In Chapter 3 you find Paul's qualifications for a bishop and deacon. Once again, both are husbands. There isn't the slightest wiggle room where Paul has left any doubt that the leadership role in a church was for the man only!

It is too clear that Paul did not believe that a woman should ever teach in church! So, how can a Christian church have women in any leadership role? They can't and still be a Christian Church. Call that church whatever you want to call it, but it isn't Christian if it is led by a woman.

It's funny, if you look back 50 years ago, woman spent more of their time at home raising their children. We had very few divorces. Woman never stood in the pulpit and most families went to church. Doing things contrary to the biblical way God wants you to live, will only be divisive in the long run.

Let's look at politics. Many churches try to either avoid politics, or they lead their congregations on a non-biblical voting quest. Jesus stated, to give unto Caesar what is Caesar's. As a member of a free democracy you are expected to vote. It isn't just your right, it is your duty. So, why wouldn't you want to vote? Who and what you vote for should be simple if you are a real Christian.

God expects you to vote your conscience, not your wallet! How can you vote for a candidate that is opposed to your Christian values even if you may have a better standard of living under his values? Abraham's nephew Lot, obviously enjoyed his standard of living and position in Sodom, but God didn't, and he lost everything.

If you believe as I do that abortion is a sin, how can you vote for any candidate that doesn't strongly oppose abortion? How can you vote for any gay rights values or open sex for that matter? Does the candidate's lifestyle really matter? Of course it does. Once elected they will vote for legislation that will make their own lives more enjoyable for themselves.

Does the environment factor into your voting values? You know, a candidate might be for the latest environmentally friendly positions. Sure, that could be a factor, but not if he or she will trounce one of your key values. Read your Bible. Man will wreck this world. God has told you in advance. Man will not save and sustain it. So, why would the environment be more important to a real Christian over the sanctity of life? Know your values. God will judge you for them!

If a candidate is attending a Church does that make him OK? What does that Church believe? I believe all candidates have their faults; you have to pick the one with the closest values to your's.

Yes, living a life that is pleasing to God isn't politically correct in today's worldly environment. You can choose to have an easier life, or you can choose to live for God.

So, What is Wrong with My Church?

These next two chapters are my personal views, but they are a compilation of the scriptures we have covered. If you don't want to be offended, this may be a great time to put this book back on your shelf. Before you can answer what's wrong with your church for yourself, you really have to master an understanding of the Bible.

Have you read it completely through yet? Should you trust anything over the Bible? Should a book like this, or an author such as myself, be influential enough to convince your heart that your present "living" is wrong? Of course not. You should go back to the Bible for that!

The purpose of this book was to show you that you need a real foundation found only in constant study of the Bible itself. There is no other document. But, you must research the information. Reading from front to back is a good start, but researching hard to understand verses or those that appear to fall out of the framework found in the Law is required.

After you think you have a basis to work from, start asking the hard questions with reference to your church's doctrine. Remember what Paul stated about doctrine: "But that we or an angel from heaven, preach any other gospel unto you than that which we have preached unto you, let him be accursed." (Galatians 1:8) And: "For such are false prophets, deceitful workers, transforming themselves into the Apostles of Christ. And no marvel, for Satan himself is transformed into an angel of light." (II Corinthians 11:13-14)

Lastly read again Acts Chapter 20. Focus on the warning by Paul starting in verse 28, about those that will come in like "wolves" not sparing the flock. Of course I would prefer that you read the entire chapters that I have referenced in the above paragraphs, but Paul makes it clear that the Church will be steered away from the truth by both Satan and those wanting control, for whatever reason.

Just ask yourself, do I really want to live a life that is Christ and God the Father focused? Do you really? I believe, if most people answered it honestly, they would have to say "no," because following the Bible is not convenient. I find that to be the same for all of the church leaders of my past. Why can I say that so definitively? Because the Bible makes it perfectly clear what we as Christians should believe and teach. When anyone takes a doctrine of their church over the truths in the Bible, they are living for themselves, and not God the Father and our Lord Jesus Christ. It has become their job, not their love and passion.

Here is a good example not used earlier in this book. God revealed it to me today while I was reading His word (just before this book went to the press). How do modern Christian churches explain "leaven" in the Scriptures? I have only heard it referred to as Sin. It is the "puffing up" that is focused on, as an analogy to pride. Self pride is wrong and sinful, but is that how "leaven" is used in the Bible. This is the problem with denominational teaching. They won't teach the Bible. If you have a preacher that teaches this way then they have never read their Bible through from front to back, so why would you listen to them?

Look at all the Jewish celebrations that used unleavened bread. Are they relevant to you today? Do you have the temple, so that you can follow these traditions? Go back and read the celebration of the Pentecost in the Old Testament located an Leviticus Chapter 23, verses 9-21. It isn't called the Pentecost, but is a 50-day period of time, hence Pentecost.

If you believe the Book of Acts, when was the Holy Spirit given out in the New Testament? It is at Pentecost. Read what was to be eaten at this celebration in Leviticus Chapter 23, verse 17. It is Leavened bread! So it is a God Ordained celebration that is performed with leavened bread. So all leaven isn't bad and that means that it can't be a representation for sin. In fact, for a Christian it is the "bringing in" of a new, better way that is celebrated with leaven. The old is out "unleavened Judaism," and the New is in "Leavened Christianity."

With all that stated, let's see how I stack up various churches. From reading this book you should understand that I will not take a tradition of man over the commandment of God. That will be the standard.

Let me make this perfectly clear. There will be saved Christians probably from all Christ centered churches of today and the past, even Catholicism. This we know by reading the Book of Revelation. So I am definitely not stating that if you are attending a church today, you will not be salvation bound. The Bible makes it perfectly clear that it is a heart issue. But, you have to ask yourself, am I living for Christ by attending and supporting the Church I am associated with?

I do believe that if you read your Bible through a couple of times you will have to agree that the Sabbath is the only day that God has ordained. Go to church on whatever day you please, but you are not allowed to "work" on the Sabbath. That makes Sabbath worship obvious. There are only three well-known organized churches that keep the Sabbath: Seventh-Day Baptist, Church of God, and the Seventh-Day Adventists.

The Church of God (CoG) has changed their stance on Sabbath, and now lets their congregation decide between Sabbath and the Lord's day worship. That comes back to the scriptural slam made on Israel in the Book of the Judges where it stated: "And Israel did what was right in their own eyes." The CoG did well until the death of Pastor Armstrong, but has since drifted to the desires of their congregation over the Commandments of God. Many other commandments have to be questioned, including the dietary laws.

The Seventh-Day Baptists do believe in the Sabbath. But, they also believe in the trappings of the Baptist belief system, such as the trinity. Any religion that believes that Jesus is "God", in any form, just isn't scriptural. They too have to evaluate the eating of unclean flesh.

I did attend a Seventh-Day Adventist church for a while, but when confronted with their printed belief that Ellen White was a prophet and that her writings were an extension to the scriptures, I had to stop attending. I still have several friends that believe as I do, but keep attending this denomination.

Why should you stop attending when you find that the church is non-biblical? If you keep attending, this tells the world that you stand for the values of that church. I believe that God expects us to vote our values with our feet and tithes.

The Seventh-Day Adventists believe that Ellen White was a prophet. Hence, her written word is elevated equal to the Bible. Unfortunately, she wrote things that contradict the Bible. Her early work, supposedly in vision, contradicts her later work. This shows that she doesn't pass the test of a true prophet of God. They believe in the dietary Laws, but have added vegetarianism to them. That is just like the Jews in Jesus Christ's day adding man's laws to God's Law to ensure that they stayed holy. As their doctrine states that Ellen's writings are an extension to scripture, and there for you to live by, I have to pass on this church. I may put out another book just focusing on so-called prophets like Ellen to show that there are no current, neither have there been, any "true" prophets in modern history.

Speaking of prophets, does your Church have a modern day prophet that has been led by an angel to deliver a gospel that is other than the one given by Paul? Take the Mormons, or as they like to be called, the Church of Jesus Christ of Latter Day Saints (LDS). Their founding Prophet, John Smith, taught many things that contradict the Bible. Since his death, they have dropped many of his controversial teachings, just to fit in.

What is the difference between a prophet and a priest? A priest can be "elected" by succession, but a prophet is always picked by God. Show me one person that made himself a "True Prophet" or was elected by man to be a prophet in the Bible. There isn't one. God picks His prophets, not man. So, as the LDS select their prophet through succession, what authority does their prophet have with God? During the 2008 US Presidential campaign, their current prophet passed away and "they" elected a new one! Does man elect the spokesperson for God?

The Bible does tell you that there will be two prophets from God to man during the end times. This is written about in the Book of Revelation. But, they haven't appeared yet. How do I know? Read Revelation and learn what they do.

Does your Church have women ministers and teachers? Does your church allow homosexuality? Worse, do homosexuals teach from the pulpit? Obviously I am talking about the Episcopal and Lutheran Churches, but many other Churches fit the mold. Read your Bible through a couple of times and you will have to agree that they have welcomed in the wolves through the front door. Their African counterparts reject these two unscriptural acts. It's funny how we have to look to Africa for a truer scriptural doctrine in these churches.

Does your church teach that you are committing blasphemy when you are performing "works?" I am zooming in on Calvary Chapels. But, they are not alone in this matter. They and other modern evangelical Christian churches try to persuade you that if you are trying to keep the law, you are trying to earn your way to heaven. They call it a "works trip." They teach against all things that are not convenient, such as the Sabbath. Look back in the New Testament and show me anyone that is a Christian and is or has broken the Law of God, and does not show remorse. This is just a softer gentler Christianity that is not scriptural.

Does your Church teach that God came down to live and die among us? That is of course referring to Jesus Christ, and will sum up most other denominations. There is no trinity. There is only one God and that is the Father. God is not the Spirit either. There are seven spirits that are before the Father in heaven, but they are not the Father. Try reading the Book of Revelation.

Catholicism. Take all the above and add idolatry. Think about it, who do Catholics pray to? Just about everyone or anything that looks like they may have had a link to God. Is that how Jesus taught His disciples to pray? It was to the Father only! Remember the Lord's Prayer. It starts like this: "Our Father, who art in heaven..."

God hates sin. God does not necessarily hate the person, but He does hate the act. How can you call yourselves a body of believers if you allow sin, as defined by God, to be allowed, or worse, acceptable in your worship and lives?

This chapter is a bit blunt, but why not? Are you adding apologetics to your church's doctrine to explain why you are not living the way "God" has dictated? Yes, He has dictated how those that are His will live. If you have a church that meets the challenges set forth in this book, send it to me and I will research it out. If it is really a truly scriptural Church, I will print it in the next addition of this book.

Churches may start with the best of intentions, but for some reason, probably convenience of their members, stray from the Commandments of God. God the Father did not give us wiggle room to decide how we would worship and honor Him. As for now, I have found no scripturally based church in America!

How do I Know if I Love God and Why Don't I Fit Comfortably into Modern Society?

As stated in the beginning of the last chapter, this chapter is really nothing but opinion and it takes a broad sweep from scripture. Very little scripture is quoted, so you may want to close the book at this point as it is only my opinion. How do you know if you love God? And, if I love God, why won't I fit comfortably into society? Let's first look at love.

A Christian's spiritual growing life should be simple and evolve through three stages. Simply put, God is Love, and so love should be reflected in a Christian's life. God made the family as an example for all loving relationships. Until you have a family of your own and experience a birth and a death of your children and parents, I don't believe you will ever understand the love God Almighty has for you. This is why He has instructed us that the commitment made when we get married is one to be worked on over the rest of our lives.

Living for God manifests it's way into your life. First, you must know in your heart that He exists and has a plan for you. If you truly believe He does, you will want to please Him, because He loves you. At this point in your life, you will do those things that you believe will bring Him pleasure. This is called obedience.

It's like when your son is 10 years old, and you ask him to mow the lawn for the first time. He understands that you need him to do this. So, he responds with a nicely cut lawn. He understood that you wanted him to do it and out of love and respect (maybe even fear) he did it. Take the husband and wife's first anniversary. At year one, he brings home a dozen roses because he wants to express his love to show he really treasures the unity. This stage is filled with knowing you are loved and doing those things that you feel are expected.

The modern evangelical church (MEC) believes that you don't have to do anything for your relationship to flourish with God. All relationships require work, if they are to grow. That includes marriage, parenting, and your relationship with God. To be a loving son, you are obedient to your earthly father. Why wouldn't you want to be obedient to your heavenly father? If you think that He doesn't expect a certain way of life from you, read your Bible. Not the choice verses set out by the MEC to conclude that you can't do anything to please Him.

Read from Genesis Chapter 1, verse 1, to Revelation Chapter 21, verse 22, and decide for yourself. You will learn that there were many people that are referred to as friends of God. Do you want to be a friend of God? How did they live? You can only know through personal study.

Stage two is where you are doing things in your worship because of the growing love you have for Him. There is a striking difference. It isn't because you know they are expected, rather it is because you are looking at better ways to express your love.

Take that 10-year-old boy. He is now 16. He knows that he is loved because his dad has been taking him driving (or some other enjoyable event). In response he mows the lawn before his dad even asks for it. In fact, dad has one of the best yards in town. Or, the husband is now married 15 years. He knows the wife has been having a hard day and so he swings by the supermarket and picks up some flowers for the evening. No special reason other than to show her how he really feels. These are ways we express our desire to please others.

With our Heavenly Father we start looking for the deeper meaning that we find as we study the Bible. Jesus Christ taught during the sermon on the mount, that the commandments given were the outward "doing" of what our Heavenly Father was looking for from our hearts. As we grow spiritually, we understand that it really is a heart issue between the Father and ourselves.

You live on this earth for about 80 years, during which time you will either become more spiritual, or desire the things of this world. Understanding that God would like you to remove those worldly thoughts as well as the deeds, is a big step to understanding real obedience. Just saying that it can't be done is a cop out!

Stage three. I'm afraid that few will ever attain this level of love. It is one where your life is an outpouring of the love within you. Think of it as your 17-year-old that learns that a neighbor has been injured and decides to do their yard too. No need for pay, no bragging to mom, just the understanding that it really needs to be done and decides to take it upon himself to do it. Or, the marriage that is a success. Where the husband and wife are truly entwined as one. Not to say they don't argue, but work together through thick and thin, for better or worse. Passing the years growing old together, taking care of each other out of love. Caring more for the pair, than they do for the other, and more for the other than they do for themselves.

Jesus Christ stated it best when he stated, "No man can show better love than to lay down one's life for another." True love is living your life for God. Caring for what He wants you to care for. Loving what He loves, and hating what He hates. Oh yes, God does hate. Read your Bible.

If you are not diligently searching your Bible to see what He requires of you, you are stagnating in stage 1. If you think it is all about salvation and a few words you utter, you are just a baby Christian and maybe not even that. Paul stated it best as a Christian that is on milk, but should be on meat.

There are many requirements that God has placed on all of us? The MEC would like you to believe that you can do nothing to add to your salvation, and theirs is a better way. If that were true, why does the MEC live so contrary to the scriptures, old or new? Did Christ accept divorce, homosexuality (sodomy), or idolatry? How then is homosexuality moving into our churches? Why is the divorce rate so high in the church? How about porn? Do you pray to anyone but God the Father? Is praying to Jesus Christ scriptural? How about borrowing (stealing pens and pencils) from work?

Look at today's notable Christian Leaders of the MEC that have all come tumbling down. Mostly, caught in sexual or financial scandals. Do you really think these people are saved? Don't forget, this is why they teach "once-saved-always-saved!" They have to believe in it, as they don't have a chance if their life was to come under the looking glass, but it will. Read Revelation again.

If you love the Lord it will be in your life. Will you still be tempted to sin? Of course, but when you realize that you are weak and need His help and ask for it, He will always pull you through. Why not read your Bible from front to back a few times and then _you_ will know!

So, if I have this love for God, why won't a real Christian fit into society?

At best, the majority of society will put up with you, if you are really living a Christian Lifestyle. What is a Christian Lifestyle? One that is focused on the Lord God Almighty through the power of Jesus Christ. Jesus stated it best. "They hated me first, and they will hate you."

If society doesn't hate you right now, what are you doing wrong? The MEC has no problem fitting into society. They pretty much believe that everything is OK. They will fight for what they believe, but only so far. God hates sin. Do you hate sin? Do you believe that most people will go to heaven? If so, where did you get that? At most funerals I hear speeches about the individual looking down from heaven at us. Where do you get that from in the scriptures?

Yes, we have produced a softer gentler Christianity. If you start explaining that we should live a righteous lifestyle, then people, even Christians, will say that you are being "Holier than Thou." It may be true. Jesus Christ stated: "Be as I, Be Holy." What is wrong with that? It is simple. By living that way, you are condemning the less righteous lifestyle. If this topic is upsetting to you, that's OK. I don't need to be accepted by man, just God.

Living a righteous lifestyle is simple. It is following the Law. You know, the one thing the MEC tells you, you can't keep (The Law). They explain that if you try to keep it, you then break it, and the more you try to keep it, the more you will fail. That is hogwash. I keep the Law. It really isn't that hard. All you have to do is understand your position. God made me, hence I listen to Him.

Sure, every now and then I fail, and He may chastise me, but more often than not, I am ashamed. And like the Prodigal son, that is enough for Him. Like Jesus Christ stated, go and sin no more. Do you know what repentance is? It is stopping from continuing to sin. You must understanding that sin is wrong and ask God for help to avoid your selfish desires. But wait, that would mean that we are keeping the Law!

So, your non-Christian friends won't like you because you don't do those dirty little deeds. And, your so-called Christian friends won't like you because you won't do those dirty little deeds. Guess what, the whole world doesn't like you. The only people that will like you are like-minded Christians that search the scriptures to understand how God wants us to live.

One last time, remember the Apostle Paul, who is so miss quoted by so-called Christians by not reading his entire letters? What does he say about the Law at the end of Romans Chapter 3? We embrace the Law! Why, because it states in the same letter that the Law shows us sin!

www.ingramcontent.com/pod-product-compliance
Lightning Source LLC
LaVergne TN
LVHW061217060426
835508LV00014B/1338